W9-AGA-426

Modern Cryptanalysis

Modern Cryptanalysis

Techniques for Advanced Code Breaking

Christopher Swenson

WILEY

Wiley Publishing, Inc.

Modern Cryptanalysis: Techniques for Advanced Code Breaking

Published by
Wiley Publishing, Inc.
10475 Crosspoint Boulevard
Indianapolis, IN 46256

Copyright © 2008 by Christopher Swenson

Published by Wiley Publishing, Inc., Indianapolis, Indiana

Published simultaneously in Canada

ISBN: 978-0-470-13593-8

Manufactured in the United States of America

10 9 8 7 6 5 4 3 2 1

No part of this publication may be reproduced, stored in a retrieval system or transmitted in any form or by any means, electronic, mechanical, photocopying, recording, scanning or otherwise, except as permitted under Sections 107 or 108 of the 1976 United States Copyright Act, without either the prior written permission of the Publisher, or authorization through payment of the appropriate per-copy fee to the Copyright Clearance Center, 222 Rosewood Drive, Danvers, MA 01923, (978) 750-8400, fax (978) 646-8600. Requests to the Publisher for permission should be addressed to the Legal Department, Wiley Publishing, Inc., 10475 Crosspoint Blvd., Indianapolis, IN 46256, (317) 572-3447, fax (317) 572-4355, or online at http://www.wiley.com/go/permissions.

Limit of Liability/Disclaimer of Warranty: The publisher and the author make no representations or warranties with respect to the accuracy or completeness of the contents of this work and specifically disclaim all warranties, including without limitation warranties of fitness for a particular purpose. No warranty may be created or extended by sales or promotional materials. The advice and strategies contained herein may not be suitable for every situation. This work is sold with the understanding that the publisher is not engaged in rendering legal, accounting, or other professional services. If professional assistance is required, the services of a competent professional person should be sought. Neither the publisher nor the author shall be liable for damages arising herefrom. The fact that an organization or Website is referred to in this work as a citation and/or a potential source of further information does not mean that the author or the publisher endorses the information the organization or Website may provide or recommendations it may make. Further, readers should be aware that Internet Websites listed in this work may have changed or disappeared between when this work was written and when it is read.

For general information on our other products and services or to obtain technical support, please contact our Customer Care Department within the U.S. at (800) 762-2974, outside the U.S. at (317) 572-3993 or fax (317) 572-4002.

Library of Congress Cataloging-in-Publication Data is available from the publisher.

Trademarks: Wiley, the Wiley logo, and are related trade dress are trademarks or registered trademarks of John Wiley & Sons, Inc. and/or its affiliates in the United States and other countries, and may not be used without written permission. All other trademarks are the property of their respective owners. Wiley Publishing, Inc., is not associated with any product or vendor mentioned in this book.

Wiley also publishes its books in a variety of electronic formats. Some content that appears in print may not be available in electronic books.

The views and opinions expressed in this book do not reflect those of the United States Department of Defense.

To Sára

About the Author

Christopher Swenson (www.caswenson.com) is currently completing his PhD in computer science at The University of Tulsa, where he has assisted with and taught courses in security, telecommunications, and cryptanalysis. He is an active researcher and has published many papers in the security field. He was the recipient of a scholarship in the Information Assurance Scholarship Program, also known as the Department of Defense Cyber Corps program.

Credits

Executive Editor
Carol Long

Development Editor
John Sleeva

Production Editor
Debra Banninger

Copy Editor
Cate Caffrey

Editorial Manager
Mary Beth Wakefield

Production Manager
Tim Tate

**Vice President and Executive
Group Publisher**
Richard Swadley

**Vice President and Executive
Publisher**
Joseph B. Wikert

Project Coordinator, Cover
Lynsey Stanford

Proofreader
Nancy Carrasco

Indexer
Melanie Belkin

Cover Image
© Yamada Taro/Digital Vision/
Getty Images

Acknowledgments

I thank the many people who helped me shape this book. First and foremost, I thank my fiancée, Thursday Bram, for her support throughout the writing of this book. I thank Sujeet Shenoi and The University of Tulsa for providing me with the venue to teach the original class (as well as all of the students in that original class). I thank John Hale, Gavin Manes, and Mauricio Papa for being great mentors over the years. And of course, I thank my mother, Glenda, and my father, Roger, as well as my sisters, Rikki and Jessi, and my step-father, Richard, for all of their continued support throughout the years.

I could not have written the book without Carol Long and John Sleeva's support at Wiley. Also, a great many thanks to Donald Knuth, Leslie Lamport, John D. Hobby, and the hundreds of other individuals who have given their support in TeX, LaTeX, MetaPost, and related typesetting projects.

Contents at a Glance

Contents

Introduction

This book, like many things, was developed in response to a problem: There is no text that explains modern advancements in the field of cryptanalysis. The field of cryptanalysis has developed significantly in the last several hundred years, and for the most part, cryptanalysis has been well-studied and documented throughout this time.

However, when we move into the 20th century, the documentation of cryptanalysis has come to a near standstill. Almost every book published on the topic of "cryptanalysis" is stuck nearly 100 years in the past, idling around the area of breaking some of the simplest ciphers, by today's standards.

The field itself has not stopped developing. On the contrary, it has been moving incredibly rapidly, especially in the past 30 years, with the rise of ever more powerful computers. While all of this research into cryptanalysis has been documented and presented at various conferences throughout the world, nobody had bothered to create a simple resource with which to learn cryptanalysis from scratch. Bruce Schneier [5] stated that such a resource would not be worthwhile, because the field changes so much, and he has a point. But, the current roads on which cryptanalysis travels are built on the same foundations, and the amount of background material needed to understand current research or participate is becoming very large and complicated. Furthermore, the important papers are written by many different individuals with many diverse goals and audiences, which can make the papers difficult to understand.

I must reiterate what Schneier says [5], though: There is only one way to become a good cryptanalyst — to practice breaking codes. However, it is my hope that this book will be a good outline of many important topics to a new or veteran cryptanalyst.

While teaching at The University of Tulsa, I had many students express their interest in learning cryptanalysis, knowing that I enjoyed the field. As I began to prepare to teach a class, I discovered that there was definitely no textbook for what I wanted to teach, although I did prepare the students mathematically using the material in Reference [7].

Therefore, I gathered up all of the material I could from various conferences and publications and hobbled together notes and summaries for the students in the class. I then realized that there might be a few other people in my situation, wanting to learn the subject on their own, or possibly even teach or take a class on cryptanalysis with a sparse foundation to build on. Hopefully, there are, or my publisher will be very disappointed with the sales of this book.

In order to properly teach modern cryptanalysis, we have to get a few things out of the way first. For one thing, we need to agree on what it is exactly that we are doing and why, which is what this Introduction is about. We are going to have to do some review of math in Chapter 2, although I will leave a more vigorous run-through for other textbooks.

I will then go through some of the older cryptanalysis methods commonly found in other cryptanalysis books, as well as many computer security books. Then we get to the good stuff.

First, I will briefly cover some aspects of ciphers based on number theory, such as RSA and Diffie-Hellman. Although these are typically instantiated in such a manner that the algorithms I discuss will take too long to actually perform, I will discuss the basic framework that is used to look at these ciphers.

Then we get into the real meat of the book: block ciphers. I start with a brief discussion of cryptography: how the algorithms themselves are built. Then I start discussing some very modern but general attacks on block ciphers, such as rainbow tables.

I will then go into linear and differential cryptanalysis, as well as the many methods derived from them. Nearly all modern cryptanalysis is based on or heavily influenced by these two concepts, thus a good deal of material will go into fully developing them and getting into contemporary research. Although this is a book on cryptanalysis, we must first understand the science behind everything: cryptology. Going even further back, cryptology is but one weapon to combat a security problem.

Concepts of Security

So what is this "security" thing people always talk about? It's all over the Internet — security lapses here, lack of security there, someone loses a laptop full of sensitive identifying information, a student hacks into another student's account, or a piece of software on your computer is allowing someone to take control of it remotely. So what does *security* mean?

Looking up *security* in a few dictionaries will give a general consensus that *security* is "freedom from danger, risk, and loss" [2,4]. This is a book related to computers, thus we are concerned with dangers, risks, and losses related to computers, especially information.

Over the past several years, we have seen or heard of many examples of violations of security, particularly with the advent of the Internet. Valuable information is often targeted by criminals, who often seek to steal credit card information, Social Security numbers (for U.S. citizens), bank accounts, login names, passwords, and corporate data. Other examples are simply data loss: Improper storage of valuable data can mean that the data is not recoverable when it is needed.

There are several fundamental cornerstones of information security that it helps to keep in mind when trying to understand any technique meant to further this concept of keeping our information free from danger, risk, and loss.

The first principle is **confidentiality**: keeping our information free from the danger of being exposed to unauthorized parties. This exposure can be through accidentally or purposefully losing the information, such as by transmitting it via insecure means or by simply misplacing a briefcase with no lock on it (a lock would provide at least some confidentiality, since not just anyone would bother to open it). Confidentiality can often be the most critical element of information: keeping it from prying eyes. Information on national defense and corporate secrets often places the most emphasis on maintaining confidentiality, since once data is in the hands of another person, it could be damaging or worthless, making any other points of security moot. Confidentiality, as in the example above, can be implemented by locking the information (such as in a briefcase), or perhaps encoding it so that it is gibberish to anyone who doesn't know how to decode it.

A second critical property is **integrity**: keeping our information free from the danger of being modified by unauthorized parties, and thus being invalid. Even if it is not necessary for the information to be secret, as with confidentiality, it may be very important that the information is correct. For example, an e-mail from your boss may not hold anything particularly sensitive and could even be sent to the entire workforce, but you need to know for sure that nobody but your boss wrote it or modified it before you saw it.

A third property of information security we may wish to protect is its **availability**: keeping our information around, that is, free from loss. For example, if someone is hosting a streaming video service for a sporting event, delivering video to every subscriber may be the most important issue: If a video packet or two is slightly jumbled when it arrives, it is not usually a very big deal. Mechanisms for availability include redundancy (e.g., power, servers) and extensive testing before actual use.

What good is our information, even if it is all there, available, and secure, if it was written by somebody other than we expect? **Authenticity** is keeping our information written only by the party that we wish to have written it. Authenticity can also be called verification, and we see it in every day life constantly. The signature on a written check, watermarks and other properties of the paper used for currency, ATM cards to access a bank account, PIN numbers on an ATM card, passwords for bank accounts, and thumbprints for logging, in all verify some property about an object to guarantee its genuineness.

Although some of the other topics are touched on a bit in this book, we are primarily concerned with the oldest and most prominently placed principle of security in this text: confidentiality. Specifically, how do we transmit information so that, if it is intercepted, no one can see what it is without great difficulty? Naturally, we need to modify or garble the message in some way, but so that the intended recipient can figure out what the original message was.

Cryptology

As mentioned, the confidential exchange of information is critical in society — from military orders to credit card numbers, for thousands of years, people have had data that must be protected from unwanted eyes. The science of securely transferring information is known as **cryptology** and is usually separated into two distinct yet related sciences: cryptography and cryptanalysis.

Cryptography is the most commonly encountered area of cryptology, consisting of the science of understanding, implementing, and using information obfuscation techniques. These techniques are called cryptographic algorithms, codes, codebooks, cryptosystems, cryptoalgorithms, or ciphers.

Cryptography can be as simple as a code a child might use to hide notes in class — an understanding with another student that the message is, say, written backwards, character-by-character. It can also be extremely complex, requiring advanced mathematics just to understand some of the basic principles, such as in elliptic curve cryptography.

The term **encryption** refers to taking information that is unobfuscated (the **plaintext**) and applying the cipher to acquire obfuscated data (the **ciphertext**). Taking ciphertext and deriving the plaintext is called **decryption**.

Sometimes, algorithms rely on an external (to the plaintext or ciphertext) piece of information to guide the encryption and decryption processes. This external piece of information is often called a **key**, or **cryptovariable**.

Cryptology

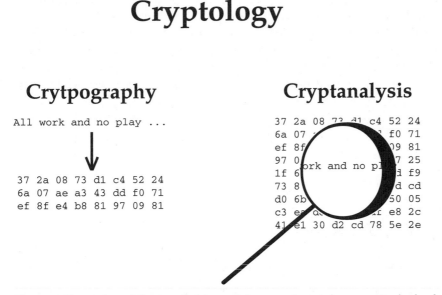

Crytpography

```
All work and no play ...
```

```
37 2a 08 73 d1 c4 52 24
6a 07 ae a3 43 dd f0 71
ef 8f e4 b8 81 97 09 81
```

Cryptanalysis

```
37 2a 08 73 d1 c4 52 24
6a 07            f0 71
ef 8f            09 81
97 0 ork and no p  7 25
1f 6             d f9
73 8             d cd
d0 6b            50 05
c3 e          f e8 2c
41 e1 30 d2 cd 78 5e 2e
```

Figure 1 Illustration of the two fundamental areas of cryptology: cryptography, how to use ciphers to encrypt and decrypt information, and cryptanlaysis, how to break ciphers.

As a very quick example, we could take a simple word, such as cat, and our cipher could be to simply transmit each letter by its position in the standard English alphabet (a = 1, b = 2, etc.). In this case, our message would be (3, 1, 20). We could use a key (say, a small number) and add this value to each character. Therefore, if our key was the number 5, we would then have the encrypted message (8, 6, 25).

The study of cryptography itself is important it has many good books covering how ciphers work and how to properly use them. Hence, we are more concerned with how well these algorithms protect the information with which they are entrusted. Hence, **cryptanalysis** is the study of defeating and strengthening cryptographic techniques; that is, finding, exploiting, and correcting weaknesses in either the algorithms themselves or in particular implementations. Understanding cryptanalytic methods helps us break bad ciphers and make good ones. As you can tell by the title of this book, our primary focus is going to be on cryptanalysis.

As long as there have been cryptographers, there have been people who have attempted to cryptanalyze the systems used to protect data. The fact that somebody bothered to protect the data at all might be an indicator that it is valuable!

A related field, although technically not directly involved with cryptology, is **steganography**. This mostly separate field is concerned with hiding data in other information, usually without altering the original information. For example, a particularly noisy image file of a photograph can have many bits changed, producing effects that will be not noticeable (or negligibly so) to the human eye, but could be interpreted into separate data.

Steganographic and cryptographic techniques can be combined to increase the security of the data hiding, though. Otherwise, known methods would be fairly easy to defeat: Tied with encryption, the encoded data would look nearly identical to random noise.

Although both cryptography and steganography are both fascinating and intricate fields, I shall not discuss either in great detail throughout this book. However, principles of steganography may be sprinkled throughout to give a more holistic view.

History of Cryptology

As soon the first person realized that it might be desirable to write down a piece of information, either for storage or for transportation, and there would be undesirable consequences should that piece of information be revealed, the challenge of cryptology arose. As people started to tackle this wide problem, either by figuring out ways to encode information or by trying to understand others' encoded information, the field started to develop.

One of the first uses of cryptography, and still one of the most important to date, is hiding information about military orders: Should the courier transporting deployments from a general in charge of managing a battle to the field commanders fighting it, be intercepted by the enemy on route to the battlefield, the enemy would then know what orders were to be given if the orders were not protected. This is a *confidentiality* problem. Furthermore, if the interceptor realizes that he can intercept the order, might he not replace that order with an erroneous order that would give the advantage to the enemy? This is an *integrity* problem, if the message can be so thwarted. Finally, by simply killing all of the couriers, no orders will get through, thereby preventing the passage of information from command, creating an *availability* problem. When evaluating security problems, it is useful to understand several properties about the system's security posture. First, there are **threats** to a system: events or entities that can potentially do harm to the security. These can be intentional or unintentional threats, including natural disasters. An earthquake destroying data is just as total a loss as an adversary deleting all of the data. Both are considered threats.

A potential ability for harm to come to a system is through a **vulnerability**. A vulnerability is merely an opportunity for harm to occur. For example, leaving your office door unlocked constitutes a vulnerability in the physical security of your office systems.

An actual **risk** occurs when threats are combined with vulnerabilities. A threat to your system that can actually use vulnerabilities to compromise the security of a system creates a risk. The cost (monetary or otherwise) along with likelihood of these vulnerabilities being exploited by threats constitutes the degree of a response necessary to counter these risks.

The entire process of risk analysis is beyond the scope of this book, but the concepts can be easily seen in our military example. In the early days of warfare, the other army might be nearly or completely illiterate — therefore, having the orders written down at all, even in the clear, may be a vulnerability, but there is no risk associated since the enemy has no ability to read the message.

Often, when performing this kind of analysis, it can be useful to create a matrix of the different vulnerabilities and threats to determine potential problems in the security of a system.

Principles of Good Cryptography

Claude Shannon proposed several criteria of good ciphers that are fairly influential in the development of cryptography [6].

1. **The amount of security necessary should dictate how much effort we put into securing or encrypting our data.**   Essentially, if a piece of information doesn't need to be protected, then don't protect that information. For example, no one would probably go so far as to encrypt and hide, say, an executable program on a computer used to play solitaire.[1]

2. **The size of the ciphertext should be less than or equal to the size of the plaintext.**   Shannon was a pioneer of information theory. From an information theory perspective, the plaintext contains some amount of information encoded into bits. If the ciphertext contains the same information, but more bits, theoretically there is more room there for us to derive the original information.

3. **The cryptographic system should be simple.**   A lot of complexity makes lots of room for errors. AES is a model of simplicity, while being extremely robust (see Chapter 4).

   As a corollary, the implementation must also be simple. If the algorithm itself is simple, but the implementation can only be programmed on an incredibly complex machine, then this can also be undesirable.

[1]That is, unless you are trying to hide the fact that you spend all day at work playing solitaire from your boss.

Also, the keys themselves shouldn't be unnecessarily complicated: if the keys rely on a computationally heavy algorithm for their generation (say, the key must be a prime greater than $2^{2,000,000}$) or have arbitrary and strange requirements (say, every other bit must zero).

4. **Errors should not propagate.**   Essentially, if there is a transmission error when sending an encrypted message, accidently leaving out a bit, or getting some part of the message wrong, should have as limited an impact as possible.

   This principle is a little less relevant nowadays than it was in 1949, as communications methods have become more robust, and the use of error detection and correction has accelerated.

   Furthermore, this principle is difficult and conflicts a bit with the concept of diffusion: If errors never propagate, then there isn't enough entropy in the cipher, and this might lead to a line of attack.

These principles are not fast and hard, but merely guidelines. Even the author disagrees with the first principle to a certain extent. For example, many people now have document shredders so that they can shred certain documents before throwing them away, in hopes of deterring potential identity thieves. The author is of the opinion that for every real treasure trove of personal information shredded (e.g., a document with a Social Security number or a bank account number on it), then *at least* one piece of absolute garbage information should be shredded. The idea is to significantly increase the difficulty in recovering any potentially important documents.

A similar argument can be made toward the storage of sensitive information, in conflict with Shannon's first principle. If all information is regularly stored with very strong encryption (all using different keys), then, with any luck, anyone attempting to get access to the original information will have to work harder.

There are a few other principles that often crop up in discussions of security.

For example, there is often the phrase "security through obscurity," applied when using an encryption method that is not publicly known. These ciphers are also known as **black box** ciphers, since we don't know what is going on in them. In general, security through obscurity is frowned upon: Although there is some sense of security in knowing that few people know how a particular system is implemented, it is possible that, without enough people evaluating the system, there will be undiscovered errors in the algorithm. This lesson was learned well with the selection of the Advanced Encryption Standard, where every candidate cryptoalgorithm went under numerous public evaluations before being selected as the choice.

Conventions Used in This Book

Throughout this book, I will use several distinctive text markings regularly. First, words that are in **bold** are important words that are being defined — they represent key concepts of the chapter they are in. Emphasized words are in *italics*.

In some of the introductory chapters, I indicate unencrypted text (plaintext) in `lowercase, in a fixed-width font`. For encrypted text (ciphertext), I put the text in `UPPERCASE, IN A FIXED-WIDTH FONT`.

Fixed-width fonts are also used to indicate hexadecimal numbers, separated on a byte or larger grouping. For example, the number `AA BB` (or `aa bb`) represents the number 43,707 (in decimal). Source code is put into listings in a fixed-width font as well.

Mathematical expressions, including variables, are in italics, such as $f(x) = x^2$.

Book Contents

This book is composed of the following chapters, some of which can be skipped, depending on your interests.

Chapter 1 presents some of the classic ideas of cryptography and cryptanalysis. It explains some of the simpler systems of cryptography and how they were broken.

In Chapter 2, I discuss some of the mathematics necessary for understanding more advanced cryptanalysis. Topics in probability theory, number theory, and algebra are covered in a fast-paced manner. The probability theory is mandatory for students studying cryptanalysis, but the more mathematical parts of number theory and algebra can be safely skipped by students more interested in block cipher analysis, rather than number theoretic ciphers.

Chapter 3 covers number theoretic and algebraic cipher techniques and focuses on some explanations for common cryptanalytic techniques.

Chapter 4 introduces many of the concepts used in building modern block ciphers, such as Feistel structures, substitution-permutation networks, and shift registers.

Chapter 5 gives some background into some of the more general-purpose cryptanalytic techniques, various "brute-force" techniques, complexity theory, and rainbow tables.

Chapter 6 is where some of the modern, advanced techniques come into play, including linear and multilinear cryptanalysis, and some of its derivative work and results.

Chapter 7 finally delves into differential cryptanalysis, including its descendants.

Students interested mostly in cryptography and basic cryptanalysis should be concerned with Chapters 1 and 4, as well as some of Chapters 2 and 5. Although this book is by no means an exhaustive covering of some of the more mathematical techniques, a good feel for them can be obtained in Chapters 2 and 3 (see, for example, References [1], [3], and [7] for more coverage, for starters). Block cipher enthusiasts should study everything, though, saving possibly Chapter 2 (except probability theory) and Chapter 3, for the less mathematically inclined.

References

[1] Henri Cohen. *A Course in Computational Algebraic Number Theory*, Graduate Texts in Mathematics. (Springer-Verlag, New York, 2000).

[2] Dictionary.com. *Definitions from Dictionary.com*; http://www.dictionary.com. Based on the Random House Unabridged Dictionary (2006).

[3] Alfred J. Menezes, Paul C. van Oorschot, and Scott A. Vanstone. *Handbook of Applied Cryptography*. (CRC Press, Boca Raton, FL, 1996).

[4] Merriam-Webster. *Merriam-Webster Online Dictionary*; http://www.m-w.com.

[5] Bruce Schneier. A self-study course in block-cipher cryptanalysis. *Cryptologia* **24**(1): 18–34 (2000); http://www.schneier.com/paper-self-study.pdf.

[6] Claude Shannon. Communication theory of secrecy systems. *Bell Systems Technical Journal* 28: 656–715 (1949).

[7] Samuel S. Wagstaff. *Cryptanalysis for Number Theoretic Ciphers*. (Chapman & Hall/CRC, Boca Raton, FL, 2003).

# CHAPTER 1

Simple Ciphers

As long as there has been communication, there has been an interest in keeping some of this information confidential. As written messages became more widespread, especially over distances, people learned how susceptible this particular medium is to being somehow compromised: The messages can be easily intercepted, read, destroyed, or modified. Some protective methods were employed, such as sealing a message with a wax seal, which serves to show the communicating parties that the message is genuine and had not been intercepted. This, however, did nothing to actually *conceal* the contents.

This chapter explores some of the simplest methods for obfuscating the contents of communications. Any piece of written communication has some set of symbols that constitute allowed constructs, typically, words, syllables, or other meaningful ideas. Some of the simple methods first used involved simply manipulating this symbol set, which the cryptologic community often calls an **alphabet** regardless of the origin of the language. Other older tricks involved jumbling up the ordering of the presentation of these symbols. Many of these techniques were in regular use up until a little more than a century ago; it is interesting to note that even though these techniques aren't sophisticated, newspapers often publish puzzles called **cryptograms** or **cryptoquips** employing these cryptographic techniques for readers to solve.

Many books have been published that cover the use, history, and cryptanalysis of simple substitution and transposition ciphers, which we discuss in this chapter. (For example, some of the resources for this chapter are References [2] and [4].) This chapter is not meant to replace a rigorous study of these techniques, such as is contained in many of these books, but merely to expose the reader to the contrast between older methods of cryptanalysis and newer methods.

1.1 Monoalphabetic Ciphers

It's certain that, as long as people have been writing, people have been using codes to communicate — some form of writing known only to the communicating parties. For example, the two people writing each other secret letters might agree to write the first letter of each word last, or to exchange some letters for alternate symbols. Even many children experiment with systems and games of writing based on similar ideas.

The most basic kind of cipher is one in which a piece of text is replaced with another — these are called **substitution ciphers**. These can be single-letter substitutions, in which each letter in each word is exchanged one at a time, or whole-block substitutions, in which whole blocks of text or data are exchanged for other whole blocks (**block ciphers**, which are discussed in detail in Chapter 4).

One family of simple substitution ciphers related to the above is the family of **monoalphabetic ciphers** — ciphers that take the original message and encrypt it, one letter (or symbol) at a time, using only a single new alphabet to replace the old. This means that each character is encrypted independently of the previous letter, following the same rule. Since these rules must always translate a character in the same way every time, a rule can be represented as a new alphabet, so that a message can be encrypted via a conversion table between the two alphabets.

The simplest example of a monoalphabetic cipher is to perform a single shift on the alphabets. In other words, replace all a's with b's, b's with c's, and so forth, and wrap around the end so that z's are replaced with a's. This means that the word cat would be encrypted as DBU, and the word EPH would be decrypted as dog.

One of the first, and certainly the most widely known, monoalphabetic ciphers was one used by ancient Romans. It is affectionately called the **Caesar cipher** after the most famous of Romans [4]. This system was reportedly used to encrypt battle orders at a time when having the orders written at all was almost good enough to hide them from the average soldier, and it is extraordinarily simple. To obtain the ciphertext for a plaintext using the Caesar cipher, it is necessary simply to exchange each character in the plaintext with the corresponding character that occurs three characters later in the common order of the alphabet (so that a encrypts to D, b encrypts to E, etc., and wrapping around, so that x encrypts to A).

Naturally, getting the plaintext back from the ciphertext is simply a matter of taking each character and replacing it with the character that appears three characters before it in the common order of the alphabet (see Table 1-1).

For example, the text retreat would be encoded as UHWUHDW.

To decrypt a message, simply reverse the table so that d →a, e →b, and so on.

Table 1-1 Caesar Cipher Lookup Table

PLAINTEXT ↔ CIPHERTEXT			
a ↔ d	h ↔ k	o ↔ r	v ↔ y
b ↔ e	i ↔ l	p ↔ s	w ↔ z
c ↔ f	j ↔ m	q ↔ t	x ↔ a
d ↔ g	k ↔ n	r ↔ u	y ↔ b
e ↔ h	l ↔ o	s ↔ v	z ↔ c
f ↔ i	m ↔ p	t ↔ w	
g ↔ j	n ↔ q	u ↔ x	

As a quick example, the text

```
the quick brown roman fox jumped over the lazy ostrogoth dog
```

can be easily encrypted by shifting each character three to the right to obtain

```
WKH TXLFN EURZQ URPDQ IRA MXPSHG RYHU WKH ODCB RVWURJRWK GRJ
```

However, as any person experienced in newspaper crypto-puzzles can tell you, one of the key features to breaking these codes is found in the placement of the spaces: If we know how many letters are in each word, it will help us significantly in guessing and figuring out what the original message is. This is one simple cryptanalytic piece of knowledge we can use right away — we are not encrypting the spaces! There are two solutions: We can either encrypt the spaces as an additional "27-th" letter, which isn't a terrible idea, or remove spaces altogether. It turns out that it makes slightly more sense, cryptanalytically speaking, to remove the spaces altogether. This does make it hard to read and write these codes by hand; thus, we often just remove the spaces but add in new ones at regular intervals (say, every four or five characters), giving us ciphertext such as

```
WKHTX LFNEU RZQUR PDQIR AMXPS HGRYH UWKHO DCBRV WURJR WKGRJ
```

When encrypted, the lack of the correct spaces in the ciphertext means nothing to either party. After decryption, though, when the party has plaintext with few spaces in the correct place, the inconvenience is usually minor, as most people can read the message anyway. The added security of removing all spaces from the plaintext before encryption is worth the small added difficulty in reading the message. The spaces added at regular intervals add no new information to the data stream and are therefore safe to keep.

With these examples, it is easier to see exactly what is meant by the term **monoalphabetic**. Essentially, to use a monoalphabetic cipher, we only need to consult a *single* lookup table. This will contrast shortly with other techniques, which consult multiple tables.

1.2 Keying

The Caesar cipher has a prominent flaw: Anyone who knows the cipher can immediately decrypt the message. This was not a concern to Caesar 2,000 years ago, as having the message in writing often provided sufficient subterfuge, considering the high illiteracy of the general population. However, the simplicity of the cipher allowed field commanders to be able to send and receive encrypted messages with relative ease, knowing that even if a message was intercepted and the enemy was literate, the opposition would have little hope of discovering the content.

As time progressed, more people became aware of the algorithm, and its security was therefore lessened. However, a natural evolution of the Caesar cipher is to change the way the letters are transformed into other letters, by using a different ordering of the alphabet.

But easily communicating an alphabet between two parties is not necessarily so easy. There are 26! = 403,291,461,126,605,635,584,000,000 different possible arrangements of a standard 26-letter alphabet, meaning that both sides would need to know the encrypting alphabet that the other was using in order to decrypt the message. If the two parties first agree on an alphabet as a **key**, then, since they both know the algorithm, either can send messages that the other can receive. However, if they number the alphabets individually, they would have an 89-bit key (since $26! \approx 2^{89}$), which is difficult to work with. Instead, most cryptographers would typically use a few simple transformations to the alphabet, and have a much smaller key.

For example, the most common method is simply to shift the letters of the output alphabet to the right or left by a certain number of positions. In this way, the Caesar cipher can be viewed as having a shift of +3. There are then 26 different keys possible, and it should be fairly easy for two parties to exchange such keys. Moreover, such a short key would also be easy to remember.

Other common transformations are typically a combination of the shifting operation above and another simple operation, such as reversing the order of the output alphabet [4].

1.2.1 Keyed Alphabets

To increase the number of alphabets available for easy use, a popular keying method is to use a keyword, such as `swordfish`, to generate an alphabet.

An alphabet can be derived, for example, by removing the letters in the keyword from the alphabet, and appending this modified alphabet to the end of the keyword. Thus, the alphabet generated by `swordfish` would be

```
swordfihabcegjklmnpqtuvxyz
```

Note that the second `s` was removed from the keyword in the alphabet and that the alphabet is still 26 characters in length.

There are a few disadvantages to using such a technique. For example, encrypting a message that contains the keyword itself will encrypt the keyword as a string of letters starting something along the lines of `ABCDEFGH`. Another, probably more severe disadvantage is that letters near the end of the alphabet will not be shifted at all unless the keyword has one or more characters appearing at the end of the alphabet, and even so, would then likely be shifted very little. This provides patterns for the experienced code breaker.

1.2.2 ROT13

A modern example of a monoalphabetic cipher is ROT13, which is still used on the Internet, although not as much as it has been historically. Essentially, this is a simple cipher in the style of the Caesar cipher with a shift of +13.

The beauty of this cipher is in its simplicity: The encryption and decryption operations are identical. This fact is simply because there are 26 letters in the Latin alphabet (at least, the way we use it in English); thus, shifting twice by 13 yields one shift of 26, which puts things back the way they were. Also note that it doesn't matter in which ''direction'' we shift, since shifting left by 13 and shifting right by 13 always yield the same results.

But why use such an easy-to-break cipher? It's, in fact, trivial to break since everyone knows the cipher alphabet! Despite the fact that this style of cipher has been obsolete for centuries, ROT13 is useful to protect slightly sensitive discussions. For example, readers of a message board might discuss the endings of books using ROT13 to prevent spoiling the conclusion for others.

Looking through articles or posts on the Internet where sensitive topics might be displayed, and suddenly having the conversation turn into strange-looking garbage text in the middle (often with other parties replying in the exact same code) often means that the posters are writing in ROT13. Plus, ROT13 often has a very distinctive look that one can recognize after a while. For example, our standard text from above,

```
the quick brown roman fox jumped over the lazy ostrogoth dog
```

would display as

```
GUR DHVPX OEBJA EBZNA SBK WHZCRQ BIRE GUR YNML BFGEBTBGU QBT
```

when encrypted with ROT13.

1.2.3 Klingon

I would like to delve into a language other than English for a moment, to show that these cryptographic (and later, cryptanalytic) techniques are not reliant on English, but can have similar properties in other languages as well, including even constructed languages. An example language that might be easy to follow is the Klingon language.

Klingon [1] (more properly, "tlhIngan Hol"), as seen in the *Star Trek* films and television shows, is an artificial language invented mostly by Marc Okrand using only common Latin characters and punctuation. This allows the use of encryption techniques similar to the ones we have used in English so far, showing some different properties of the language.

Table 1-2 shows all of the characters of tlhIngan Hol as they are commonly spelled in the Latin alphabet. From this table, we can then determine that the 25 characters, `abcDeghHIjlmnopqQrStuvwy´`, are the only ones we should be seeing and therefore need to encrypt (note that English has 52 characters, if you include capital letters).

Using the character ordering of the previous paragraph, we can perform a ROT13 of the Klingon text:

```
Heghlu'meH QaQ jajvam
```

(In English, this translates as "Today is a good day to die.")
After the ROT13, we obtain the enciphered text:

```
trStyIn'rt DoD wowjo'
```

Table 1-2 Sounds of tlhIngan Hol [1]

b	ch	D	gh	H
j	l	m	n	ng
p	q	Q	r	S
t	tlh	v	w	y
'	a	e	I	o
u				

1.3   Polyalphabetic Ciphers

We can naturally think of several ways to make the monoalphabetic cipher a more powerful encryption scheme without increasing its complexity too much. For example, why not use two different ciphers, and switch off every other letter? Or use three? Or more?

This would be an example of a **polyalphabetic cipher**. These began to be widely adopted over the past 500 years or so owing to the increasing awareness of how weak monoalphabetic ciphers truly are. There are a few difficulties in managing the alphabets. A key must be used to select different alphabets to encrypt the plaintext.

However, this necessitates an increase in key complexity. If a key represents some set of k alphabets, then there are $(26!)^k$ different sets of alphabets that could be chosen. (This is 26 factorial to the k-th power. In other words, take the number 26 and multiply it by 25, 24, and so on down to 2, and take *that* number, and multiply it by itself k times. With $k = 1$, this is about four hundred million billion billion, or a 4 followed by 23 zeros. The number of zeros roughly doubles with each increment of k.) To reduce this number, cryptographers often use a small number of alphabets based on easily remembered constructions (such as shifts and reversals of the normal alphabetic ordering), and use parts of the key to select alphabets used for substitution.

1.3.1   Vigenère Tableau

The most common table used to select alphabets is the famous Vigenère Tableau, as shown in Table 1-3. The Vigenère Tableau is a pre-selected set of alphabets, along with some guides to help encrypt and decrypt text characters if you know the key. When using the Vigenère Tableau to select alphabets for a polyalphabetic cipher, we obtain the Vigenère cipher. For this polyalphabetic cipher, the key is a word in the alphabet itself.

Encrypting a message using the Vigenère Tableau is fairly easy. We need to choose a keyword, preferably of short length to make it easy to remember which alphabet we are using at every point in the message. We then take our message and encrypt it character by character using the table and the current character of the keyword (start with the first of each). We merely look up the current character of the keyword in the left column of the Tableau.

To show an example, we can use our favorite phrase:

```
the quick brown roman fox jumped over the lazy ostrogoth dog
```

We then encrypt it with the key `caesar` to obtain the ciphertext:

```
VHI IUZEK FJONP RSEAE HOB BUDREH GVVT TLW LRBY SKTIQGSLH UQG
```

Table 1-3 The Vigenère Tableau

	a	b	c	d	e	f	g	h	i	j	k	l	m	n	o	p	q	r	s	t	u	v	w	x	y	z
a	a	b	c	d	e	f	g	h	i	j	k	l	m	n	o	p	q	r	s	t	u	v	w	x	y	z
b	b	c	d	e	f	g	h	i	j	k	l	m	n	o	p	q	r	s	t	u	v	w	x	y	z	a
c	c	d	e	f	g	h	i	j	k	l	m	n	o	p	q	r	s	t	u	v	w	x	y	z	a	b
d	d	e	f	g	h	i	j	k	l	m	n	o	p	q	r	s	t	u	v	w	x	y	z	a	b	c
e	e	f	g	h	i	j	k	l	m	n	o	p	q	r	s	t	u	v	w	x	y	z	a	b	c	d
f	f	g	h	i	j	k	l	m	n	o	p	q	r	s	t	u	v	w	x	y	z	a	b	c	d	e
g	g	h	i	j	k	l	m	n	o	p	q	r	s	t	u	v	w	x	y	z	a	b	c	d	e	f
h	h	i	j	k	l	m	n	o	p	q	r	s	t	u	v	w	x	y	z	a	b	c	d	e	f	g
i	i	j	k	l	m	n	o	p	q	r	s	t	u	v	w	x	y	z	a	b	c	d	e	f	g	h
j	j	k	l	m	n	o	p	q	r	s	t	u	v	w	x	y	z	a	b	c	d	e	f	g	h	i
k	k	l	m	n	o	p	q	r	s	t	u	v	w	x	y	z	a	b	c	d	e	f	g	h	i	j
l	l	m	n	o	p	q	r	s	t	u	v	w	x	y	z	a	b	c	d	e	f	g	h	i	j	k
m	m	n	o	p	q	r	s	t	u	v	w	x	y	z	a	b	c	d	e	f	g	h	i	j	k	l
n	n	o	p	q	r	s	t	u	v	w	x	y	z	a	b	c	d	e	f	g	h	i	j	k	l	m
o	o	p	q	r	s	t	u	v	w	x	y	z	a	b	c	d	e	f	g	h	i	j	k	l	m	n
p	p	q	r	s	t	u	v	w	x	y	z	a	b	c	d	e	f	g	h	i	j	k	l	m	n	o
q	q	r	s	t	u	v	w	x	y	z	a	b	c	d	e	f	g	h	i	j	k	l	m	n	o	p
r	r	s	t	u	v	w	x	y	z	a	b	c	d	e	f	g	h	i	j	k	l	m	n	o	p	q
s	s	t	u	v	w	x	y	z	a	b	c	d	e	f	g	h	i	j	k	l	m	n	o	p	q	r
t	t	u	v	w	x	y	z	a	b	c	d	e	f	g	h	i	j	k	l	m	n	o	p	q	r	s
u	u	v	w	x	y	z	a	b	c	d	e	f	g	h	i	j	k	l	m	n	o	p	q	r	s	t
v	v	w	x	y	z	a	b	c	d	e	f	g	h	i	j	k	l	m	n	o	p	q	r	s	t	u
w	w	x	y	z	a	b	c	d	e	f	g	h	i	j	k	l	m	n	o	p	q	r	s	t	u	v
x	x	y	z	a	b	c	d	e	f	g	h	i	j	k	l	m	n	o	p	q	r	s	t	u	v	w
y	y	z	a	b	c	d	e	f	g	h	i	j	k	l	m	n	o	p	q	r	s	t	u	v	w	x
z	z	a	b	c	d	e	f	g	h	i	j	k	l	m	n	o	p	q	r	s	t	u	v	w	x	y

1.4   Transposition Ciphers

The preceding encryption mechanisms are all substitution ciphers, in which the primary operation is to replace each input character, in place, with some other character in a reversible way. Another general class of ciphers mentioned briefly above is **transposition ciphers** (or **permutation ciphers**), in which instead of characters being substituted for different ones, they are shuffled around without changing the actual characters themselves. This preserves the actual contents of the characters but changes the order in which they appear. For example, one of the simplest transposition ciphers is simply to reverse the characters in the string — `cryptology` becomes `YGOLOTPYRC`.

In order for a transposition cipher to be secure, its encryption mechanism can't be so obvious and simple as merely reversing the string, since even an amateur eye can easily see what is happening. In the following sections, we explore some of the more popular and effective methods of implementing transposition ciphers.

1.4.1   Columnar Transpositions

Probably the most common, simple transposition cryptographic method is the **columnar transposition** cipher. A columnar transposition works in the following way: We write the characters of the plaintext in the normal way to fill up a line of a rectangle, where the row length is referred to as k; after each line is filled up, we write the following line directly underneath it with the characters lining up perfectly; to obtain the ciphertext, we should read the text from top to bottom, left to right. (Often, spaces can be removed from the plaintext before processing.)

For example, to compute the ciphertext of the plaintext `all work and no play makes johnny a dull boy` with $k = 6$, write the message in a grid with six columns:

```
a l l w o r
k a n d n o
p l a y m a
k e s j o h
n n y a d u
l l b o y
```

Now, reading from the first column, top to bottom, then the second column, and so forth, yields the following message. Spaces are added for clarity.

AKPKNL LALENL LNASYB WDYJAO ONMODY ROAHU

To decrypt such a message, one needs to know the number of characters in a column. Decryption is then just writing the characters in the same order that we read them to obtain the ciphertext, followed by reading the text left to right, top to bottom.

The key can then be viewed as the integer k, the number of columns. From this, we can calculate the number of rows (r) by dividing the message length by k and rounding up.

1.4.2 Double Columnar Transpositions

It does not take an advanced cryptanalyst to see an immediate problem with the above columnar transposition cipher — we can easily guess the number of columns (since it is probably a low number for human-transformable messages), or just enumerate all possibilities for k and then check to see if any words are formed by taking characters that are k.

To protect messages more without increasing the complexity of the algorithm too much, it is possible to use two columnar transpositions, one right after the other. We simply take the resulting ciphertext from the single columnar transposition above and run it through the columnar transposition again with a *different* value of k. We refer to these values now as k_1 and k_2.

For example, if we take the encrypted string, shown earlier, from all work and no play makes johnny a dull boy, encrypt it with $k = 6$ (as above), obtaining the ciphertext from the previous section), and encrypt it *again* with $k_2 = 8$, we get:

```
ALYOA KEBNH PNWMU KLDON LYDLN JYLAA RASOO
```

To show how jumbled things get quite easily, we will take the plaintext P to be the alphabet:

```
abcde fghij klmno pqrst uvwxy z
```

Encrypting with $k_1 = 5$, we get the ciphertext C_1:

```
AFKPU ZBGLQ VCHMR WDINS XEJOT Y
```

And we encrypt the ciphertext C_1 with $k_2 = 9$ to obtain the next and final ciphertext C_2:

```
AQNFV SKCXP HEUMJ ZROBW TGDYL I
```

1.5   Cryptanalysis

In the previous sections, we explored the evolution of several simple cryptographic systems, many of which were used up until the previous century (and some still find limited use, such as ROT13). Now we will discuss the weaknesses in the above methods and how to defeat these codes.

1.5.1   Breaking Monoalphabetic Ciphers

The first topic we covered was monoalphabetic ciphers. These simple ciphers have several weaknesses, a few of which were alluded to previously. There are a few important tools and techniques that are commonly used in the evaluation and breaking of monoalphabetic ciphers, which we explore in the following sections.

1.5.1.1   Frequency Analysis

The most obvious method is called **frequency analysis** — counting how often individual letters appear in the text.

Frequency analysis is based on patterns that have evolved within the language over time. Most speakers of English know that certain letters occur more often than others. For example, any vowel occurs more often than X or Z in normal writing. Every language has similar character properties like this, which we can use to our advantage when analyzing texts.

How? We simply run a counter over every character in the text and compare it to known samples of the language. For the case of frequency analysis, monoalphabetic ciphers should preserve the *distribution* of the frequencies, but will not preserve the matching of those relative frequencies to the appropriate letters. This is how these ciphers are often broken: trying to match the appropriate characters of a certain frequency in the underlying language to a similarly acting character in the ciphertext. However, not all ciphers preserve these kinds of characteristics of the origin language in the ciphertext.

A distribution of English is shown in Figure 1-1, which is derived from *The Complete Works of William Shakespeare*. The graph shows the frequency of each character in the Latin alphabet (ignoring case) in *The Complete Works of William Shakespeare* [3].

Each language has a unique footprint, as certain letters are used more than others. Again, in Figure 1-1, we can see a large peak corresponding to the letter E (as most people know, E is the most common letter in English). Similarly, there are large peaks in the graph around the letters R, S, and T.

For monoalphabetic substitution ciphers, the graph will be mixed around, but the frequencies will still be there: We would still expect to see a large

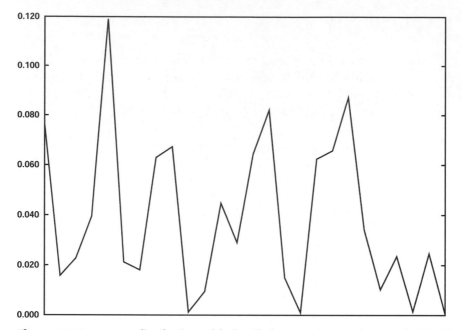

Figure 1-1 Frequency distribution table for Shakespeare's complete works [3]. The letters are shown left to right, *A* through *Z*, with the *y*-value being the frequency of that character occurring in *The Complete Works of William Shakespeare* [3].

peak, which will probably be the ciphertext letter corresponding to *E*. The next highest occurring letters will probably correspond to other high-frequency letters in English.

Frequency distributions increase in utility the more ciphertext we get. Trying to analyze a five-letter word will have practically no information for us to derive any information about frequencies, whereas several paragraphs or more will give us more information to derive a frequency distribution.

Note, however, that just as frequency distributions are unique to languages, they can also be unique to particular samples of languages. Figure 1-2 shows a frequency analysis of the Linux kernel source code that has a different look to it, although it shares some similar characteristics.

1.5.1.2   Index of Coincidence

One of the first questions we might ask is if a particular message is encrypted at all. And, if it is encrypted, how is it encrypted? Based on our discussion above about the different kinds of cryptography, we would want to know whether the message was encrypted with a mono- or polyalphabetic cipher so that we can begin to find out the key.

We can begin with the **index of coincidence** (the I_C), a very useful tool that gives us some information about the suspect ciphertext. It measures

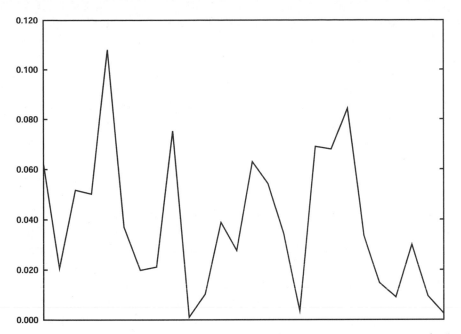

Figure 1-2 Frequency distribution table for "vanilla" Linux 2.6.15.1 source code (including only alphabetic characters). The total size is approximately 205 megabytes.

how often characters could theoretically appear next to each other, based on the frequency analysis of the text. You can think about it as a measure of how evenly distributed the character frequencies are within the frequency distribution table — the lower the number, the more evenly distributed. For example, in unencrypted English, we know that letters such as E and S appear more often than X and Z. If a monoalphabetic cipher is used to encrypt the plaintext, then the individual letter frequencies will be preserved, although mapped to a different letter. Luckily, the I_C is calculated so that the actual character does not matter, and instead is based on the ratio of the number of times the character appears to the total number of characters.

The index of coincidence is calculated by the following:

$$I_C = \sum_{c \in \text{alphabet}} \frac{\text{count}(c) \times [\text{count}(c) - 1]}{\text{length} \times (\text{length} - 1)}$$

This means that we take each character in the alphabet, take the number of them that appear in the text, multiply by that same number minus one, and divide by the ciphertext length times the ciphertext length minus one. When we add all of these values together, we will have calculated the probability that two characters in the ciphertext could, theoretically, be repeated in succession.

How do polyalphabetic ciphers factor into this? In this case, the same letter will not be encrypted with the same alphabet, meaning that many of the letter appearances will be distributed to other letters in a rather random fashion, which starts to flatten out the frequency distribution. As the frequency distribution becomes flatter, the I_C becomes smaller, since the amount of information about the frequencies is decreasing.

An adequate representation of the English language is *The Complete Works of William Shakespeare* [3]. We can easily calculate the index of coincidence, ignoring punctuation and spaces, by counting the occurrences of each character and applying the above formula. In this case, we calculate it to be approximately 0.0639.

While Shakespeare provides an interesting reference point and is fairly representative of English, it is necessary to consider the source of the message you are analyzing. For example, if your source text likely is C code, a better reference might be a large collection of C code, such as the Linux kernel. The Linux 2.6.15.1 kernel has an $I_C \approx 0.0585$. Or, if the text is in Klingon, we can take a sample size of Klingon with a few English loan words (taken from about 156 kilobytes of the *Qo'noS Qonos*), and find the $I_C \approx 0.0496$.

The theoretically perfect I_C is if all characters occurred the exact same number of times so that none was more likely than any other to be repeated. This can be easily calculated. For English, since we have 26 characters in our Latin-based alphabet, the perfect value would be that each character occurs exactly 1/26-th of the time. This means that, in the above equation, we can assume that length $= 26 \times$ count(c) for all c.

This gives us the following formula to calculate the perfect theoretical maximum. We can assume that the count is n, to make the formula easier to read. To see what happens as we get more and more ciphertext, the counts will be more precise; therefore, we will assume that the amount of ciphertext is approaching an infinite amount.

$$I_C = \lim_{n \to \infty} \sum_{c \,\in\, \text{alphabet}} \frac{n(n-1)}{26n(26n-1)}$$

We can simplify this a little (since we know that each part of the sum is always the same):

$$I_C = \lim_{n \to \infty} \frac{26n(n-1)}{26n(26n-1)}$$

And we can even simplify a little further:

$$I_C = \lim_{n \to \infty} \frac{n-1}{26n-1}$$

Most calculus courses teach L'Hôpital's Rule, which tells us that the above limit can be simplified again, giving our theoretical best:

$$I_C = 1/26 \approx 0.03846$$

This can be seen intuitively by the fact that, as n gets very large, the subtraction of the constant 1 means very little to the value of the fraction, which is dominated by the $n/26n$ part. This is simplified to $1/26$.

Note that this technique does not allow us to actually break a cipher. This is simply a tool to provide us more information about the text with which we are dealing.

1.5.1.3 Other Issues

There are some proposed methods of strengthening basic ciphers (monoalphabetic, polyalphabetic, transposition, or others). See Reference [5] for some of these examples.

One very simple method is to throw meaningless characters called **nulls** into the ciphertext. For example, the character X does not appear very often in texts. Therefore, we could just throw the letter X randomly into the plaintext before encrypting. This technique isn't terribly difficult to spot: Frequency analysis will show a fairly normal distribution of characters, except for an extra, large spike in the distribution. Once any suspected nulls are removed, the analysis should be easier. Another common null is to remove spaces from the plaintext and add them to the ciphertext in a random, English-like manner.

Another popular mechanism is to use **monophones** — where one plaintext letter can be represented by more than one ciphertext letter. They can be chosen randomly or with some certain pattern. This is slightly more difficult to detect, since it will have the property of flattening the distribution a bit more. Since using monophones quickly depletes the normal alphabet, extra symbols can often be introduced.

The opposite of a monophone is a **polyphone** — where multiple plaintext characters are encoded to the same ciphertext character. This requires the receiver to know this is happening and be a bit clever about decrypting the message, since there may be multiple interpretations of the characters.

There are no good ways of automatically detecting and removing these security measures — a lot of them will involve a human using the preceding and following tools, along with practice, and simply trying out different ideas.

1.5.2 Breaking Polyalphabetic Ciphers

The key to breaking a polyalphabetic cipher of a keyed type (such as Vigenère) is to look for certain patterns in the ciphertext, which might let us guess at the key length. Once we have a good guess for the key length, it is possible to break the polyalphabetic ciphertext into a smaller set of monoalphabetic ciphertexts (as many ciphertexts as the number of characters in the key), each a subset of the original ciphertext. Then, the above methods, such as frequency analysis, can be used to derive the key for each alphabet.

The question is, how do we guess at the key length? There are two primary methods: The first is a tool we described above — the index of coincidence.

As stated above, the index of coincidence is the probability of having repeated characters and is a property of the underlying language. After a text has been run through a monoalphabetic cipher, this number is unchanged. Polyalphabetic ciphers break this pattern by never encrypting repeated plaintext characters to be the same character in the ciphertext. But the index of coincidence can still be used here — it turns out that although the ciphers eliminate the appearance of repeated characters in the plaintext being translated directly into the ciphertext, there will still be double characters occurring at certain points. Ideally (at least from the point of view of the person whose messages are being cracked), the index of coincidence will be no better than random (0.03846). But, luckily (from the viewpoint of the cryptanalyst), the underlying language's non-randomness comes to the rescue, which will force it into having a non-perfect distribution of the repeated characters.

Just as longer keys for polyalphabetic ciphers tend to flatten out the frequency distributions, they also flatten out the non-random measurements, such as the index of coincidence. Hence, a smaller key will result in a *higher* index of coincidence, while a longer key gives us an index of coincidence closer to 0.03846. Table 1-4 shows us the relationship between the number of characters in the key and the index of coincidence.

As can be seen, the measurement starts to get pretty fuzzy with key lengths of around six or so characters. Without a great deal of ciphertext, it becomes very difficult to tell the difference between a polyalphabetic key length of six and seven, even.

We clearly cannot rely completely on the I_C for determining the key length, especially for smaller amounts of ciphertext (since it is only effective with large amounts of text, and not very precise for larger keys). Luckily, we have another method for guessing at the likely key length.

Friedrich Kasiski discovered that there is another pattern that can be seen, similar to the index of coincidence [4]. In English, for example, *the* is a very common word. We would, therefore, assume that it will be encrypted multiple times in a given ciphertext. Given that we have a key length of *n*, we can hope that we will have the word *the* encrypted at least *n* times in a given ciphertext. Given that it is encrypted at least that many times, we will be guaranteed to have it be encrypted to the *exact same* ciphertext at least twice, since there are only *n* different positions that *the* can be aligned to with regard to the key.

We know that we can expect there to be repetitions of certain strings of characters of any common patterns (any common trigraphs, e.g.). But what does this reveal about the key? This will actually give us several clues about the length of the key.

Table 1-4 Relationship between Key Length of a Polyalphabetic Cipher and the Resulting Index of Coincidence of the Ciphertext in *The Complete Works of William Shakespeare* [3]

KEY LENGTH	APPROXIMATE I_C
1	0.0639
2	0.0511
3	0.0468
4	0.0446
5	0.0438
6	0.0426
7	0.0423
8	0.0417
9	0.0412
10	0.0410
. . .	. . .
∞	0.0384

If we are very certain that two repetitions of ciphertext represent the exact same plaintext being encrypted with the same pieces of the key, and we know that the key is repeated (such as in Vigenère) over and over again, this means that it must be repeated over and over again in between those two pieces of ciphertext. Furthermore, it means that they were repeated an integral number of times (so that it was repeated 15 or 16 times, but not 14.5). Therefore, we calculate the difference in the positions of the two pieces of ciphertext, and we know that this *must* be a multiple of the length of the ciphertext. Given several of these repetitions, and several known multiples of the length of the cipher key, we can start to hone in on the exact length of the key.

A good example may help clear up what is going on. The following plaintext is from the prologue to *Romeo and Juliet* [3]:

```
twoho useho ldsbo thali keind ignit yinfa irver
onawh erewe layou rscen efrom ancie ntgru dgebr
eakto newmu tinyw herec ivilb loodm akesc ivilh
andsu nclea nfrom forth thefa tallo insof these
twofo esapa irofs tarcr ossdl overs taket heirl
```

We can encrypt this using the key romeo (the key in this case has length 5), to obtain the following ciphertext:

```
KKALC LGQLC CREFC KVMPW BSURR ZUZMH PWZJO ZFHIF
FBMAV VFQAS COKSI IGOIB VTDSA RBOMS EHSVI UUQFF
VOWXC ESIQI KWZCK YSDIQ ZJUBP CCAHA RYQWQ ZJUPV
RBPWI EQXIO ETDSA WCDXV KVQJO KOXPC ZBEST KVQWS
KKAJC VGMTO ZFAJG KODGF FGEHZ FJQVG KOWIH YSUVZ
```

These repetitions occur at the paired positions:

$$(0, 160), (34, 169), (61, 131), (99, 114), (140, 155), (174, 189)$$

This corresponds to differences of 160, 135, 70, 15, 15, and 15. We can factor these, giving us $160 = 2 \times 2 \times 2 \times 2 \times 2 \times 5$, $135 = 3 \times 3 \times 3 \times 5$, $70 = 2 \times 5 \times 7$, and $15 = 3 \times 5$.

The only common factor of all of them is 5. Furthermore, the sequence with difference 15 occurs many times (once with five-character repetition), and 70 occurs with a four-character repetition, giving us strong evidence that the key length is a common factor of these two numbers.

Now that we know how many different alphabets are used, we can split the ciphertext into many ciphertexts (one for each character in the key), and then perform frequency analysis and other techniques to break these ciphers. Note that each of these ciphertexts now represents a monoalphabetic substitution cipher.

1.5.3   Breaking Columnar Transposition Ciphers

Breaking the simple transposition ciphers is not incredibly difficult, as the **key space** is typically more limited than in polyalphabetic ciphers (the **key space** being the total possible number of distinct keys that can be chosen). For example, the key space here is limited by the size of the grid that the human operator can draw and fill in reliably.

The preferred method is performing digraph and trigraph analysis, particularly by hand.[1] A **digraph** is a pair of letters written together. Similarly, a **trigraph** is a set of three letters written together. All languages have certain letter pairs and triplets that appear more often than others. For example, in English, we know that characters such as *R, S, T, L, N,* and *E* appear often — especially since they appear on *Wheel of Fortune*'s final puzzle — thus it should come as no shock that letter pairs such as *ER* and *ES* appear often as well, whereas letter pairs such as *ZX* appear very infrequently. We can exploit this property of the underlying language to help us decrypt a message. Tables 1-5 and 1-6 show some of the most common digraphs and trigraphs for English (again, from Shakespeare) and Klingon, respectively.

---

[1]A computer program could easily try every value of the key and analyze each decrypted text to see if it makes sense in the language, for example, by dictionary lookups. This method would also work on any other small key space, such as monoalphabetic shift ciphers.

Table 1-5 Most Common Digraphs and Trigraphs in *The Complete Works of William Shakespeare*

DIGRAPH	PROBABILITY	TRIGRAPH	PROBABILITY
th	3.16%	the	1.45%
he	2.28%	and	0.87%
an	1.63%	you	0.58%
er	1.62%	her	0.53%
ou	1.47%	hat	0.50%
in	1.45%	tha	0.48%
ha	1.27%	ing	0.48%
es	1.27%	eth	0.41%
nd	1.24%	our	0.40%
st	1.24%	his	0.38%
re	1.24%	thi	0.37%
en	1.19%	for	0.35%
ea	1.14%	ere	0.34%
or	1.07%	ith	0.33%
at	1.02%	ent	0.32%
is	1.01%	oth	0.31%

How exactly do we exploit these language characteristics? This isn't terribly difficult, even without a computer. The trick is to write out two or more copies of the ciphertext *vertically*, so that each ciphertext strip looks like

```
A
K
:
:
```
.

We take out the two or more copies of this sheet we have made, and line them up side by side. We then use the **sliding window technique** — essentially moving the sheets of paper up and down with respect to each other. Then we measure how common the digraphs (and trigraphs with three letters, or 4-graphs with four letters, etc.) found in the resulting readout are. Next, we measure how far apart they are (in characters), and this length will be the number of *rows* (represented as r) in the matrix used to write the ciphertext. We then calculate the number of columns (based on dividing the ciphertext

Table 1-6 Most Common Digraphs and Trigraphs in Klingon, Taken from *Qo'noS QonoS* Sample

DIGRAPH	PROBABILITY	TRIGRAPH	PROBABILITY
ch	2.53%	tlh	1.44%
gh	2.27%	wI'	0.71%
u'	1.71%	atl	0.58%
a'	1.57%	be'	0.57%
tl	1.49%	mey	0.53%
lh	1.44%	cha	0.50%
e'	1.21%	'ej	0.50%
I'	1.15%	chu	0.49%
wI	1.14%	pu'	0.45%
ng	1.13%	ach	0.41%
aH	1.13%	'e'	0.41%
'e	1.02%	nga	0.38%
ej	0.99%	Daq	0.37%
me	0.91%	ogh	0.36%
Da	0.91%	vam	0.35%
ha	0.87%	taH	0.34%

size by the number of rows and rounding up), so that we have the original key (k, the number of columns).

To show this method, let's take the first transposition-cipher example ciphertext (from Section 1.4.1) and show how to break it using the sliding window technique. The ciphertext obtained from encrypting "all work and no play..." was

AKPKNL LALENL LNASYB WDYJAO ONMODY ROAHU

The sliding windows for this ciphertext are shown in Figure 1-3.

Examining the example in Figure 1-3 can reveal a great deal about the best choices. Looking at $r = 1$, we have letter pairs in the very beginning such as *KP* and *PK*. We can consult a table of digraphs and trigraphs to check to see how common certain pairs are, and note that these two letter pairs are very

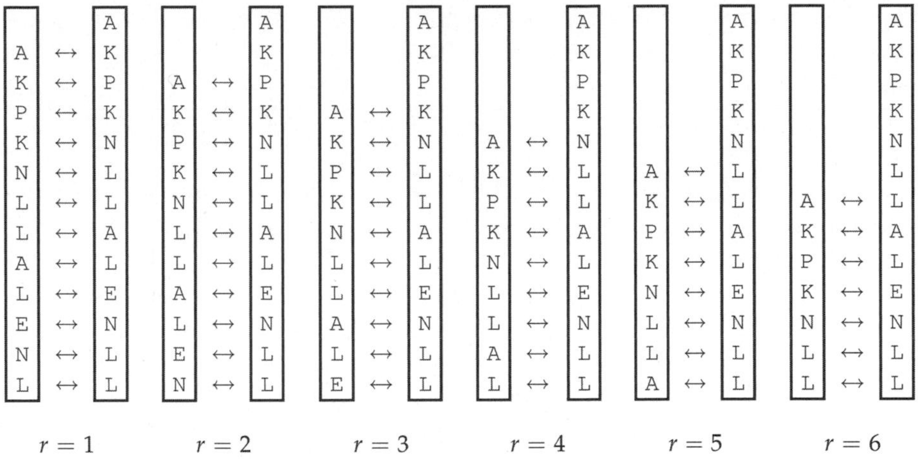

Figure 1-3 represents the sliding window technique for $r = 1, \ldots, 6$:

$r = 1$
```
      A
A ↔ K
K ↔ P
P ↔ K
K ↔ N
N ↔ L
L ↔ L
L ↔ A
A ↔ L
L ↔ E
E ↔ N
N ↔ L
L ↔ L
```

$r = 2$
```
      A
      K
A ↔ P
K ↔ K
P ↔ N
K ↔ L
N ↔ L
L ↔ A
L ↔ L
A ↔ E
L ↔ N
E ↔ L
N ↔ L
```

$r = 3$
```
      A
      K
      P
A ↔ K
K ↔ N
P ↔ L
K ↔ L
N ↔ A
L ↔ L
L ↔ E
A ↔ N
L ↔ L
E ↔ L
```

$r = 4$
```
      A
      K
      P
      K
A ↔ N
K ↔ L
P ↔ L
K ↔ A
N ↔ L
L ↔ E
L ↔ N
A ↔ L
L ↔ L
```

$r = 5$
```
      A
      K
      P
      K
      N
A ↔ L
K ↔ L
P ↔ A
K ↔ L
N ↔ E
L ↔ N
L ↔ L
A ↔ L
```

$r = 6$
```
      A
      K
      P
      K
      N
      L
A ↔ L
K ↔ A
P ↔ L
K ↔ E
N ↔ N
L ↔ L
L ↔ L
```

Figure 1-3 Sliding window technique example for $r = 1, \ldots, 6$.

infrequent. For $r = 2$, letter pairs such as *KK* and *PN* are also fairly uncommon. It would not be too difficult to create a simple measurement of, say, adding up the digraph probabilities with all of the pairs in these examples, and comparing them.

However, a word of caution is necessary — since we removed all of the spaces, there is no difference between letter pairs *inside* a word and letter pairs *between* words. Hence, the probabilities will not be perfect representations, and we cannot simply always go for the window with the highest probability sum.

It is also useful to note that digraphs and trigraphs can also be easily used for helping to break substitution ciphers. If we calculate the most common digraphs and trigraphs appearing in a ciphertext, then we can see if those correspond to common digraphs and trigraphs in the assumed source text.

1.5.4 Breaking Double Columnar Transposition Ciphers

Breaking double columnar transposition ciphers is still possible by hand, but a little more complex to work out visually, as we did with the sliding window technique for single columnar ciphers. The operations required are much more suited to computers, because of the large amount of bookkeeping of variables and probabilities.

The primary technique for breaking the double transposition ciphers is the same, in theory, as the sliding window technique: We want to simulate different numbers of columns and calculate the digraph, trigraph, and so on probabilities from these simulations. For double (or even higher-order) transposition ciphers, we simply have to keep track of which character winds up where.

It is best to examine these ciphers slightly more mathematically to understand what is going on. Let's assume that we have ciphertext length n, with k_1 being the number of columns in the first transposition and r_1 being the number of rows in the first transposition (and similarly, k_2 and r_2 for the second transposition).

In all cases, to our luck, the character in position 0 (computer scientists all start to count from 0) always stays in position 0. But after the first transposition, the character in position 1 ends up in position r_1. The character in position 2 ends up in position $2r_1$. Going further, the character in position $k_1 - 1$ ends up in position $(k_1 - 1)r_1$. The next position, k_1, falls under the next row, and therefore will end up in position 1. Then $k_1 + 1$ ends up in position $r_1 + 1$. In general, we might say that a ciphertext bit, say, $P[i]$, ends up in position $C_1[\lfloor i/k_1 \rfloor + (i \bmod k_1)r_1]$. Here, "mod" is simply the common modulus operator used in computer programming, that is, "$a \bmod b$" means to take the remainder when dividing a by b. The $\lfloor x \rfloor$ operation (the **floor** function) means to round down to the smallest integer less than x (throwing away any fractional part), for example, $\lfloor 1.5 \rfloor = 1$, $\lfloor -2.1 \rfloor = -3$, and $\lfloor 4 \rfloor = 4$.

Things start to get jumbled up a bit more for the next transposition. Just as before, the character in position 1 ends up in position r_2, but the character that starts up in position 1 is $C_1[1]$, which corresponds to $P[k_1]$.

We can draw this out further, but it's needlessly complex. Then we can simply write out the two formulas for the transformation, from above:

$$P[i] = C_1[\lfloor i/k_1 \rfloor + (i \bmod k_1)r_1]$$
$$C_1[i] = C_2[\lfloor i/k_2 \rfloor + (i \bmod k_2)r_2]$$

Now we have equations mapping the original plaintext character to the final ciphertext character, dependent on the two key values k_1 and k_2 (since we can derive the r-values from the k-values). In order to measure the digraph (and other n-graph) probabilities, we have to check, for each k_1 and k_2 guess, the digraph possibility for $P[i]$ and $P[i + 1]$ for as many values of i as we deem necessary.

For example, to check values $i = 0$ and $i = 1$ for, say, $k_1 = 5$ and $k_2 = 9$, we then run through the numbers on the previous double columnar transposition cipher used (the alphabet, thus $n = 26$). We know that $P[0] = C_1[0 + 0] = C_1[0] = C_2[0 + 0] = C_2[0] = $ A, just as it should be. We can then calculate $P[1] = C_1[0 + 1 \times r_1] = C_1[r_1] = C_2[\lfloor r_1/9 \rfloor + (r_1 \bmod 9) \times r_2]$. Knowing that $r_1 = \lceil 26/k_1 \rceil = \lceil 26/5 \rceil = 6$ and $r_2 = \lceil 26/k_2 \rceil = \lceil 26/9 \rceil = 3$, we have $P[1] = C_2[0 + 6 \cdot 3] = C_2[18] = $ B. Although performing digraph analysis would be useless on this ciphertext (since the plaintext is not from common words, but simply the alphabet), we could easily then calculate the digraph probability for this pair. Also, this pair ensures that the calculations came out correctly, since the alphabet was encrypted with those two keys in that order, and we know that the first two characters in the plaintext were ab.

1.6   Summary

In this chapter, we discussed many techniques used regularly throughout civilization until the start of the twentieth century. As can be seen from the demonstrated analysis, the encryption techniques are very weak from a modern standpoint, although easy to implement. However, the ideas behind these ciphers, including substitutions and transpositions, represent the core of modern ciphers, and we can learn a lot by studying the analyses of these now mostly defunct ciphers.

Furthermore, we looked at many of the simple cryptanalytic methods used to break apart these cryptographic schemes. Although modern ciphers are not this easy to break, analyzing these ciphers illustrates ideas that resonate throughout the rest of the book. Particularly, it is important to know that ciphers are not broken by accident — it takes a lot of work, patience, cleverness, and sometimes a bit of luck.

Exercises

Exercise 1. The following message is encrypted with a monoalphabetic cipher. Ignoring spaces and punctuation, decrypt the message.

WKH FDW LQ WKH KDW VWULNHV EDFN

Exercise 2. Write a program to find the most common digraphs in a Latin-based alphabet, ignoring everything except alphabetic characters.

Exercise 3. Write a program to find the most common trigraphs in a non-Latin-based language (say, using Unicode).

Exercise 4. Write a program to use a dictionary file (a listing of valid words in the appropriate language) to break single transposition ciphers. Your program should work by choosing the decryption with the highest number of dictionary words formed. Such dictionary files can either be compiled (by finding a large enough source of similar text to the kind being analyzed, and making a list of the words found in it), or by using a pre-constructed dictionary file.

Exercise 5. Implement Kasiski's method for breaking polyalphabetic ciphers. The first step should be producing a candidate list of numbers that could be the key length. Then, assuming that the underlying cipher is a Vigenère polyalphabetic cipher, attempt to break the ciphertext into multiple ciphertexts and perform a frequency analysis on each. The program should produce a reasonable guess to a certain selection of keys, as well as accompanying plaintexts. Use of a dictionary file is encouraged to increase the precision.

References

[1] Marc Okrand. *The Klingon Dictionary*. (Pocket Books, New York, 1992).

[2] Charles P. Pfleeger. *Security in Computing*, 2nd ed. (Prentice-Hall, Upper Saddle River, NJ, 2000).

[3] William Shakespeare. *The Complete Works of William Shakespeare*. (Project Gutenberg, 1994); `http://www.gutenberg.org`.

[4] Simon Singh. *The Code Book*. (Anchor, New York, 2000).

[5] Jeff Thompson. Monoalphabetic cryptanalysis. Phrack Magazine, **51** (September 1997); `www.phrack.org/issues.html?issue=51`.

# CHAPTER 2

Number Theoretical Ciphers

In recent years, many cryptographic algorithms have been based on mathematical structures designed to hide information: Information is very easy to obscure if you know the correct trick. This trick is knowing the scheme and a key of some sort, as is the case for the previously studied simple ciphers.

All ciphers are based on tricks: Those in Chapter 1 were more mechanical in nature. A person or computer can perform the encryption and decryption by using a table or a very simple algorithm, and translating the result. This chapter introduces cryptographic algorithms in which the encryption and decryption algorithms are very mathematical, using recent advances in number theory and algebra to make finding the information difficult.

This is not a mathematics book, but it is necessary to know a little bit about mathematics in order to understand some of these ciphers. Regardless, I do not want to drown you with math notation or obscure notions. This explanation is not exhaustive (or formal), but it should eliminate any reader confusion about the subject.

I am also torn between two desires: the desire to explain everything, but also the desire to not lose the reader in details and in lots of tedious mathematics. I will try to explain everything necessary in as simple terms as possible, but I will understand if you gloss over some of the mathematics and get straight to the juicy stuff. Just know that the math is there if you want or need to read it, although for more comprehensive looks into these topics, you will need to look elsewhere (such as in some of the books in the references).

2.1   Probability

This section constitutes a quick review of definitions and a few principles of probability, which most likely will be review or just plain common sense.

We normally define the **probability** of an occurrence as being the likelihood that it happens, on a scale of 0 to 1: 0 meaning that it never happens, and

1 meaning that it always happens. Furthermore, if we have some set of occurrences, say X, then the sum of the probabilities of each of the occurrences happening has to be 1, since something *must* happen. We can define situations to be more complex, where several things can happen at once, but it is best to consider a more basic set of occurrences and build more complicated events out of it. Because we want only one occurrence to happen at a time, we want each particular occurrent at this level to be mutually exclusive.

For example, if we flip a standard, two-sided coin, we have a set of two events that could happen, {heads, tails}. We denote the probability with a capital letter P. When we flip a **fair** (ideal) coin, we have an equal probability of either side facing up after flipping it, so that $P(\text{heads}) = 0.5$ and $P(\text{tails}) = 0.5$, and their sum is 1.

The fact that the probability has to be between 0 and 1 is also convenient, because we can calculate a negative probability as well. If we have a standard deck of 52 cards, then the probability of drawing the jack of diamonds is $1/52$. The probability of drawing anything but the jack of diamonds is therefore $1 - (1/52) = 51/52$.

2.1.1 Permutations and Choices

As we start calculating probabilities, it becomes necessary to have a clearer understanding of counting. Specifically, we need to remember a few basic ideas about counting arrangements and ways to choose objects.

Sometimes we will want to know the number of **permutations** of a given set of objects — the number of ways they can be written down in an order. For example, with two objects, say, the numbers 1 and 2, we can write them as (1 2) and (2 1), so there are two permutations. With three objects, say 1, 2, and 3, we can write them down in six different orders: (1 2 3), (1 3 2), (2 1 3), (2 3 1), (3 1 2), and (3 2 1). A clever thought would be that we started with 2, and when we added a third object, we get $6 = 3 \times 2$. If we want to know all of the permutations of four objects, we have to consider all of the cases above, with the fourth object being placed in at different places. This means that four can be placed at the beginning of all of the above:

$$(4\,1\,2\,3), (4\,1\,3\,2), (4\,2\,1\,3), (4\,2\,3\,1), (4\,3\,1\,2), (4\,3\,2\,1)$$

Or we can add the number 4 in between the first and second entries, as in

$$(1\,4\,2\,3), (1\,4\,3\,2), (2\,4\,1\,3), (2\,4\,3\,1), (3\,4\,1\,2), (3\,4\,2\,1)$$

as well as in between the second and third, and after the third. This is four different places, with each of them having six arrangements, for a total of 24 different arrangements. Note that $24 = 4 \times 3 \times 2 \times 1$.

For five items, we would then have five places to put the fifth object, and each would have 24 places to go, for a total of $24 \times 5 = 120$. The pattern continues on forever. These numbers $(2, 6, 24, 120, \ldots)$, obtained by multiplying successive numbers together, are results of the **factorial** function. The factorial of a number is usually denoted with an exclamation mark, as in $6! = 6 \times 5 \times 4 \times 3 \times 2 \times 1$. It should be obvious, but worth saying, that there is only one way to organize a set of one thing: it, by itself. Similarly, there is only one way to specify the arrangement of a set of nothing: with a set of nothing. Thus, by definition, $1! = 0! = 1$.

Another important concept is the idea of **permuted choices** — how many different ways there are of selecting two objects from a set of four objects, where order does not matter. For example, from the set of numbers 1, 2, 3, and 4, how many pairs can we pick? We can easily see that there are the following six pairs:

$$(1\ 2), (1\ 3), (1\ 4), (2\ 3), (2\ 4), (3\ 4)$$

where order doesn't matter, so $(1\ 2)$ is equivalent to $(2\ 1)$.

The number of such sets that are being picked can be calculated using a **binomial coefficient** — it is a function of two variables, n and k, where n is the number of objects in the larger set, and k is the size of the sets that are desired to be picked from the n objects, where order does not matter. In this book, we denote this binomial coefficient as $\binom{n}{k}$, although it can also be denoted as $C_{n,k}$ and $C(n, k)$ or even $_nC_k$. When read out loud, it is almost always pronounced, "n choose k." (I say "almost always" because most mathematicians and scientists frown upon saying "always" unless there is proof.)

The simple way to calculate these binomial numbers is to use the following formula, based on the concept of permutations and factorials above:

$$\binom{n}{k} = \frac{n!}{(n-k)!\, k!}$$

For example, say we have five cars to choose from, and we need to pick two. How many ways are there to pick two of them? In this case, we don't care about the order in which they are picked, just the number of ways to choose two items from five. Calculating "5 choose 2":

$$\binom{5}{2} = \frac{5!}{(5-2)!\, 2!} = \frac{5 \times 4 \times 3 \times 2 \times 1}{3 \times 2 \times 1 \times 2 \times 1} = 10$$

meaning we have 10 different pairs of cars that could be chosen.

2.1.2 Dependence

Probabilities can be more complicated, as mentioned above. For example, sometimes events are not so easily modeled as a set that adds up to 1. For example, say we are rolling a six-sided die, and we define a simple game: Alice scores if the number that comes up is even, and Bob scores if the number is prime (see Figure 2-1). Whoever scores wins, except if both or neither scores,

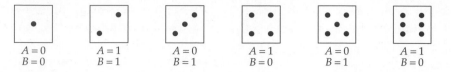

Figure 2-1 The Alice and Bob dice game. Here, $A = 1$ if Alice scores, and $B = 1$ if Bob scores.

in which case it is a draw. This means that in the sticky situation when we roll a 2, which is both even and prime, both score, and therefore it is a draw. In this case, if Alice scores, then that affects the probability of Bob scoring — Alice scores on a 2, 4, or 6, which means that Bob now has a 1/3 chance of scoring instead of the 1/2 chance he had before (since Bob scores on a 2, 3, or 5).

The preceding example can be broken into a normal set of occurrences of the die rolling a number in the set $\{1, 2, 3, 4, 5, 6\}$, and the above rules constituting subsets of this, so that the probabilities will again add up to 1. (For example, we would have the rolls $\{1, 2, 3, 4, 5, 6\}$ represent $\{D, D, B, A, B, A\}$, where D means draw, B means Bob wins, and A means Alice wins.) The particular situation we are analyzing might dictate one representation or another to use (such as if we are interested in who wins or who scores).

Measuring the probability of a draw, which in the above happens when a 2 is thrown on the die, is more complicated because the events are **dependent** — the outcome of one event happening affects the probability of another event happening. If events are **independent** of one another, then one happening will have no influence on the probabilities in another event. For instance, if we threw the die a second time, the second throw would have the same probabilities again, since they are not affected by the previous throw. However, if we threw four dice, calculating how many times a 6 was rolled, and rerolled any dice that did not roll a 6 a second time, then the outcome of the first roll will affect the second one — the throwing of the dice would then no longer be independent.

2.1.2.1   *Fun with Poker*[1]

Maybe a more concrete example or two might solidify a few of the above ideas — at least, more than the preceding, slightly abstract examples.

Poker is a game played with a standard 52-deck of playing cards (see Figure 2-2). There are four **suits** (shapes associated with particular cards), each having an equal number of 13 cards: (in increasing order of power) numbered cards 2 through 10, a Jack, a Queen, a King, and an Ace (which doubles as a virtual 1 as well).

---

[1] Another optional section. But hopefully a fun one.

Figure 2-2 Standard deck of 52 playing cards. Graphics licensed under LGPL [1].

A quick rundown of the basic rules: The goal of nearly every kind of poker is to obtain a hand of five cards. The makeup of these five cards determines your strength. If the particular poker game allows a player to have more than five cards, the player then will typically have to select the best five-card poker hand out of those cards. In the event of a tie — say, two players both have flushes — then the player with the highest card in the flush wins. If that is also tied, then the next card, and so forth. Similarly, if players both have a pair, then the higher pair wins (thus, a pair of Kings beats Queens, and a pair of Aces beats Kings). If both players have the same pair, then the one with the next highest card in his hand wins, and then the next highest (in the case of a tie), and so forth. The listing of five-card poker hands is shown in Table 2-1.

Texas Hold 'Em has been a particularly popular poker variant for quite a while, and a rather simple one to explain. We won't get into the betting structure, but some of the mechanics will be of interest. Also, in Texas Hold 'Em, no suit is better than any others, so there can be ties.

Every player (usually between 2 and 10 players) is dealt two cards, which only that player sees. Next, three **community cards** are placed in the middle (the **flop**). Then, a fourth additional card is placed in the middle as a community card (the **turn**). Finally, a fifth card is added to the community cards (the **river**).

Each player can use the community cards, as well as the cards in his or her hand, to make the best five-card hand possible. The player with the highest hand wins.

Texas Hold 'Em is an interesting game to analyze. It's *just* on the edge of computationally feasible to calculate exact probabilities for many of our scenarios.

A first question we might ask is, how many different seven-card combinations can there be? Well, in our case, since order doesn't matter, there are going to be 52 cards, and we want a set of 7 of them. This can be calculated with

$$\binom{52}{7} = \frac{52!}{45! \, 7!} = 133,784,560$$

Table 2-1 Ranking of Poker Hands

HAND	DESCRIPTION OF THE HAND	HAND	DESCRIPTION OF THE HAND
High Card	If you have nothing else in this list, the value of your highest card. The best this person has is the King.	Flush	All five cards are of the same suit. Ties broken on the highest card. The player has an "ace-high" flush.
Pair	A pair of the same value card. Here, the player has a pair of jacks.	Full House	Three of a kind and a separate pair. The three of a kind is used as the tiebreaker. Here is a full house, "8's over Jacks."
Two Pair	Two distinct pairs, same-valued cards. The player has two pairs: 10's and 7's.	Four of a Kind	Four cards of the same value. The player has four 2's.
Three of a Kind	Three cards of the same value. The player has "trip 9's."	Straight Flush	All cards are of the same suit and are sequential. This straight flush is the "Royal Flush."
Straight	All five card values are sequential. Aces play as below 2's or above Kings, but not both. The player has a "5-high" straight.		

Hands are arranged top to bottom in increasing order of strength.

Note this doesn't even take into account the fact that suits are built equally. Many of these hands will be repeats. How many? We'll leave this as an exercise to the reader.

As we'll see more of, later, solving cryptanalytic problems involves a lot of probability. Indeed, much of cryptanalysis is figuring out how the probabilities in one part of a cipher affect the probabilities of another part, then measuring actual outcomes to attempt to learn information about parts that we cannot see, such as the plaintext or the key. In many ways, this is not unlike analyzing some poker situations.

Let's analyze some poker scenarios. One thing someone usually wants to know is, what is the probability that a player will get a pair in his or her own private hand (not in community cards) to start out with? This is usually considered to be a good thing. To start out with, it doesn't matter who is sitting where, or how many players there are. Since the player we are concerned with can't see anyone else's cards, then there is no information to be had, so we can ignore the fact that other people are playing.

The first card is dealt to the player, and it can be any one of the 52 cards in play, so it won't affect the player. But, to get a pair, the second card has to be one of the only other three cards left in the deck of (now) 51 cards in order to pair with the first card dealt. Thus, our probability is

$$\frac{52 \times 3}{52 \times 51} = \frac{3}{51} = \frac{1}{17} \approx 5.88\%$$

This means that a player can expect to receive a pair dealt at the beginning about 1 out of every 17 hands, on average.

A situation people often see themselves in playing poker is what is called a **draw** — where a person needs certain cards in order to get a stronger hand, and there are still cards to be dealt.

For example, if a person has two cards of the same suit as his own personal cards (his "down" cards), it is easy to calculate that it is fairly improbable that the person will get a flush immediately on the flop. But what if two of the three cards dealt are the same as the player's down cards? What is the probability then that the player will obtain a flush?

The only information known to the player is the identities of the down cards and community cards. Knowing this, 4 of the 13 cards in the desired suit are already in play, and 1 additional card that is not, for a total of 5 cards in play. The player has two opportunities to get a card of the desired suit: the turn and the river cards, which will be picking cards from 47 and 46 cards, respectively.

But the probability isn't quite so simple. There's the possibility that both cards are of the suit, none are, or just the first or the second one is. Rather than try to add up the probabilities of each of these events occurring, we can take the probability that neither card is of the desired suit, and reverse it (by subtracting it from 1). In this case, we have 9 cards that we are avoiding out of 47, and therefore $47 - 9 = 38$ cards that are desired. We then have to try our luck again, and attempt to get none of those 9 out of the 46 left, so we have 37 to choose from. Since these happen in succession, we multiply

$$\frac{38}{47} \times \frac{37}{46} \approx 0.6503$$

This is the probability that we fail in our endeavor to get the flush. Therefore, the probability that we get it is the above subtracted from 1, which is about 0.3497, or 34.97%.

We won't venture further into poker probabilities here (although there is some more investigation in the exercises), but cryptanalysis is much like poker in some regards. In cryptanalysis, we often are trying to get a key, which can be like trying to figure out the other person's hand, or trying to figure out how to win the game. Nearly every technique in cryptanalysis is probabilistic and statistical: It works, statistically, some of the time, and the trick is figuring out how much of that time it does work, and adjusting the algorithms appropriately.

2.1.3   The Birthday Paradox

The **birthday paradox** is an important concept in cryptanalysis. This "paradox" shows that the probabilities aren't always what they first seem.

The traditional telling of the paradox is to ask someone, "How likely is it that two people have the same birthday?" Here, we are interested in the probability of a **collision** occurring, where two events have the same result. In theory, the correct answer is not too difficult to figure out — $1/365 \approx$ 0.274% (not including leap years, or taking into account any other factors that will skew this number in real life). The two events are **independent** — the first person's birthday doesn't influence the birthday of the second person. Assuming uniform distribution of birthdays, then the first person's birthday will be a random day. This means that we can just assume that the first person's birthday is fixed: It won't be changing. We take the second person's birthday as being random as well. The probability that it is going to happen to coincide with the first person's birthday is the same probability that it would happen to be any other day as well, since they are all equally probable: $1/365$.

But what happens if you ask the question, "What is the probability that at least two people out of three have the same birthday?" This is where things start to get a bit messier. If we are just concerned with collisions in general (not caring which particular pair of people shares a birthday, as long as one pair does), then we now have three different pairs to consider: 1–2, 2–3, and 1–3. Any of these pairs might share a birthday.

What is now the probability that a collision occurs in these three pairs? We might also naively answer, "Just add the probabilities of one collision together three times!" This does seem logical at first, but this does not scale well. We have to start considering cases such as if there were, say, 400 people. This would mean $\binom{400}{2} = 79{,}800$ different pairs, and therefore a $79{,}800 \times (1/365) = 218.63\%$ probability, which is ludicrous. Hence, this is definitely not the right way.

This is because, once you add a third person, you aren't just adding one more day to check; you are adding two possible days, since the third person could match the first or the second. Therefore, adding a second day significantly increases the probability that a collision occurs. However, eventually this will slow down to the point where adding an additional person is unlikely to greatly affect the probability. For example, if you have a group of 363 people and another group of 364 people, there is nearly no difference in the two groups' possibility of having a repeat birthday.

To model these situations, it's often convenient to look at the situation in reverse; that is, rather than trying to ascertain the probability that, say, of n people, there is at least one birthday collision, let's look at the probability that there are *no* birthday collisions with n people.

In this case, we are going to assume that a person's birthday has a completely even chance of occurring on any given day out of 365. We will generalize this to be any of n particular objects we might pick, so that this is not specific to birthdays — it could be anything that someone has a finite number of choices for, such as cryptographic keys. For birthdays, we just note that $n = 365$.

To reiterate, in this case we are interested in the probability of no repetition. For the first object, we will just pick any object (in our birthday example, this is a day of the year), as we are guaranteed to have no repetitions; thus, we can consider the probability of no repetition to be n choices out of n total choices, which is 1. The second choice we make is slightly dependent on the first one. Since we picked one of the objects (or birthdays in this case), we have $n - 1$ choices left in order for there to be no repetition, for which we have a probability of $(n - 1)/n$. If we have a third person, then we have a probability of $(n - 2)/n$, since we now have two birthdays that would cause a collision if chosen.

If we extrapolate this out to, say, k people, then this would be

$$\frac{n - (k - 1)}{n} = \frac{n - k + 1}{n}$$

Now, for every birthday we add on, we want there to be no repetitions. Thus, we start with one birthday, add another (and calculate the probability), add another (and calculate the probability), and so on. In order to calculate the likelihood of all of these events occurring in sequence, we *multiply* the probabilities together, since we need the first one to happen, and then the second, and then the third, and so forth.

To look at it more simply, take fair coin tosses again. If we want to know the probability that we get heads three times in a row, we take the probability that we have heads after the first throw (0.5); since we are already in this situation with this probability, then the probability of both events happening is the probability of the first times the probability of the second. Therefore, we multiply the first outcome by the probability that we have heads the second time ($0.5 \times 0.5 = 0.25$), and then multiply that by the probability that we have heads the third time ($0.25 \times 0.5 = 0.125$). Each successive event always leads to a multiplication of the previous probability with the next.

For our probabilities in the birthday paradox above, we then have a probability of

$$\frac{(n)(n-1)(n-2)\cdots(n-k+1)}{n^k}$$

Note that the leftmost n in the numerator cancels out one of the n's in the denominator. We can then pair each number in the numerator with an n in the denominator, such as $(n-1)/n$, which can be rewritten as $1 - (1/n)$, with $(n-2)/n = 1 - (2/n)$, and so forth, to rewrite the product as

$$\left(1 - \frac{1}{n}\right)\left(1 - \frac{2}{n}\right)\cdots\left(1 - \frac{k-1}{n}\right)$$

Here we have to use some calculus trickery to get this in a form more easily manipulatable. The concept of Taylor polynomials allows us to use the approximation that

$$e^{-1/n} \approx 1 - \frac{1}{n}$$

This approximation holds true when $1/n$ is very small, and therefore when when n is large. (Note that e is the Euler constant, approximately equal to 2.71828.) For birthdays, $n = 365$ is perfectly sufficient for the approximation to hold. The reader can easily verify this voodoo math by verifying in a calculator that $1 - (1/365) \approx 0.9972603$ and $e^{-1/365} \approx 0.9972640$, which are pretty close.

We now have the previous quantity rewritten, approximately, as

$$e^{-1/n}e^{-2/n}\cdots e^{-(k-1)/n}$$

Combining the exponents by adding them yields

$$e^{[-1-2-3-\cdots-(k-1)]/n}$$

This might remind us of the familiar identity that $1 + 2 + 3 + \cdots + n = n(n+1)/2$, allowing us the further simplification

$$e^{-k(k-1)/(2n)}$$

Now this is something we can use. Specifically, we will want to know the value of k, relative to n, for us to have a certain probability of no repetition (and, therefore, the probability of at least one repetition). It's easy to know when there is a 100% chance: Just let $k = n$ (for birthdays, pick 365 people, and there will be a repetition). Something more useful to know would be the tipping point: When will the probability be about half (0.5)? In this case, the probability of no repetition is the same as the probability of at least one repetition (since $1 - 0.5 = 0.5$), thus we can just set the previous approximation for our probability equal to 0.5 and solve for k in terms of n:

$$1/2 = e^{-k(k-1)/(2n)}$$

If we take the natural logarithm of both sides, we get

$$\ln(1/2) = \frac{-k(k-1)}{2n}$$

Since $\ln(1/x) = -\ln x$, because of the rules of exponents, we have

$$\ln 2 = \frac{k(k-1)}{2n}$$

And multiplying both sides by $2n$:

$$k(k-1) = n(2\ln 2)$$

We can solve this for k exactly (using the quadratic formula from college algebra), but the results look a little inelegant. Since we already have made one approximation, there's not too much harm in making another one, especially if it simplifies our final result. In this particular case, we are already assuming that n is large. We can kind of gauge then that k is going to be a bit large too, but not quite as much so as n. But if k is still pretty large, then $k \approx k - 1$, so that $k(k-1) \approx k^2$. For example, if k were about 100, then there would be very little difference between $100(100 - 1) = 9,900$ and $100^2 = 10,000$: The difference is only 1%.

This allows us to write the preceding statement as

$$k^2 = n(2\ln 2)$$

Taking the positive square root of both sides (since a negative k would not make sense):

$$k = \sqrt{n(2\ln 2)}$$

We can take the $\sqrt{2\ln 2} \approx 1.1774$ outside, and substitute its approximation:

$$k \approx 1.1774\sqrt{n}$$

This is pretty significant. It means that if we have n possibilities, we need only to look at a constant times the square root of that number of events in order to have about a 50% chance of having a repetition. For birthdays (with $n = 365$), this means that $k \approx 22.494$. Rounding up to get a better than half chance, we get $k = 23$. That is, if you have a roomful of at least 23 people, then you have a pretty decent chance that there is at least one repeated birthday. (This often works well when attempting to demonstrate the birthday paradox principle to the said roomful of people.) Figure 2-3 shows a plot of the birthday paradox probabilities, giving a good idea of how the probabilities increase with more samples (in our case, people's birthdays).

We can use the birthday paradox as a tool to use against certain cryptographic algorithms. For example, we may be concerned with finding two particular plaintexts that result in some certain bit pattern in some (or all) of the ciphertext. If this is a bit pattern of n bits, we would normally have to acquire 2^n plaintexts and ciphertexts in order to guarantee having the same ciphertext pattern twice. However, the birthday paradox tells us that, if we store each of the pairs, we only have to look at about $\sqrt{2^n} = 2^{n/2}$ ciphertexts to expect to find the pattern twice. (We normally ignore the multiplicative constant in these cases.)

The next section expands one this idea for a certain class of algorithms.

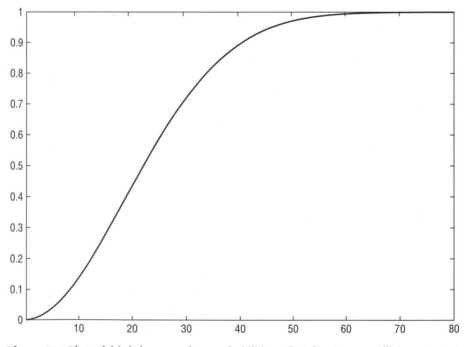

Figure 2-3 Plot of birthday paradox probabilities of at least one collision at up to 80 people. The function increases very rapidly after the first few samples are taken, and hit above 50% at about the 23rd person.

2.1.4   Cryptographic Hashes

Let's discuss a very basic side effect that the birthday paradox has on hashing algorithms, such as MD5 and SHA-1 [7, 8].

For starters, a **hashing algorithm** takes as input a (usually large) stream of data and produces a **digest** (also called a **checksum**), which is some unique characteristic of that data. For example, the string `all work and no play`, when transmitted using standard ASCII encoding of Latin characters, results in the transmitted bytes (in hexadecimal):

```
61 6c 6c 20 77 6f 72 6b 20 61 6e 64 20 6e 6f 20 70 6c 61 79
```

We can calculate a simple checksum of this data by performing normal integer addition of each byte together, and taking only the least significant byte as the result (the last 8 bits). In the previous bytes, this checksum would be `42`.

What does this give us? Well, it's a condensed representation of some parts of the image, with the hope that any other random message would have a different checksum. This way, if one person receiving a message knew to look for a certain checksum, and only accept messages with that checksum, then the communicating parties would have a little more confidence in their communications.

But what if an intruder wanted to break through this confidence and send a false message? How difficult is that? Just using random messages, then we can use the birthday paradox to look at the problem statistically. A random message is going to have a (hopefully) random checksum. Ignoring any possible patterns to be found or other clever ways to circumvent this problem, we want to know how many of these we need to calculate to have a match for a message.

Since this hash is 8 bits long, for a total of 256 values, then the birthday paradox says that if we have

$$1.1774\sqrt{256} = 18.8384$$

or about 19 hashes, then we have a better than half chance of having a repeated hash of the random messages. Unfortunately, this doesn't give us any particular value — it will be random. However, sometimes the goal is merely to demonstrate the weakness of the algorithm by finding random messages that have the same hash — this is called a **collision attack**.

Getting messages that hash to a *particular* value is, in general, a bit harder. This is the goal if we wanted to spoof the preceding message, but knowing only its hash value (this is called a **preimage attack**). A clever reader should be able to figure out how to spoof a message that has the same checksum as before.

Owing to the insecurity of this simple hash algorithm, it is not used for secure communications, although similar additive checksums are used to check the message for errors in transmission, since a message that has been corrupted will, we hope, have a different checksum. For hash algorithms with a little more robustness, we need to turn to MD5 and SHA-1, two of the leading **cryptographic hash algorithms**, with digest sizes of 128 bits and 160 bits, respectively. A **cryptographic hash algorithm** is one that is not based on a simple trick, but tries to obfuscate all of the information so that the outputted digest is as random as possible, with no possible way to figure out much of anything in the original message. It is their goal to be true **one-way** hashes, where it is impossible to extract any information about the original input from the hash's output.

For example, MD5 (see Section 4.12.3), which is the fifth in a series of message digest algorithms created by Ronald Rivest, works on messages represented as bits, of arbitrarily large (and small) length. It then does some pre-processing, and finally, on each 512-bit block, it churns through 64 operations to make it as much of an unrecognizable mush as possible, including using the output of the previous operation of 512 bits. SHA-1 works in a similar fashion (see Section 4.12.4).

Both hashes take a lot longer than our previous additive sum. However, the confidence in both algorithms is also incredibly higher, since both are still used to protect value information. Cryptographic sums are often powerful enough to be combined with some of the forms of cryptography (covered below in this chapter), to provide assurances of the authenticity and integrity of the message without having the message itself encrypted, providing a form of digital signature. (This is because doing mathematical operations on a very large input text can be cumbersome, but the hashes are a small, fixed size.)

2.2   Number Theory Refresher Course

We have now covered some basic knowledge of probability. Fortunately, we need to know a bit more math to understand a lot of cryptanalysis, so we get the pleasure of a run-through of number theory, and later algebra, as well.

The foundation of many modern cryptographic algorithms lies in **number theory** — the mathematical study of integers, especially relating to topics in divisibility (such as prime numbers). Cryptanalysts definitely need a working knowledge of these topics in order to properly understand the workings of many cryptographic algorithms (such as RSA) and cryptanalytic methods (such as factoring algorithms, like Pollard's Rho).

Before we dive in too deeply, let's go through a few quick definitions. The basic classes of numbers that we are concerned with are integers, rational numbers, real numbers, and complex numbers. **Integers** ($\mathbb{Z}$) are the class of numbers that we could theoretically count to, as well as zero and the negative of these counting numbers: $\{\ldots, -3, -2, -1, 0, 1, 2, 3, \ldots\}$. These are positive and negative numbers with no fractional part, including zero. **Rational numbers** ($\mathbb{Q}$), or just **rationals**, are the class of numbers that can be represented in the form p/q, where p and q are both in $\mathbb{Z}$, as with $1/2$ or $2/3$. Note that if $q = 1$, then the rational number is also an integer, thus all integers are rational. **Real numbers** ($\mathfrak{R}$), or just the **reals**, include the integers and the rationals, as well as any other numbers that can be numerically compared (less than, greater than) with integers and rationals, but that may not have rational form, or even a finite representation. This includes numbers such as π, $\sqrt{3}$ that, if written out, would take an infinite number of digits to express their exact value. The real numbers that are not rational are called, logically, **irrational**. However, the reals do not include numbers that have a component with a square root of a negative number: These numbers cannot be compared with, say, the integer 2, to say which one is "greater," for example. The class of numbers that do include these are the **complex numbers** ($\mathbb{C}$), which all have the form $a + bi$, where a and b are in $\mathfrak{R}$, and $i = \sqrt{-1}$.

2.2.1 Divisibility and Prime Numbers

We'll assume everyone understands what it means for an integer (say, c) to be **divisible** by another non-zero integer (say, a). The definition we will use is that if c is **divisible** by a, then there exists another integer (say, b) such that $c = a \times b$. Hence, there is no remainder when c is divided by b or when c is divided by a. Although I will try to avoid confusing notation, mathematicians often denote the fact that a divides into c with no remainder by writing $a \mid c$, or "a divides c."

Now for a few properties of divisibility: It should come as no shock that division is transitive — that is, if a divides c and c divides another number (say, e), then a divides e. This can be easily shown by noting that $c = a \times b$. And by our previous definition of divisibility, there must be a number d such that $e = c \times d$. Then, by simple substitution, $e = a \times b \times d$, which shows that a will divide into e.

Another concept that is important is the **greatest common divisor** (GCD) of two numbers, a and b, often written as a math function $\gcd(a, b)$. This number is defined to be the largest positive integer that divides both a and b. In the special case that the GCD of two numbers is 1, then these two numbers are called **relatively prime**. If a number shares no common divisors with any numbers less than it, other than 1, then that number is defined to be **prime**.

2.2.2 Congruences

An important aspect of computers, which we will ultimately use to implement any cryptographic or cryptanalytic algorithm, is that they are **finite**; they do not contain unlimited memory, so we can't operate on *all* of the integers, but smaller sets of them. We need to have some mathematics that understands this restriction. Luckily, the theory of congruences allows us to perform operations on subsets of the integers. In fact, many of the modern crypto-algorithms actually rely on certain properties of congruences in order to perform their magic.

The basic definition of a **congruence** (although it is actually three definitions) is that if we have three integers, a, b, and m, then we say that a is **congruent** to b, **modulo** m, if m divides $(a - b)$. This is written in the more compact form, $a \equiv b \pmod{m}$. We also refer to m as the **modulus**.

An important corollary to the definition is that, if $a \equiv b \pmod{m}$, then we know that m divides $(a - b)$, and therefore we know that there is some integer k such that $mk = a - b$, or $a = b + km$.

As a quick, historical example, computers before the year 2000 had a problem: They would store only the last two digits of the year, since it was assumed that all dates were in the 1900s. This was known as the Y2K problem. Since we consider only two digits, this is the same as considering all numbers modulo 100 (since, if we take any number's remainder when divided by 100, we would be left with the last two decimal digits). The problem then arose that $2000 \equiv 1900 \equiv 0 \pmod{100}$. This caused some computer programs to have erratic behavior, such as suddenly transition from the year 1999 to 1900, with unpredictable results.

A similar problem might occur again in 2038. It turns out that the POSIX standard section 4.14 and standard header file `<sys/time.h>`'s `time_t` construct [4] use the original time definition from the first edition of UNIX [12], which measures time as a signed 32-bit integer containing the number of seconds since 1 January 1970. This gives us a total of 2,147,483,647 seconds to work with, so that we are working modulo 2,147,483,648. When we divide this by 60 seconds per minute, 60 minutes per hour, 24 hours per day, and 365.25 days per year,[2] the result is a little more than 68 years from 1970, or sometime in 2038, before the congruence between 0 and 2,147,483,648 kicks us back to 1970.

It also turns out that numbers that are congruent with a certain modulus can be used interchangeably for many mathematical operations also in that modulus. These operations include addition, subtraction, and multiplication, but *not* division. These three operations work exactly like they do with normal numbers: Addition is still addition, and $5 + 5$ is still going to be 10 modulo 20, but it will be congruent to an infinite number of other integers in the modulus, including 30, 50, and even -10.

---

[2]Technically, there are about 365.26 days per year, not counting leap seconds. This is because we normally skip leap years every 100 years, except when we don't every 400 years. However, since we aren't skipping leap years for the next 93 years, we can just ignore this. Also, the POSIX time standard doesn't include leap seconds.

For example, in modulo 10, 12 and 2 are congruent to each other. If we performed, say, $2 + 2 \bmod 10$, we know that the answer is congruent to 4 modulo 10. And if we compute $12 + 12$ modulo 10, we know that we will get 24, which is congruent to 4 as well. Subtraction and multiplication work similarly.

But division is not so straightforward. For example, let's take modulo 10 again. Computing $20 \div 5 = 4$, if division worked as we expect it to, we should be able to replace 20 with 0 and then divide by 10, since $20 \equiv 0 \pmod{10}$. However, in that case, we get 0, which is not congruent to 4.

A little more terminology: A set of numbers that are all congruent to each other in a particular modulus are often grouped together in a set called its **congruence class** or **residue class**. As such, any particular number is referred to as a **residue**.

Furthermore, if we have a **complete set of residues** (CSR), then every integer will be congruent to *exactly* one residue in the set. This can work as a basis to do any arithmetic for the modulus. All operations can be computed for the elements of the CSR, and the results written also as elements of the CSR. For example, a complete set of residues for modulo 10 is

$$\{1, 2, 3, 4, 5, 6, 7, 8, 9, 10\}$$

which we will often use as our standard CSR. However, another complete set is

$$\{0, 1, 2, 3, 4, 5, 6, 7, 8, 9\}$$

or even

$$\{101, 102, 103, 104, 105, 106, 107, 108, 109, 110\}$$

There is another important set of residues we need to discuss: a **reduced set of residues** (RSR). With a CSR, we have every integer congruent to exactly one element of the CSR. With an RSR, however, we only care about numbers that are relatively prime to the modulus. A set of numbers that has the property that every integer relatively prime to the modulus is congruent to exactly one of the numbers in the set is an RSR.

For example, say we have a CSR of 10 again, $\{1, 2, 3, 4, 5, 6, 7, 8, 9, 10\}$. We calculate the RSR by going through each item in the list and deleting every number that is *not* relatively prime to 10. Since $10 = 2 \times 5$, then we have 2, 5, and 10 taken out, as well any multiples (which then eliminates 4, 6, and 8, since they are multiples of 2), giving us an RSR of

$$\{1, 3, 7, 9\}$$

There are many such RSRs. For example, if we multiply each number in an RSR by, say, a (with the condition that a is relatively prime to m, so that they share no divisors), then the new numbers will also form an RSR. This is because each number, which was already relatively prime to m, was multiplied by a number that is relatively prime to m and hence will continue to be relatively prime (since the numbers won't grow new prime factors).

We now have another important definition based on the RSR. The **Euler totient** (or just the **totient**) of a number is the size of the RSR of the set of all integers less than it. In the previous example, we calculated the Euler totient of 10. We typically write the totient of an integer n as $\phi(n)$. The previous example tells us that $\phi(10) = 4$.

Another equivalent definition of the Euler totient of n is the number of positive integers less than n that are relatively prime to n.

An important property of totients is called **Euler's totient theorem** (since Euler had many theorems). It states that if $m > 1$, and a and m are relatively prime, then $a^{\phi(m)} \equiv 1 \pmod{m}$.

To show how this is true, let's take a reduced set of residues, $\{r_1, r_2, \ldots, r_{\phi(m)}\}$ (since the totient is involved with how many numbers are in this set). Then we also know that $\{ar_1, ar_2, \ldots, ar_{\phi(m)}\}$ is a reduced set of residues (if the GCD of a and m is 1). Furthermore, we also know that for any number in the first set, there will be exactly one number in the second set that is congruent to the first (since any two sets of reduced sets of residues are equivalent modulo m), since every number that is relatively prime to m must be congruent to exactly one number in each set.

Now consider the number $a^{\phi(m)} \times r_1 \times r_2 \times \cdots \times r_{\phi(m)}$. There is exactly one copy of a for each of the r's, thus we can write this as

$$(a \times r_1) \times (a \times r_2) \times \cdots \times (a \times r_{\phi(m)})$$

We also know that any set of RSRs is congruent modulo m, element by element, to any other set. This means that we can replace the previous expression, so that our original number can be written

$$a^{\phi(m)} \times r_1 \times r_2 \times \cdots \times r_{\phi(m)} \equiv r_1 \times r_2 \times \cdots \times r_{\phi(m)} \pmod{m}$$

We also know that each r is relatively prime to m, meaning that we can divide by them, obtaining

$$a^{\phi(m)} \equiv 1 \pmod{m}$$

This is exactly the result we wanted.

We have three corollaries to this statement. Specifically, since

$$a^{\phi(m)} \equiv 1 \pmod{m}$$

we have to multiply both sides by a to obtain

$$a^{\phi(m)+1} \equiv a \pmod{m}$$

Also, we can split off one of the a's from the former, to get

$$a^{\phi(m)-1} \times a \equiv 1 \pmod{m}$$

We can therefore see that $a^{\phi(m)-1}$ is the inverse of a (modulo m).

The other corollary might take a slight bit more convincing. If we have $x \equiv y \pmod{\phi(m)}$, then $g^x \equiv g^y \pmod{m}$. Why? We know that, from the definition of a congruence, $x = y + k\,\phi(m)$. We can just rewrite g^x to get

$$g^x = g^{y+k\,\phi(m)} = g^y \left(g^{\phi(m)}\right)^k \equiv g^y \pmod{m}$$

since $g^{\phi(m)} \equiv 1 \pmod{m}$.

After we get through a bit more algebra, we will see how we can use the Euler totient theorem and its corollaries for cryptography.

2.3 Algebra Refresher Course

"Algebra? Why study algebra in a book about cryptanalysis? Let's just break some codes already!" the reader might exclaim. And a very valid set of concerns this is.

In the preceding section, we did a quick refresher on number theory and probability, and it seems natural to express most of the operations in cryptography and cryptanalysis based on them. After all, we know how to do arithmetic and other operations on numbers, and computers are constructed for working well with integers represented in binary.

It turns out, however, that many important mathematical properties of cryptography and cryptanalysis are based on algebraic concepts. Furthermore, many modern cryptographic algorithms are based on algebraic constructs, such as elliptic curves, that are not easy to manipulate using normal kinds of mathematical operations. Even understanding some of these algorithms requires at least some knowledge of algebra, and attempting to break them even more so! Furthermore, many algebraic techniques can be used to break cryptographic algorithms based on numbers too. Hence, familiarity with algebra is important to cryptanalysis.

Again, however, this is not a math textbook; if the reader wishes to understand the subject of algebra more deeply, then he or she should consult a more thorough source than this. Here, we provide a crash course in algebra to help *refresh* your knowledge, or at least provide enough of an understanding that you can attempt to understand the methods of cryptography presented in this chapter.

2.3.1 Definitions

The study of collections of objects and operations on those objects is called **algebra**. In algebra, these **operations** are constructs that take as input two objects and return an object, usually (but not always) with all three objects belonging to the collection with which we are concerned. These operations are examples of **functions**, which formally means that there has to be an output for every possible input, and there can be only one output for every input (so you can't run the function twice with the same input and get different outputs). For example, a simple function from the integers to the integers is $f(x) = x^2$, so that $f(1) = 1$, $f(2) = 4$, $f(3) = 9$, and so forth. Note that every integer has a square, and that you can't square the same integer twice and get different results, therefore this is definitely a function.

In general, we often denote these collections of objects, or **sets**, that we are operating on with capital letters, such as A, F, or G, with the operations being symbols such as $\circ$, $+$, or $\times$, although this is merely convention. A set is normally written with curly braces around the objects contained in it. For example, $A = \{0, 1, 2\}$ is a set containing three objects: the numbers 0, 1, and 2. The objects need not be numbers: $B = \{\text{cat, dog, 18, } \oplus\}$ is a set containing much more arbitrary objects, but it is still a set.

We also often want more compact and unambiguous ways of writing operations so that everyone is on the same page. We write an operation often as

$$\circ : A \times B \to C$$

to mean that the operation $\circ$ acts on pairs of objects, one from A and one from B, and will *act* on them somehow to return a result from the set C. In a shorter hand, this can also be written as $a \circ b = c$, where a is an element of A, b is from B, and c is from C.

These operations can be very diverse. For example, say we have a set of people ($P = \{\text{Tom, Sara}\}$), a set of chairs ($C = \{\text{Stool, Recliner}\}$), and a set of emotions ($E = \{\text{Happy, Sad}\}$). We will use the symbol $\oplus$ for the operations. We could have the operation define a relationship between the objects, such as the fact that a person from P has an emotion from E toward an object in C, defined abstractly as $\oplus : P \times C \to E$. We can define the fact that Mary is Happy to sit in the Recliner, by stating that Mary $\oplus$ Recliner $=$ Happy.

If this seems too elementary, then don't worry — things will get complicated soon enough.

As a special case, if we have that operation consist of operations on two objects from the same set, and churning out an element of that same set (so that $\circ : A \times A \to A$, for example), then we are getting somewhere. We want a few properties to be satisfied for these operations to be useful. First, we want to have an **identity** element (say, e) — where any operation involving, say, a and the identity element gives us back a. For example, if we had addition as the operation, then $a + e = a$, and for addition we have the identity 0, as 0 plus anything is that anything. For multiplication, the identity is 1.

We want two more properties: **inverse elements** and **associativity**. For every element, we want to have an opposite, or **inverse**, element so that when the two are operated on together, the result is e, the identity. With integer addition, 3 and −3 are inverses. Integers with multiplication don't have this property — for example, there is no inverse of $1/2$.

Associativity is merely the property that, given three elements (say, a, b, c), we have the equality

$$(a + b) + c = a + (b + c)$$

meaning that it doesn't matter in which order we perform two simultaneous operations. Addition and multiplication of integers both satisfy this property. Subtraction and division do not, though, since $(1 - 2) - 3 = -1 - 3 = -4$ and $1 - (2 - 3) = 1 + 1 = 2$, which are clearly not equal.

If we have a set with an operation with all three properties, then they are both collectively called a **group**, and would be written as a pair, $(A, \circ)$ or $(\mathbb{Z} + 1)$. If we have an operation on a group $(A, \circ)$, and any two elements from A (say, a and b) satisfy $a + b = b + a$, then it is called a **commutative group**, or an **abelian group**.

There is just one more consideration to make for an operation to be valid. The operation needs to be **well-defined**; we cannot have a valid group of $(\mathbb{Z}, \div)$, since $1 \div 2 = 0.5$, which is not an integer, and therefore does not qualify as a valid operation on the integers.

Two more definitions: If we have two operations, like addition and multiplication together, then we have some other structures. A **ring** is where we have two operations on a set, say $(A, +, \times)$. In the ring, $(A, +)$ must form an abelian group, while the second operation (usually multiplication) has, at least, the property of associativity, although it need not have an identity or inverses for any elements. For the integers, we can have a ring $(\mathbb{Z}, +, \times)$, since the addition property is abelian, but we don't have as strict rules on $\times$.

Finally, if we have a ring $(A, +, \times)$, and furthermore have every element of A (except the additive identity, usually 0) form an abelian group under $\times$, then this ring is a **field**. This means that we do have to have an identity and multiplicative inverses; therefore $(\mathbb{Z}, +, \times)$ is *not* a field. However, $(\mathbb{Q}, +, \times)$ *is* a field, since every element (except 0) will have an inverse.

A particularly interesting kind of field to cryptologists is the **finite field**, where the underlying set has a finite number of elements. We could, of course, have counterintuitive definitions, such as to define a new finite field, say, $(A, \oplus, \odot)$, and $A = \{\pi, e\}$. We can then define the rules as being

$$\pi + e = e$$
$$\pi + \pi = \pi$$
$$e + e = \pi$$
$$\pi \odot \pi = 0$$
$$\pi \odot e = \pi$$
$$e \odot e = e$$

Here, essentially, π is the additive identity (like 0), and e is the multiplicative identity (like 1).

Normally, however, we usually have a set of integers to work on, like $\{0, 1, \ldots, n-1\}$, with normal integer addition and multiplication, but modulo n to reduce everything back to the finite field.

However, not every value of n works very well, at least with normal addition and multiplication (taken modulo n). If we have the set $\{0, 1, 2, 3, 4, 5\}$ (often abbreviated as $\mathbb{Z}_6$), then it is difficult to find multiplicative inverses of every number. Only when the number n is prime do we find nice, easy-to-work-with numbers. We can also work with $n = p^m$, where p is a prime and m is a positive integer, but the math gets a little ugly and complicated in explaining how it works, so we won't go into it here.

As a short example of finite fields, we can check to see if $(\mathbb{Z}_7, +, \times)$ satisfies the desired properties. Since normal addition and multiplication modulo 7 will work as expected, then the only thing to check is to make sure that we have multiplicative inverses for everything but 0. It should be easy to verify that

$$1 \times 1 \equiv 1 \ (\mathrm{mod}\ 7)$$
$$2 \times 4 \equiv 1 \ (\mathrm{mod}\ 7)$$
$$3 \times 5 \equiv 1 \ (\mathrm{mod}\ 7)$$

Therefore, all of the elements, except for 0, have multiplicative inverses, thus we indeed have a finite field.

Finite fields are also called **Galois fields**, and the primary integer Galois fields are often abbreviated as $GF(n) = (\{0, 1, \ldots, n-1\{, +, \times)$, where n is an integer.

2.3.2 Finite Field Inverses

We have glossed over one last detail: how to calculate the multiplicative inverse in a finite field, say, $(\mathbb{Z}_p, +, \times)$? It turns out that there is a simple algorithm for calculating this — the **Euclidean algorithm**. This algorithm wasn't made to solve for these numbers, as Euclid lived long before finite fields were conceived, but is instead an algorithm to compute the greatest common divisor of two integers. In our case, we will use the Euclidean algorithm to calculate the GCD of p and the number we wish to find the inverse of, say a. We should note that the GCD should be 1, since p is supposedly prime.

Let's define our goal a little more clearly before we get into the nitty gritty algorithm itself. The multiplicative inverse of a will be some number a^{-1} such that

$$a \times a^{-1} \equiv 1 \ (\mathrm{mod}\ p)$$

Or, if we rewrite this in terms of normal integer operations, using the previous definition of equivalence,

$$a \times a^{-1} = 1 + kp$$

where k is some other integer.

The Euclidean algorithm works by simply dividing numbers over and over, keeping track of the remainder each time. In the case of a and p, we start by dividing p by a (although it doesn't really matter which we start with),

$$p = n_0 \times a + r_0$$

where n_0 is an integer (which we just throw away) and r_0 is less than p and greater than or equal to zero. This way, n is as big an integer as possible. If $r_0 = 0$, then the problem is that p is divisible by a, so p isn't prime. (In the normal version of the algorithm where we want the GCD, we would stop here and return a as the GCD, since it divides both a and p.) Otherwise, we continue the algorithm by dividing a by r_0:

$$a = n_1 \times r_0 + r_1$$

Again, n_1 is just some integer, and r_1 is the remainder ($0 \leq r_1 < a$).

We iteratively repeat this process until at some point we have the last two equations:

$$r_{i-1} = n_i \times r_i + r_{i+1}$$
$$r_i = n_{i+2} \times r_{i+1} + 0$$

In the normal algorithm, where we want the GCD, we just found it: r_{i+1}. Since one of our original numbers was prime, though, then the GCD, and hence r_{i+1}, should be 1 (otherwise, it wouldn't be a prime number, so something would be wrong with the number of the implementation of the algorithm).

How, then, do we get the inverse from this mess? Well, we know, from the second to last step of the algorithm, by replacing $r_{i+1} = 1$, that

$$r_{i-1} = n_{i+1} \times r_i + 1$$

Rewriting this, we have

$$1 = r_{i-1} - n_{i+1} \times r_i$$

We can then use the previous equation in the algorithm, $r_{i-2} = n_i r_{i-1} + r_i$, to substitute in the above for r_i:

$$1 = r_{i-1} - n_{i+1} \times (r_{i-2} - n_i r_{i-1}) = -n_{i+1} r_{i-2} + n_{i+1} n_i r_{i-1}$$

We then keep repeating the substitutions back up, eventually obtaining an expression for $1 = a \times a^{-1} - np$.

Let's run through a quick example by computing the inverse of 17 mod 31 using the Euclidean algorithm:

$$31 = 1 \times 17 + 14$$
$$17 = 1 \times 14 + 3$$
$$14 = 4 \times 3 + 2$$
$$3 = 1 \times 2 + 1$$
$$2 = 2 \times 1 + 0$$

Just as we stated above, we start with the second to last equation and work our way backward. To make the work a little easier to follow, we underline the next number to be substituted:

$$1 = 3 - \underline{2}$$
$$1 = 3 - (14 - 4 \times 3) = -1 \times 14 + 5 \times \underline{3}$$
$$1 = -1 \times 14 + 5 \times (17 - 1 \times 14) = 5 \times 17 - 6 \times \underline{14}$$
$$1 = 5 \times 17 - 6 \times (31 - 1 \times 17) = 11 \times 17 - 6 \times 31$$

This last equation is of exactly the correct form, revealing that $17^{-1} \equiv 11 \pmod{31}$. We can easily multiply these out to check our answers.

There are algorithms to keep track of these successive multiplications and combinations as you go down the Euclidean algorithm so that you don't have to "run backward" through it. Such an algorithm, used to calculate inverses modulo p, is called an **extended Euclidean algorithm**.

Cohen [2] gives one such algorithm (his Algorithm 1.3.6). This iterative algorithm takes just a few steps (note that $\lfloor x \rfloor$ means to convert x to an integer by rounding down, throwing away any fractional part).

Extended Euclidean Algorithm. For the following, assume that we are computing the GCD of two numbers, a and b. The output of the algorithm is three integers: u, v, and d, such that d is the GCD of a and b, and u and v satisfy $au + bv = d$.

1. Set $u \leftarrow 1$ and $d \leftarrow 0$.

2. If $b = 0$, then set $v \leftarrow 0$ and stop.

3. Set $v_1 \leftarrow 0$ and $v_3 \leftarrow b$.

4. If $v_3 = 0$, then set $v \leftarrow (d - a \times u) \div b$ and stop.

5. Set $q \leftarrow \lfloor d/v_3 \rfloor$ and $t_3 \leftarrow d \bmod v_3$.

6. Set $t_1 \leftarrow u - qv_1$, $u \leftarrow v_1$, $v_1 \leftarrow t_1$, $v_3 \leftarrow t_3$.

7. Go to Step 4.

The proof that this algorithm correctly computes the desired numbers can be found in Reference [2].

Finite fields are used quite often throughout cryptography. For example, Rijndael [3] (the algorithm that makes up the Advanced Encryption Standard, AES) uses finite field arithmetic for some of its calculations. In fact, Neal Koblitz has an entire book devoted to the connections between algebra and cryptography [5].

Now that we have some mathematics under our belt, let's review some cryptographic schemes based on these principles.

2.4   Factoring-Based Cryptography

One very popular problem to use as the basis for cryptography is the **factoring problem**: Given an arbitrary (and typically very large) number n, it is very difficult to calculate all of its prime factors in a reasonable amount of time. The difficulty typically increases as the number of prime factors shrinks, reaching the most difficult case when n is the product of two large primes. Several cryptosystems are based on the current knowledge that there is no very good algorithm to calculate these prime numbers easily.

2.4.1   The RSA Algorithm

The **RSA algorithm**, first published in the 1970s by Ronald Rivest, Adi Shamir, and Leonard Adleman, remains the most popular algorithm currently in use whose security is based on the factoring problem.

Specifically, RSA is based on a particular assumption. First, assume p and q to be very large prime numbers (many hundreds of digits long). If we let $n = pq$ be their product, then we assume that, knowing n, it is very difficult to derive p and q. The larger the values of p and q, theoretically, the more difficult it is to factor n.

The trick is to use some number theory principles to form a way to encode information using these numbers. RSA works by the following method:

1. Let $n = pq$, where p and q are two distinct, large prime numbers.

2. Calculate $t = \phi(n) = (p - 1)(q - 1)$, which is the Euler totient of n.

3. Let e be a positive integer, greater than 1 and less than t, that is relative prime to t. Mathematically, $e \in \mathbb{Z}$, $1 < e < t$, $\gcd(e, t) = 1$. One way to do this, for example, is to make e also be prime.

4. Calculate $d = e^{-1}$ in $\mathbb{Z}_t$, that is, such that $ed \equiv 1 \pmod{t}$.

Now, these numbers we have calculated, e and d, have an interesting property. Assume we have a message, M, represented as an integer less than n. Here we derive that

$$M^{ed} \equiv M^{de} \equiv M^{t+1} \equiv M^1 \equiv M \pmod{n}$$

Why does this work? It's just using Euler's totient theorem (specifically, the last corollary). Here, t is the totient of n, and we know that $ed \equiv 1 \pmod{t}$ from the construction of e and d. The last corollary from Euler's theorem lets us state that

$$M^{de} \equiv M^1 \pmod{n}$$

The significance is that if we represent our message as an integer, then we can use e as an encryption exponent, and d as a decrypting exponent, and have ciphertext

$$C \equiv M^e \pmod{n}$$

We will then be able to calculate back the plaintext

$$M \equiv C^d \equiv M^{ed} \pmod{n}$$

The real slickness comes in the fact that we can have *anybody* know e and n, so that they can encrypt messages, but it is extremely difficult to compute d knowing these two numbers without being able to factor n. Most proposed methods of breaking this algorithm simply involve factoring n to obtain p and q, so that the totient can be calculated.

We now use the pair (e, n) as the public key and the pair (d, n) as a private key.

Let's do a quick example of some cryptography using RSA. Let's say $p = 11$ and $q = 17$, two prime numbers. In real-life scenarios, we would have these numbers be hundreds of digits long; otherwise, factoring the resultant product would be very easy. For this case, we can see that $n = 11 \times 17 = 187$, and $t = \phi(187) = 10 \times 16 = 160$. Let's pick e to be a nice prime number, say, 3.

Now, we can calculate $d = 3^{-1}$ using the extended Euclidean algorithm from before, getting the result $d = 107$.

Let's encrypt our message. Here, consider our message to be encoded as the number 15 (for example, it could be the 15th letter of the Latin alphabet, O). It should be easy to see that $15^3 = 3,375 \equiv 9 \pmod{187}$, so that our encrypted number is $C = 9$. Going the other way is a bit trickier. We don't really want to multiply 9 by itself 107 times. It turns out there is a shortcut, using the binary representation of 107, that is to say, representing 107 as the sum of powers of 2. In binary, 107 is 1101011, meaning $107 = 2^6 + 2^5 + 2^3 + 2^1 + 2^0 = 64 + 32 + 8 + 2 + 1$. We can then write

$$9^{107} \equiv 9^{64+32+8+2+1} \pmod{187}$$

It's easy to see that $9^1 = 9$, thus we have

$$9^{107} \equiv 9^{64+32+8+2} \times 9 \pmod{187}$$

From the last equation, we know that $9^1 \equiv 9 \pmod{187}$, so then $9^2 \equiv (9^1) \times (9^1) \equiv 9 \times 9 \equiv 81 \pmod{187}$, and we have

$$9^{107} \equiv 9^{64+32+8} \times 81 \times 9 \pmod{187}$$

Even though we don't have a 9^4 term, we will go ahead and calculate the value for it anyway, by taking $9^4 = 9^2 \times 9^2 \equiv 81 \times 81 \equiv 16 \pmod{187}$. Repeating again, we know that $9^8 = 9^4 \times 9^4 \equiv 16 \times 16 \equiv 69 \pmod{187}$. So far, we then have

$$9^{107} \equiv 9^{64+32} \times 69 \times 81 \times 9 \pmod{187}$$

Repeating again, we have $9^{16} = 9^8 \times 9^8 \equiv 69 \times 69 \equiv 86 \pmod{187}$. But we have no 9^{16} term, so we repeat, getting $9^{32} = 9^{16} \times 9^{16} \equiv 86 \times 86 \equiv 103 \pmod{187}$. We then have, so far

$$9^{107} \equiv 9^{64} \times 103 \times 69 \times 81 \times 9 \pmod{187}$$

Finally, we can calculate $9^{64} = 9^{32} \times 9^{32} \equiv 103 \times 103 \equiv 137 \pmod{187}$, giving us

$$9^{107} \equiv 137 \times 103 \times 69 \times 81 \times 9 \pmod{187}$$

Not much of a shortcut is left here, so we just multiply it out and take the remainder, with the result:

$$9^{107} \equiv 137 \times 103 \times 69 \times 81 \times 9 \equiv \underline{15} \pmod{187}$$

Therefore, the decryption worked, since $C^d \equiv M \equiv 15 \pmod{187}$.

2.5 Discrete Logarithm-Based Cryptography

From high school mathematics, we might recall that a normal logarithm takes an exponential and "reverses" it, so that if we know that $10^x = 100$, then we can take the logarithm of both sides to know that $x = \log 100$.

The **discrete logarithm** has the exact same goal, except instead of acting on continuous numbers, such as the reals or the complex numbers, we are concerned with solving algebraic equations of the form

$$a^x = b$$

where a and b are known elements of a finite field **F** (instead of $\Re$ or $\mathbb{C}$), with a^x representing a operating on itself x times with the field operation. Solving for x is known as "calculating the discrete logarithm."

Another difference between the continuous and the discrete logarithm is that there are known, simple formulas to compute arbitrary logarithms of real-valued or complex-valued numbers. There is currently no known way to easily solve the discrete logarithm problem for x even if a and b are known. In fact, the difficulty of this problem is such that many cryptosystems rely on the difficulty of calculating discrete logarithms for their security.

2.5.1 The Diffie-Hellman Algorithm

Probably one of the simplest and most widely used cryptosystems that relies on the discrete logarithm being hard is the **Diffie-Hellman Key Exchange Protocol**.

Key exchange algorithms, in general, suffer from a fatal flaw. If we have a foolproof, secure way to exchange a key between two users, then why not just exchange the message we want to send through this channel? Normally, this is simply because the key is a small, fixed-size object, and only has to be exchanged once. But any messages may not have these properties.

Furthermore, we may not have any way of securely communicating a key! Diffie and Hellman devised a way for two parties to securely acquire the same key over an insecure channel, where anyone could be listening.

Let's say we have two parties communicating, A and B.

1. A and B agree on a finite field $\mathbf{F}$, as well as a generator g, which are both publicly known.

2. A picks a secret integer a, and B picks a secret integer b.

3. A sends to B (in the open) the number g^a computed in $\mathbf{F}$.

4. B sends to A (in the open) the number g^b computed in $\mathbf{F}$.

At the end of this exchange, A can compute $(g^a)^b = g^{ab}$ in $\mathbf{F}$, and B can compute $(g^b)^a = g^{ab}$ in $\mathbf{F}$ as well, so they both share a secret g^{ab} known only to each other. Anybody listening would know g, $\mathbf{F}$, g^a, and g^b, but thanks to the discrete logarithm being difficult, knowledge of g^a and g^b does not let any listener easily derive either a or b, and the properties of the fields do not allow one to use both g^a and g^b to easily calculate g^{ab} either.

2.6 Elliptic Curves[3]

There has been a significant trend in cryptography over the last few years toward elliptic curve-based algorithms, and away from normal (integer-based) number theoretic algorithms. Using elliptic curve cryptography gives us one primary advantage over the previous number theoretic methods: We can use much smaller numbers (by an order of magnitude) and achieve the same level of security. Smaller numbers mean less to transmit, and fewer operations to manipulate them. For example, 2048- and 4096-bit moduli are common for RSA, compared to the 256- and 384-bits common for the size of prime number p of the underlying field in elliptic curves.

This will be a very elementary go-through of very basic elliptic curve theory. For a more thorough look, see References [10], [11], and [13].

Broadly speaking, **elliptic curves** are sets of points formed by equations that are quadratic in the y-term and cubic in the x-term. These equations, in the most general form, are represented by the points (x, y) that satisfy the general equation:

$$ax^3 + bx^2y + cx^2 + dxy^2 + exy + fx + gy^3 + hy^2 + iy + j = 0$$

where x and y are variables ranging over fields (usually the rationals, the reals, complex numbers, or a finite field), and $a, b, \ldots, j$ are elements of the same

---

[3]This section is even more optional, as the material is a bit more abstract and advanced.

field. However, as will be explained shortly, there is always an additional point, often called the **point at infinity**, denoted ∞ [14].

We are usually not concerned with every type of elliptic curve. We want curves that are easier to manipulate, since we will be using them for cryptographic and cryptanalytic algorithms; the preceding form is a bit unwieldy for easy use. As such, we are concerned with elliptic curves that are simplified in what is called the **Weierstrass form** of an elliptic curve [13]:

$$y^2 = x^3 + ax + b$$

Not all elliptic curves in all fields can be represented in this form, but the simplicity of this form makes up for it. The restriction the form makes on the underlying field is that the field cannot have a characteristic of 2 or 3, because in those fields, division by 2 or 3, respectively, is equivalent to dividing by 0 in normal arithmetic, and we need to divide by 2 and 3 to construct the Weierstrass form.

Figure 2-4 shows some elliptic curves plotted in $\Re$. Note how there are three different shapes of these elliptic curves. The shape of the curve is dependent on the values of a and b. If $4a^3 + 27b^2 > 0$, then the curve will be shaped like Figure 2-4(a). If $4a^3 + 27b^2 = 0$, then the curve will be shaped like Figure 2-4(b); however, in this case, we have a double or even triple root, which tends to spoil some of the mathematics. We don't consider this case when constructing any of our algorithms. Finally, if $4a^3 + 27b^2 < 0$, then the curve will be shaped as in Figure 2-4(c).

2.6.1 Addition of Points

In order to do many of the elliptic curve cryptographic algorithms, we need to have some way to use these curves. In fact, we are actually going to perform operations on the *points* that satisfy the curve equation.

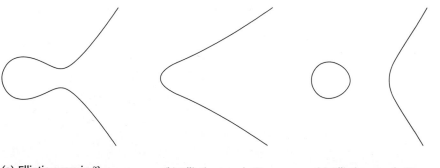

(a) Elliptic curve in $\Re$ representing the equation $y^2 = x^3 - 3x + 3$.

(b) Elliptic curve in $\Re$ representing the equation $y^2 = x^3$.

(c) Elliptic curve in $\Re$ representing the equation $y^2 = x^3 - x$.

Figure 2-4 Elliptic curves in $\Re$.

We will do this by defining operations on the points. First, assume that a point is represented by its coordinates, $P = (x, y)$. We want to define the **negative** to a point by negating the y component (that is, taking $0 - y$ in the appropriate field), so that $-P = (x, -y)$.

We also want to define the addition of two points. Assume that we have two points, $P = (x_1, y_1)$ and $Q = (x_2, y_2)$. Graphically, we want to calculate $P + Q$ by the following construction:

1. Draw a line $\overline{PQ}$ through $P + Q$.

2. There will be a third intersection of the line $\overline{PQ}$ with the elliptic curve, say, R.

3. The **sum of the two points** is then defined to be the negative of the third intersection, so that $P + Q = -R$.

This definition of addition isn't too difficult to grasp. But as we can see in graphs of the curve, such as in Figure 2-5, we have some difficulties. What if we add together two points that are inverses of each other, that is, $P + (-P)$? Graphically, this creates a vertical line.

This is where the point at infinity we mentioned comes into play. Graphically speaking, we want to include the "top" of the y-axis as a virtual point on the curve, so that the vertical line "intersects" this point ∞. When we work with non-graphically representable elliptic curves, such as those on finite fields, we merely have to treat the point at infinity as a construct that helps us deal with these special cases.

We can also see that this point, given our usage thus far, fulfills the role of the algebraic identity, if we consider the points on the elliptic curve together with addition as a potential group. This is exactly what we want! We already

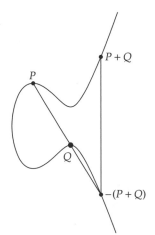

Figure 2-5 Elliptic curve addition of two points, P and Q.

have that $P + (-P) = \infty$. It should also make sense that $\infty + \infty = \infty$, as well as $\infty = -\infty$. By our construction, we can also see that $P + \infty$ is found by drawing a vertical line through P, and finding the third intersection, which will be $-P$. We take the inverse of $-P$, which is P, and thus $P + \infty = P$.

For more generic groups, we add this point at infinity to the potential group, with the previous properties defined, since we can't have a more drawing-focused version — it's not very easy to "draw" lines if our field is the integers 0–12.

Now, let's refine our above definition of addition of points to be more algebraically generic. When we draw a line, that normally means taking the two points and writing an equation expressing a linear relationship between the two points. Finding the third intersection is a matter of solving a system of two equations (one linear, one cubic) and two unknowns, which it turns out has a general solution on a field.

For the following calculation of $P + Q$, assume that we have an elliptic curve represented by the points satisfying the equation $y^2 = x^3 + ax + b$ in some field F, with $P = (x_1, y_1)$ and $Q = (x_2, y_2)$.

1. Check the special case $P = -Q$, in which case $P + Q = \infty$.

2. Check the other special case $P = Q$. In this case, our equation of $y = mx + c$ is **tangent** to the curve (intersects, but does not pass through). From calculus, we can calculate the derivative via implicit differentiation of the curve at P as the slope of the tangent curve, which will be $(3x_1^2 + a) \times (2y_1)^{-1}$. **Be very careful here**: We are calculating the inverse of $2y_1$ in the field; this does **not** mean division of integers or real numbers.

3. If $P \neq Q$, then we can calculate the slope the old-fashioned way: $m = (y_2 - y_1) \times (x_2 - x_1)^{-1}$ ("rise over run," but on a field). Again, **be careful**, since we are not necessarily doing normal division.

4. We now need to calculate the value c (our y intercept). We have two equations:

$$y_2 = mx_2 + c \tag{2.1}$$
$$y_1 = mx_1 + c \tag{2.2}$$

We can solve for c by taking twice the first equation and subtracting the second equation, that is, $2 \times$ Equation (2.1) − Equation (2.2), which gives us $c = 2y_2 - 2mx_2 - y_1 + mx_1$.

5. We now want to solve for $P + Q = (x_3, y_3)$ on the curve, thus we have two equations:

$$y = mx + c \tag{2.3}$$
$$y^2 = x^3 + ax + b \tag{2.4}$$

Substituting the first into the second, we get that $(mx + c)^2 = x^3 + ax + b$, or $x^3 - m^2x^2 + (a - 2mc)x + (b - c^2) = 0$. Now, this is not too much fun to factor. However, some basic algebra might conjure up the fact that the x^2 coefficient is the negative of the sum of the three solutions of the equation. Since we already know two of the solutions (they had better be x_1 and x_2), we can calculate $-m^2 = -x_3 - x_2 - x_1$, giving us $x_3 = m^2 - x_2 - x_1$. Plugging this into the above equations will reveal that the other coefficients come out as they should.

To calculate y_3, we use the fact that $y_3 = mx_3 + c$ and that we know what x_3 and c are. Since we had to calculate x_3 anyway, we'll just use that value, but we can simplify the c term a little. Plugging in $mx_3 + c$ for y_3, we get

$$
\begin{aligned}
y_3 &= mx_3 + 2y_2 - 2mx_2 - y_1 + mx_1 \\
&= m(x_3 - 2x_2 + x_1) + (y_2 - y_1) + y_2 \\
&= m(x_3 + (x_1 - x_2) - x_2) + (y_2 - y_1) + y_2 \\
&= m(x_3 - x_2) + (y_1 - y_2) + (y_2 - y_1) + y_2 \\
&= m(x_3 - x_2) + y_2
\end{aligned}
$$

Thus, we have found that

$$P + Q = (x_3, -y_3) = (m^2 - x_2 - x_1, m(x_2 - x_3) - y_2)$$

This addition procedure has identical properties to the above geometrical construction — it doesn't matter which point is "first": $P + Q = Q + P$. We also know that we have an identity element of ∞. It also turns out that if we have three points, say $P, Q,$ and R on the elliptic curve, then we are guaranteed that $(P + Q) + R = P + (Q + R)$, so that addition of points on the elliptic curve is associative. This fact is non-trivial to prove; thus, I refer the reader to Reference [13] for more details.

Since we have all of these properties, we find that the elliptic curve points, together with addition, form an abelian group, often denoted as $(E(F), +)$, where F is the field that the coordinates for the points on the elliptic curves come from.

Let's do a quick example of the addition of two rational points, so that we can make sure that we have the concept down (and also as a simple test case for any computer implementation of elliptic curve point addition). Our curve will be defined by $y^2 = x^3 - 25x$ (therefore, $a = -25, b = 0$), with two points $P = (x_1, y_1) = (-4, 6)$ and $Q = (x_2, y_2) = (1681/44, -62{,}279/178)$.

Following the steps of the algorithm, we note that it does not fall into the cases where $P = Q$ or $P = -Q$, so we proceed to Step 3 — calculating m. For the rational numbers, the multiplicative inverse is found just by flipping the numerator and denominator, thus

$$m = \frac{y_2 - y_1}{x_2 - x_1} = \frac{6 + \frac{62{,}279}{178}}{-4 - \frac{1{,}681}{44}} = -\frac{1{,}393{,}634}{165{,}273}$$

Step 4 was used just for the purposes of demonstration, so we skip ahead to the end of Step 5 and note that

$$x_3 = m^2 - x_2 - x_1 = \left(-\frac{1,393,634}{165,273} \right)^2 + 4 - \frac{1,681}{44} = \frac{44,348,169,325,919}{1,201,867,239,276}$$

and

$$y_3 = m(x_3 - x_2) + y_2$$

... I'm just going to leave out the calculation of those huge numbers and tell you that the answer is

$$y_3 = \frac{2,831,284,656,048,990,661}{9,028,918,374,402,834}$$

Trust me. Or better yet, don't trust me, and verify yourself.

One concept that we introduced in the addition formulation above is that we can add a point to itself, that is, calculating $P + P$. We could even add a point to itself multiple times, getting $P + P + P$, and so forth. Since we have no concept of multiplying points by each other, we can use the notation nP to mean "add n P's together" (which is $n - 1$ addition operations), so that $0P = \infty$, $1P = P$, $2P = P + P$, $3P = P + P + P$, and so forth.

Taking a closer look at the previous example, you might note that $Q = 2P$, and therefore the result is $P + 2P = 3P$.

Some of our algorithms we will be developing later involve computing very large multiples of points. The above construction doesn't seem to lend itself well to computing, say, $1048577P$. It turns out we can use a shortcut based on powers of two. Once we have computed $P + P = 2P$, we can easily calculate $2P + 2P = 4P$. And then, in a single additional operation, we have $4P + 4P = 8P$, and so forth. Therefore, the trick is to take the multiple that we want and to express it as a sum of powers of two. Once we have such a representation, we can simply calculate each multiple of P that is a power of two and add them together. We can save even more time by caching intermediate values.

Thus, in our above example, we can write $1,048,577 = 1,048,576 + 1 = 2^{20} + 2^0$, meaning that $1,048,577P = (2^{20} + 2^0)P = 2^{20}P + P$. It takes 20 point-additions to calculate $2^{20}P$, and one final one to add in the last P, for a total of 21 additions. That's definitely a far cry less than adding P to itself 1,048,576 times.

2.6.2 Elliptic Curve Cryptography

Any operation, including cryptography, that can be performed on integers or any other type of number can also be applied to points on an elliptic curve. There are two challenges to overcome: How do we represent information as points on an elliptic curve, and how do we adapt our operations to be more tailored toward elliptic curves?

To answer the first question, I take the following construction from Reference [13]. Assume that we have an elliptic curve in a finite field $(\mathbb{Z}_p, +, \times)$, represented by the equation $y^2 = x^3 + ax + b$. First, we represent our message as an integer m between greater than or equal to 0 and less than $p/100$. We will then try up to 100 points on the elliptic curve to represent the message, starting with $j = 0$:

1. Let $x_j = 100m + j$.

2. Compute $u = x_j^3 + ax_j + b$. The value of u may end up being our y_j value, or help us to find one.

3. Check to see if $u^{(p-1)/2} \equiv 1 \pmod{p}$. If not, then go back to Step 1. If the above congruence is true, then u is a square in F_p, so $y_j \equiv \sqrt{u} \pmod{p}$.

4. If $p \equiv 3 \pmod{4}$, we can calculate a square root of u, and hence y_j, with $u^{(p+1)/4} \bmod p$.

5. Else if $p \equiv 5 \pmod{8}$, then we can calculate the square root by calculating $a^{(p-1)/4} \bmod p$. If this is $+1$, then the square root is $y_j \equiv u^{(p+3)/8} \pmod{p}$. Otherwise (if the calculated number is -1), then $y_j \equiv 2u \cdot (4u)^{(p-5)/8} \pmod{p}$ [2].

6. Else if $p \equiv 1 \pmod{8}$, then we can calculate a square root of u as well, but it is quite a bit more involved. Cohen [2] recommends using Shanks's algorithm [9], even though it is probabilistic. Shanks's algorithm works as follows [2, 9]:

    (a) Take $p - 1 = 2^e q$, by continually dividing $p - 1$ by 2 until we get a non-integer. The result immediately before the non-integer is q, and the number of times we divided will be e.

    (b) Compute $z \leftarrow u^q \bmod p$.

    (c) Set $y \leftarrow z$, $r \leftarrow e$, $x \leftarrow a^{(q-1)/2} \bmod p$, $b \leftarrow ax^2$, $x \leftarrow ax \bmod p$.

    (d) If $b \equiv 1 \pmod{p}$, then x is the answer, and we stop here.

    (e) Find the smallest integer m (greater than or equal to 1) such that $b^{2^m} \equiv 1 \pmod{p}$. If $m = r$, then we have a problem, because a is not a quadratic residue of p.

    (f) Assign $t \leftarrow y^{2^{r-m-1}} \bmod p$, $y \leftarrow t^2 \bmod p$, $r \leftarrow m \bmod p$, $x \leftarrow xt \bmod p$, $b \leftarrow by \bmod p$.

    (g) Go back to Step 6d.

    (Note that p will never be congruent to 2 or 4 mod p, since that would mean that 2 would be a factor of p, which is not possible because p is prime.)

After we have represented a message as a point, we can then perform operations on it, similar to a normal additive or multiplicative group. Instead of using exponentiation by integers, as we did for finite fields over integers, we will instead use addition on the points, that is, multiplying points by integers.

2.6.3 Elliptic Curve Diffie-Hellman

A very commonly used elliptic curve cryptographic algorithm is the Diffie-Hellman key exchange, but using elliptic curves instead of normal finite fields.

In this variant, Alice and Bob both agree on an elliptic curve to operate with, over the same finite field (usually $(\mathbb{Z}_p, +, \times)$, where p is a large prime). They also agree on a particular point, say P. Just as before, they both choose secret integers a (for Alice) and b (for Bob).

1. Alice sends Bob aP.

2. Bob sends Alice bP.

Since nP is shorthand for "add n copies of P together," then we know that $b(aP) = baP = abP$ and $a(bP) = abP$, so Alice and Bob can both compute abP. Furthermore, only Alice and Bob can compute these numbers.[4]

2.7 Summary

This chapter covered a great deal of material fundamental to cryptography and cryptanalysis.

We studied the basics of probability, which are critical in many types of cryptanalytic attacks. (As we shall see, many attacks are probabilistic in nature, relying on intricate chains of events to work out.)

We then explored algebra, and number theory, including elliptic curves. This material is critical to public-key cryptographic algorithms (such as RSA) and key exchange algorithms (such as Diffie-Hellman), which are often based on these simple mathematical constructs. In the next chapter, we also use these concepts with algorithms designed to compromise public-key cryptographic and key exchange systems.

Exercises

Exercise 1. Write a program to calculate the inverse of a number modulo another number, p, by implementing the extended Euclidean algorithm.

Exercise 2. Write a program that adds two points on an elliptic curve in the standard Galois field of size p (over $\mathbb{Z}_p$), where p is a prime number.

Exercise 3. Extend your work from the previous exercise to include calculating large multiples (tens of digits) of points.

Exercise 4. Write a program that encodes an ASCII text message as a point on an elliptic curve.

---

[4]When actually implementing this algorithm, we need to be fairly careful about our choices of P, the curve, as well as the field. For more information, see, for starters, References [6] and [13].

References

[1] David Bellot. Svg-cards 2.0.1, September 2006; `http://david.bellot` `.free.fr/svg-cards/`.

[2] Henri Cohen. *A Course in Computational Algebraic Number Theory*, Graduate Texts in Mathematics (Springer-Verlag, New York, 2000).

[3] John Daemen and Vincent Rijmen. *The Design of Rijndael: AES — The Advanced Encryption Standard*, Information Security and Cryptography (Springer, New York, March 2002).

[4] Institute of Electrical and Electronics Engineers, Inc. and The Open Group. The single unix specification version 3, 2004; `http://www.unix.org/` `single_unix_specification/`.

[5] Neal Koblitz. *Algebraic Aspects of Cryptography*, 1st ed., volume 3 of *Algorithms and Computation in Mathematics* (Springer, New York, June 2004).

[6] National Institute of Standards and Technology. Recommended elliptic curves for federal government use, July 1999; `http://csrc.nist.gov/` `CryptoToolkit/dss/ecdsa/NISTReCur.pdf`.

[7] National Institute of Standards and Technology. *Secure Hash Standard* (Federal Information Processing Standards Publication 180-1, April 1995).

[8] Ronald L. Rivest. *The MD5 Message-Digest Algorithm* (Network Working Group, Request for Comments: 1321, April 1992).

[9] Daniel Shanks. Five number-theoretic algorithms. *Congressus Numerantium 7* (Utilitas Mathematica, 1973).

[10] Joseph H. Silverman. *The Arithmetic of Elliptic Curves*, 1st ed., GTM (Springer, New York, December 1985).

[11] Joseph H. Silverman. *Rational Points on Elliptic Curves*, 2nd ed., UTM (Springer, New York, November 1994).

[12] Kenneth L. Thompson and Dennis M. Ritchie. *Unix Programmer's Manual*, 1st ed. (Bell Telephone Laboratories Inc., Murray Hill, NJ, November 1971); `http://cm.bell-labs.com/cm/cs/who/dmr/1stEdman.html`.

[13] Lawrence C. Washington. *Elliptic Curves: Number Theory and Cryptography* (Chapman & Hall/CRC, Toronto, Canada, May 2003).

[14] Eric W. Weisstein. *Elliptic* Curve. From *MathWorld*–A Wolfram Web Resource.; `http://mathworld.wolfram.com/EllipticCurve.html`.

Factoring and Discrete Logarithms

The previous chapter used a hefty dose of mathematics to develop some nice cryptographic algorithms, which are still used today. Now, we are going to look at methods used to break these algorithms.

To quickly review from the end of the last chapter, factoring and discrete logarithms represent two classes of problems of growing importance in crypt-analysis. A growing number of ciphers rely on the difficulty of these two problems as a foundation of their security, including number theoretic ciphers such as RSA and algebraic ciphers such as the Diffie-Hellman key exchange algorithm. The methods themselves aren't secure; they rely on the fact that both factoring and the discrete logarithm are difficult to do for very large numbers. To date, no methods are known to solve them very quickly for the key sizes typically used.

The algorithms here may not be suitable for breaking many in-use imple-mentations of algorithms like RSA and Diffie-Hellman, but it is still important to understand how they work. Any future developments in the fields will likely build on this material.

3.1 Factorization

Factorization refers to the ability to take a number, n, and determine a list of all of the prime factors of the number. For small numbers, we can just start going through the list of integers and seeing if they divide into n. However, this method doesn't scale well, since the numbers we are often concerned with are hundreds of digits long — of course, these numbers are hundreds of digits long merely because that is the time-security tradeoff point, since the algorithms presented here start to drag their feet, so to speak, around that point.

In the previous chapter we learned about RSA, which uses exponentiation of numbers by public and private exponents. If we recall, the first step in the RSA algorithm to create these exponents is to construct a number $n = pq$, where p and q are both large prime numbers. Since we know p and q, we can calculate the totient of n, $\phi(n) = (p - 1)(q - 1)$, which we then use to find two numbers, e and d, such that $ed \equiv 1 \pmod{(p - 1)(q - 1)}$. The numbers e and n will be made public and can be used to communicate securely with anyone who knows d and n. However, if anyone were to be able to factor n into its two prime factors, then they could easily calculate d using the extended Euclidean algorithm (as that is exactly how d was originally derived), allowing them to read any messages encrypted with e and n.

RSA is therefore very reliant on factoring large values of n to be a difficult problem, or its security will be compromised. The following sections discuss the fundamental algorithms for factoring numbers.

Note that there are, theoretically, other ways to break RSA. For instance, since an attacker has access to the public key, (e, n), then he could take a message (perhaps a very cleverly constructed message) and encrypt it, knowing that when this encrypted message is encrypted again with the private key, and therefore exponentiated by d modulo n, there may be some clever way to derive d. However, at this time, no such method is known.

3.2   Algorithm Theory

Just as this is not a book on mathematics, it is also not a book on the algorithm theory. Hence, we will not require the reader to have a great deal of understanding of the methods used to determine the exact running time and storage requirements of any of the algorithms we will be discussing. However, it is important to have a decent understanding of how the various algorithms compare to each other.

Algorithmic running time and storage space are often written in terms of **order**, also known as "Big-Oh" notation, like $O(1)$ and $O(n^2)$, where n is usually our input size. For an algorithm to have a worst-case running time of, say, $O(n)$, means that, roughly speaking, the algorithm will terminate within some fixed multiple of n steps (i.e., proportional to the size of the input). Naturally, if an algorithm has, say, $O(n^2)$ storage requirements in the worst-case scenario, it will require, at most, some fixed multiple of n^2 (i.e., proportional to the square of the size of the input).

For example, suppose we devised a method for testing to see if a number is even by dividing it by 2, using the long-division method everyone learned in elementary school. For the sake of this, and other algorithms in this chapter, we let n be the size of the number in terms of digits. For example, 12345 has length 5 in decimal, or length 14 in binary; the two numbers will always differ by about $1/\log 2 \approx 3.322$, because of using logarithms[1] to convert bases;

---

[1] As my friend Raquel Phillips pointed out, "logarithm" and "algorithm" are anagrams!

thus, it doesn't affect our running time to use one or the other, since an order expressed in one will always be a constant multiple of the other, and hence have the same order in Big-Oh notation. In this book, we typically use key size in terms of the number of bits.

The previous simple division algorithm has a running time of $O(n)$ and storage requirements of $O(1)$. Why? Because the standard division algorithm we learn early on is to take each digit, left to right, and divide by 2, and then take the remainder, multiply by 10, and add it to the next digit, divide again, and so on. Each step takes about three operations, and there will about the same number of steps as there are digits, giving us about $3n$ operations or thereabouts — this is a simple multiple of n; thus, our running time is $O(n)$. Since we didn't have to keep track of more than one or two variables other than the input, we have a constant amount of storage. Algorithms with $O(n)$ running time are typically called **linear** algorithms.

This is a suboptimal algorithm, though. We might also recall from elementary school that the last digit can tell us if a number is even or odd. If the last digit is even, the entire number is even; otherwise, both are odd. This means that we could devise an $O(1)$ even-checking algorithm by just checking the last digit. This always takes exactly two operations: one to divide, and one to check if the remainder is zero (the number is even) or one (the number is odd). Algorithms that run in less than $O(n)$ time are called **sublinear**.

Who needs all that input anyway, right? It's just taking up space.

If an algorithm runs in $O(n^p)$ time, where p is some fixed number, then it is said to be a **polynomial-time algorithm**. This is an important class, often denoted simply as P. The reason this class is important is because it is *merely* a polynomial-time algorithm — other worse-performing classes of algorithms exist, known as **superpolynomial-time algorithms**. For example, the class of algorithms that can be bounded in $O(a^n)$ time (for some number a) is called an **exponential-time algorithm**. In general, superpolynomial- and exponential-time algorithms take significantly longer to run than polynomial-time algorithms. Algorithms that take less than an exponential of n to finish are called **subexponential**. Figure 3-1 shows the running time of the various classes of algorithms.

There is also another way to analyze an algorithm: by its storage complexity. Storage complexity is, for most of the algorithms we are considering, not too much of a concern. However, requiring large amounts of storage can quickly become a problem. For example, we could just pre-compute the factors for all numbers up to some extremely large value and store this, and then we would have a very small running time (only as long as it takes to search the list) for finding the factors of a number. However, the pre-computation and storage requirements make this technique silly.

We will see this kind of concept used in a more clever way in Chapter 5.

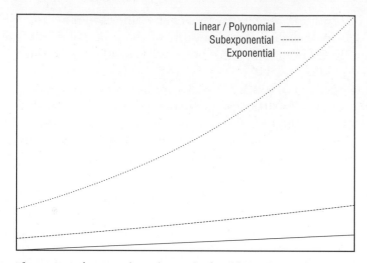

Figure 3-1 The running time of algorithms for order $O(n)$ (linear and polynomial), $O(4e^{\ln n \ln \ln n})$ (subexponential), and $O(2^n)$ (exponential) for various values of n.

3.2.1 Notation

There is another important notion in understanding algorithms: writing them out clearly, and unambiguously. For doing so, authors typically take one of three approaches: picking a programming language du jour to write all examples in, inventing a programming language, or writing everything in various forms of pseudocode (writing out the instructions in some mesh of natural language and a more formal programming language).

The first approach, picking a popular or well-known language, has an obvious disadvantage in that it dates a book immediately: a book written 40 years ago might have used FORTRAN or ALGOL to implement its algorithms, which would be difficult for many readers to understand. The second approach can be all right, but it requires that the reader learn some language that the author thinks is best. This approach can have mixed results, with some readers distracted so much by learning the language that they do not comprehend the text.

The final approach is often used, especially in abstract books. While usually very clear, it can sometimes be a challenge for a programmer to implement, especially if important details are glossed over.

The approach we use in this book is to have a combination of pseudocode and writing out in an actual programming language. The pseudocode in this and the following chapters is very simple: I merely state how a program would operate, but in mostly plain English, instead of some abstract notation. The intent of this book is not to alienate readers, but to enlighten.

For some examples, I will like a reader to be able to easily see an algorithm in action and to have some kind of source code to analyze and run. When these situations arise, I implement in a language that, in my opinion, has a complete, free version available over the Internet; is easy to read even if the reader is not fluent in the language; and in which the reader won't get bogged down in housekeeping details (like `#include <stdio.h>`-like statements in C, `import java.util.*;` statements in Java, etc.). A few languages fulfill these requirements, and one that I like in particular is Python.

If you are not familiar with Python, or Python is long forgotten in the tomes of computing history when this book is read, the implementations in Python should be simple enough to easily reproduce in whatever language you are interested in.

3.2.2   A Crash Course in Python

We shall start with a very, *very* short course in Python syntax and a few tricks. This is by no means representative of all of Python, nor even using all of the features of any given function, but merely enables us to examine some simple programs that will work and are easy to read.

A typical Python program looks like that shown in Listing 3-1.

```
x = 5
y = 0
print "x⎵=", x, "⎵⎵y⎵=⎵", y
for i in range(0, 4):
 y = y + x
 print "x⎵=", x, "⎵⎵y⎵=", y, "⎵⎵i⎵=", i

print "x⎵=", x, "⎵⎵y⎵=", y
```

Listing 3-1 A simple program in Python. The brackets inside quotes indicate a space character

The output of the program in Listing 3-1 will be

```
x = 5    y = 0
x = 5    y = 5    i = 0
x = 5    y = 10    i = 1
x = 5    y = 15    i = 2
x = 5    y = 20    i = 3
x = 5    y = 20
```

We don't want to get bogged down in too many details, but a few things are worth noting. Assignments are done with the simple = command, with the variable on the left and the value to put in on the right.

Program structure is determined by white space. Therefore the `for` loop's encapsulated code is all the code following it with the same indentation as the line immediately following it — no semicolons or braces to muck up.

The `for` loop is the most complicated thing here. It calls on the `range` function to do some of its work. For our uses, `range` takes two arguments: the starting point (inclusive) and the ending point (not inclusive), so that in Listing 3-1, `range(0, 4)` will expand to `[0, 1, 2, 3]` (the Python code for an array).

The `for` loop uses the `in` word to mean "operate the following code one time for each element in the array, assigning the current element of the array to the `for`-loop variable." In Listing 3-1, the `for`-loop variable is `i`. The colon is used to indicate that the `for` line is complete and to expect its body immediately after.

The only other thing to mention here is the `print` statement. In the case I provided above, we can print a literal string, such as `"x = "`, or a value (which will be converted to a string). We can print multiple things (with spaces separating them) by using a comma, as is shown above.

Let's go through one more quick example to illustrate a few more concepts.

```
def factorial(n):
 if n == 0 or n == 1:
  return 1
 else:
  return n * factorial(n - 1)

x = 0
f = 0
while f < 100:
 f = factorial(x)
 print f
 x = x + 1
```

Listing 3-2 A factorial function written in Python.

The program shown in Listing 3-2 will have the following output:

```
1
1
2
6
24
120
```

This program gives a taste of a few more tools: functions, conditionals, and the `while` loop.

Functions are defined using the def statement, as in the above example (its parameters specified in parentheses after the function name). Values of functions are returned using the return statement.

Conditionals are most commonly performed using if statements. The if statement takes an argument that is Boolean (expressions that return true or false), such as a comparison like == (equals) and < (less than), and combinations of Booleans, combined using and and or. There can be an optional else statement for when the if's condition evaluates to false (and there can be, before the else, one or more elif, which allow additional conditionals to be acted on).

Finally, we have another loop, the while loop. Simply put, it evaluates the condition at the beginning of the loop each time. If the condition is true, it executes the loop; if false, it breaks out and continues to the next statement outside the loop.

Python automatically converts fairly well between floating point numbers, arbitrarily large numbers, strings, and so on. For example, if we used the above code to calculate factorial(20), we would simply obtain

```
2432902008176640000L
```

The L on the end indicates that the result is a large integer (beyond machine precision). No modification of the code was necessary — Python automatically converted the variables to these large-precision numbers.

I'll spread a little Python here and there throughout this and later chapters to have some concrete examples and results. The rest of this chapter is devoted to algorithms for factoring integers and solving discrete logarithm problems, of different complexities and speeds.

3.3   Exponential Factoring Methods

When we refer to the speeds of the factoring methods, we are usually concerned not so much with the number itself, but with its size, typically in binary. For example, the number 700 (in decimal) would be written in binary as

```
10 1011 1100
```

Thus, 700 takes 10 bits to represent in binary. In general, we can use the logarithm function to calculate this. The base 2 logarithm calculates what power of 2 is required to get the desired number. With the above example, we can calculate

$$\log_2 700 \approx 9.4512$$

We round this up to determine the number of bits needed to represent the number, which is 10 bits.[2]

Since, by nature, we do not know the actual number to be factored, but we can generally tell the size of the number, this is how we categorize factorization algorithms. Categorizing them by this method also lets us see how well the algorithms do when the numbers start to get very large (hundreds or thousands of digits).

This chapter is concerned with exponential-time algorithms. As we defined earlier, this means that the algorithm running time will be $O(a^n)$, where n is the size of the number (in bits) and a is some number greater than 1.

Exponential factoring methods are often the easiest to understand. Unfortunately, while they are simple and often elegant, they are also incredibly slow. Nevertheless, some have advantages over even the fastest algorithms in some circumstances.

3.3.1 Brute-Force

Brute-force algorithms are usually the simplest method to solve most problems with a known set of solutions: just try every possible solution. Brute-force's motto is, if we don't know where to start, just start trying. Throw all of your computing power at the problem, and hope to come out on top!

The natural way to brute-force factors? *Just try them all.* Well, maybe not every number. If you have divided a number by 2 and found it is not divisible, it's fairly pointless to divide it by 4, 6, 8, and all the rest of the multiples of 2. It is similarly pointless to divide by 3 and then by 6, 9, 12, and the rest of the multiples of 3, and if we follow suit, then with the multiples of the rest of the numbers we try.

Therefore, we will limit ourselves to merely trying all of the *prime* numbers and dividing our target number by each prime. If the division succeeds (i.e., no remainder), then we have a factor — save the factor, take the result of the division (the quotient), and continue the algorithm with the quotient. We would start with that same factor again, since it could be repeated (as in $175 = 5 \times 5 \times 7$).

This technique provides an upper-bound on the amount of work we are willing to do: If any technique takes more work than brute forcing, then the algorithm doesn't work well.

An immediate assumption that many make when naively implementing this algorithm is to try all prime numbers between 1 and $n - 1$. However, in general, $n - 1$ will never divide n (once $n > 2$). As the numbers get larger, then

---

[2]Sometimes, you may only have the natural logarithm (ln) or the base 10 logarithm (plain log). In these cases, you can convert to the base 2 logarithm by using the equation $\log_2(x) = \log(x)/\log(2) = \ln(x)/\ln(2)$.

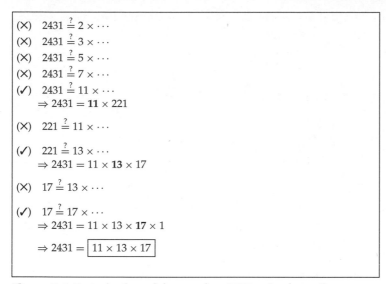

Figure 3-2 Factorization of the number 2431 using brute-force.

$n - 2$ will never divide n, and so forth. In general, the largest factor that we need to try is $\sqrt{n}$. Why? The simple reason is that if n has a factor greater than its square root, it will have to have a factor less than its square root as well; two numbers larger than its square root multiplied together will be larger than the number itself! Therefore, searching up to $\sqrt{n}$ will be sufficient for finding all the factors.

The only other small trick is the ability to find all of the prime numbers in order to divide by them. Figure 3-2 shows an example of brute-force factorization using such a list. Although for smaller numbers (only a few digits), the list of primes needed would be small, it would be prohibitive to have a list of all the prime numbers required for large factorization lying around. Furthermore, even checking to see if a large number is prime can be costly (since it would involve a very similar algorithm to that above).

The answer is that we would just hop through the list of all integers, skipping ones that are obviously not primes, like even numbers, those divisible by three, and so forth. For more details on implementations and behavior of this algorithm, see Reference [6].

We leave it as an exercise to the reader to implement the brute-force algorithm.

3.3.1.1 *Analysis*

In order to see how much time this takes to run, we need to know how many prime numbers there are. We could simply count them, which would be the only exact method. But there is a well-known rough approximation, saying that if we have a number a, then there are approximately

$$\frac{a}{\log a}$$

prime numbers less than or equal to a. In reality, there are a bit more than this, but this provides a good lower bound. In terms of the length of a (in binary digits), we have $n = \log_2 a$ digits.

The running time will then be one division operation per prime number less than the square root of the number a, which has $n/2$ digits. Therefore, dividing by every prime number of less than $\sqrt{a}$ will involve time complexity of about $O(\sqrt{a}/\log(\sqrt{a}))$, which, when converted to terms of n (the number of digits), gives us

$$O\left(\frac{2^{n/2}}{n/2}\right)$$

The storage requirements for this are simply storing the factors as we calculate them, and keeping track of where we are. This won't take up too much space; thus, we need not be worried at this point.

As terrible as this may seem when compared to other algorithms in terms of time complexity, it has the advantage that it *always* works. There is no randomness in its operation, and it has a fixed, known upper-bound. Few other algorithms discussed here have these properties. Also, other algorithms are not guaranteed to find complete prime factorizations (whereas this one does) and often rely on trial division to completely factor numbers less than some certain bound.

3.3.2   Fermat's Difference of Squares

A method attributed to Fermat in 1643 [6] uses little more than normal integer arithmetic to siphon large factors from numbers. In fact, it doesn't even use division.[3]

The algorithm works from a fact often learned in basic algebra:

$$(x + y)(x - y) = x^2 - y^2$$

for any integers x and y. Fermat theorized using this to factor a number: If we can discover two squares such that our target number (a) is equal to the difference of the two squares ($x^2 - y^2$), we then have two factors of the n, namely, $(x + y)$ and $(x - y)$.

Fermat's method just tries, essentially, to brute-force the answer by going through the possible squares and testing them. The algorithm is written out

---

[3]Division by 2 in computers is different from normal division. With numbers written in binary, simply removing the least significant bit is equivalent to dividing by 2. For example, 24 is 11000 in binary. If we remove the last bit, we get 1100, which is 12 — the same result as dividing by 2.

concisely in Reference [15], although I have changed some of the variable names for the following:

Fermat's Difference of Squares. Take an integer, a, to factor. The goal is to calculate x^2 and y^2 so that $(x+y)(x-y) = x^2 - y^2 = a$. In the following, $d = x^2 - a$ (which should, eventually, be equal to y^2).

1. Set x to be $\sqrt{a}$, rounding up (the ceiling function).
2. Set $t = 2x + 1$.
3. Set $d = x^2 - a$.

   In the algorithm, d will represent $x^2 - a$, the difference between our current estimate of x^2 and a, and thus will represent y^2 when we have found the correct difference of the squares. This means that d is positive (if a is not a perfect square in the first step) or zero (if a is a perfect square).

   Make t the difference between x^2 and the next square: $(x+1)^2 = x^2 + 2x + 1$, and hence the difference is $2x + 1$ to start with. The next square will be $(x+2)^2 = x^2 + 4x + 4$, which is $2x + 3$ more than the last. Following this trend (which can be verified using calculus), the difference between the squares increases by 2 each time.

4. (a) If d is a square ($\sqrt{d}$ is an integer), then stop and go to Step 5, because the difference is a square.

   (b) Set d to $d + t$. We are adding in the distance to the next x^2 attempt to the difference of $x^2 - a$.

   This works because we already have $(x+c)^2 - a$ (for some c, the current step), and we wish to calculate $[(x+c)+1]^2 - a = (x+c)^2 + 2(x+c) + 1 - a = (x+c)^2 - a + 2x + (2c+1) = d + 2x + 2c + 1$, the next value of d. We use the value of t to stand in for $2x + 2c + 1$, which increases by 2 every time, since c increases by 1 with each step.

   (c) Set t to $t + 2$. The distance between the next pair of squares is increased by 2 each time.

   (d) Go to Step 4a.

5. Set x to $\sqrt{d+a}$. Since $d = x^2 - a$, then $x = \sqrt{d+a}$.
6. Set y to be $\sqrt{d}$, since $d = x^2 - a$ is a perfect square, and is now our y^2.
7. Return two factors, $x + y$ and $x - y$.

For a simple example, Figure 3-3 shows this algorithm being run on the number 88.

$a = 88$

1. $x = \lceil \sqrt{88} \rceil$ (rounded up) $= 10$

2. $t = 2 \cdot 10 + 1 = 21$

3. $d = 10^2 - 88 = 12$

4(a). $d = 12 + 21 = 33$ (representing $x^2 = 121, y^2 = 33$)

4(b). $t = 21 + 2 = 23$

4(a). $d = 33 + 23 = 56$ (representing $x^2 = 144, y^2 = 56$)

4(b). $t = 23 + 2 = 25$

4(a). $d = 56 + 21 = 81$ (representing $x^2 = 169, y^2 = 81$)

4(b). $t = 25 + 2 = 27$

5. $x = \sqrt{81 + 88} = 13$

6. $y = \sqrt{81} = 9$

7. $x + y = 22, x - y = 4$

Figure 3-3 Fermat's difference of squares method for finding factors of 88.

3.3.2.1 *Analysis of Fermat's Difference of Squares*

The running time of Fermat's difference of squares method is on the order of $\sqrt{a}$ running time with constant space requirements. Although this algorithm provides essentially no improvement to trial division, the concept it uses is a fundamental building block upon which other factoring methods are built.

3.3.3 Pollard's ρ

Pollard has come up with several very clever mechanisms for factoring integers, as well as other ones we shall study below in this chapter.

Pollard's rho (ρ) method works by finding cycles in number patterns. For example, using the modular arithmetic from the previous chapter, we may want to successively square the number, say, 2, repeatedly modulo 14. This would result in a sequence

$$2, 4, 8, 2, 4, 8, \ldots$$

This sequence repeats itself forever. Pollard figured out a way to have these sequences give us clues about the factors of numbers.

We'll show the algorithm, and then explain the nifty trick behind it.

Pollard's ρ. Factors an integer, a.

1. Set b to be a random integer between 1 and $a - 3$, inclusive.

2. Set s to be a random integer between 0 and $a - 1$, inclusive.

3. Set $A = s$.

4. Set $B = s$.

5. Define the function $f(x) = (x^2 + b)$ mod a.

6. Let $g = 1$.

7. If $g \neq 1$, then go to Step 8.

   (a) Set $A = f(A)$.

   (b) Set $B = f(f(B))$.

   (c) Set $g = \gcd(A - B, a)$.

   (d) Repeat (go to Step 7).

8. If g is less than a, then return g. Otherwise, the algorithm failed to find a factor.

Why does this work? Well, the first leap of faith is that the function $f(x)$ will randomly jaunt through the values in the field. Although it is fairly simple (just a square with a constant addition), it will work, in general.

The second notion here is what is going on with the function calls. The value B is "moving" through the values of the field (values modulo a) twice as "fast" (by calling the function f twice). This will give two pseudorandom sequences through the elements of the field.

Listing 3-3 shows a simple implementation of this program in Python, and Figure 3-4 shows an example run of the program.

The reason this algorithm is called the ρ algorithm is because, if drawn out on paper, the paths of the two values, A and B, chase each other around in a way that resembles the Greek letter ρ (see Figure 3-5).

3.3.3.1   Analysis of Pollard's ρ

The Pollard ρ algorithm has time complexity of approximately $O(n^{1/4})$ for finding a factor and no significant amount of storage [15]. Completely factoring a number will take slightly more time, but finding the first factor will usually take the longest.

Step	A	B	gcd(A-B, a)
0	2	2	
1	7	52	1
2	52	85,004	1
3	2,707	89,854	1
4	85,004	200,638	1
5	33,783	133,971	1
6	89,854	29,653	1
7	2,850	183,898	1
8	200,638	145,817	1
9	84,202	114,064	1
10	133,971	186,158	1
11	225,161	69,655	1
12	29,653	212,261	113

Figure 3-4 Pollard's ρ factorization of 2,262,599, with $b = 2$, $s = 2$.

Figure 3-5 Figure showing the path of a run of the Pollard ρ algorithm. The path will eventually loop back upon itself, hence the name "ρ." The algorithm will detect this loop and use it to find a factor.

```python
# Euclidean algorithm for GCD

def gcd(x, y):
 if y == 0:
  return x
 else:
  return gcd(y, x % y)


# Stepping function

def f(x, n):
    return (x * x + 3) % n


# Implements Pollard rho with simple starting conditions

def pollardrho(a):
    x = 2
    y = 2
    d = 1

    while d == 1:
        x = f(x, a)
        y = f(f(y, a), a)
        d = gcd(abs(x - y), a)

        if d > 1 and a > d:
            return d
        if d == a:
            return -1
```

Listing 3-3 Python code for Pollards ρ algorithm for factoring integers.

3.3.4 Pollard's $p - 1$

John M. Pollard also has another method attributed to him for factoring primes [12]. Pollard's $p - 1$ method requires that we have a list of primes up to some bound B. We can label the primes to be, say, $p_1 = 2$, followed by $p_2 = 3$, and $p_3 = 5$, and so on, all the way up to the bound B. There are already plenty of lists of primes to be found on the Internet, or they could be generated with a simple brute-force algorithm as described above, since we don't need very many of them (only a few thousand in many cases).

The algorithm works by **Fermat's little theorem**, that is, given a prime p and any integer b, then

$$b^{p-1} \equiv 1 \ (\text{mod } p)$$

We want to find p such that p is a prime factor of a, the number we are trying to factor. If L is some multiple of $(p - 1)$, then $p \mid \gcd(b^L - 1, a)$. The best way to try to get L to be a multiple of $(p - 1)$ is to have L be a multiple of several prime factors. We can't compute $b^L \bmod p$, but we can compute $b^L \bmod a$. The algorithm works by computing $L = p_1^{e_1} \cdots p_k^{e_k}$ (more specifically, b^L), where $e_i = \lfloor (\log B)/(\log p_i) \rfloor$, and trying to see if $(b^L - 1)$ and n have common factors.

Pollard's $p - 1$. Factors an integer, a, given a set of primes, $p_1, \ldots, p_k$.

1. Set $b = 2$.

2. For each i in the range $\{1, 2, \ldots, k\}$ (inclusive), perform the following steps:

   (a) Set e to be $\lfloor \log(B)/\log(p_i) \rfloor$ (the logarithm, base 10, of B divided by the logarithm of the i-th prime), rounded down.

   (b) Set f to be p_i^e (the i-th prime raised to the power of the above number).

   (c) Set $b = b^f \bmod a$.

3. Set g to be the GCD of $a - 1$ and b.

4. If g is greater than 1 and less than b, then g is a factor of b. Otherwise, the algorithm fails.

I won't show an implementation of this algorithm, since it requires such a large list of primes.

3.3.4.1 Analysis of Pollard's $p - 1$

Pollard's $p - 1$ algorithm runs in time relative to the size of the upper-bound B. For each prime number less than B ($\approx B/\ln B$ of them), we calculate e (assume this is negligible), then f (this takes $\log_2 e$ operations), and then b (this takes

$\log_2 f$ operations). This gives us a total of a bit more than $B \ln B$ operations to complete. This, therefore, grows very large very fast, in terms of the largest prime number we are concerned with.

One optimization to this can be to pre-compute the values of e and f, since they will not change between runs, saving us a little bit of time.

3.3.5   Square Forms Factorization

A method of factoring based on square forms, to be discussed in this section, was devised by Shanks in References [9] and [14].

Before we dive in to the Square Forms Factorization method (SQUFOF), I'll first set up a little of the mathematics.

Let the ordered triple of integers (a, b, c) correspond to all values of

$$ax^2 + bxy + cy^2$$

for all integers x and y. We say that (a, b, c) **represents** some value m if, and only if, we can find two values x and y such that $ax^2 + bxy + cy^2 = m$.

We say that two forms of (a, b, c) are **equivalent** if the two forms represent the same set of numbers. One way in which this can be done is by a linear change of variables of x and y, where $x' = Ax + By$, $y' = Cx + Dy$, and $AD - BC = 1$ or -1. For example, if $A = 1$, $B = 3$, $C = 1$, and $D = 4$, then we would have $x' = x + 3y$, $y' = x + 4y$, and

$$\begin{aligned} ax^2 &+ bxy + cy^2 \\ &= a(x' + 3y')^2 + b(x' + 3y')(x' + 4y') + c(x' + 4y')^2 \\ &= ax'^2 + 3ax'y' + 9ay'^2 + bx'^2 + 7bx'y' + 12by'^2 + cx'^2 + 8cx'y' + 4cy'^2 \\ &= (a + b + c)x'^2 + (3a + 7b + 8c)x'y' + (9a + 12b + 4c)y'^2 \end{aligned}$$

For example, $(1, 1, 2)$ and $(4, 26, 29)$ are equivalent.

This has two implications: The two forms represent the same set of numbers, and their discriminants of the form

$$D = b^2 - 4ac$$

will be the same.

A **square form** is a form of (a, b, c), where $a = r^2$ for some integer r — that is, a is a perfect square.

We will want to find a **reduced square form**, similar to finding the smallest CSR earlier. This is not hard if $D < 0$, but if $D > 0$, then we define a form as **reduced** if $\left| \sqrt{D} - 2|a| \right| < b < \sqrt{D}$ (here, the vertical bars indicate to take the absolute value of the number inside, i.e., throw away the sign).

The SQUFOF algorithm works by finding equivalent reduced forms related to the integer we want to factor.

For more information on implementing the square form factorization, see, for example, Stephen McMath's SQUFOF analysis paper [9].

3.3.5.1   *Analysis of SQUFOF*

The SQUFOF algorithm is one of the most powerful yet. Given a number to factor, a, the running time of the algorithm will be about $a^{1/4}$. This is still exponential (in terms of the digits of a), but a bit better than other methods.

3.3.6   Elliptic Curve Factorization Method

The **elliptic curve factorization method** (ECM) works similarly to Pollard's $p - 1$ algorithm, only instead of using the field of integers modulo p, we use an elliptic curve group based on a randomly chosen elliptic curve. Since many of the same principles work with elliptic curve groups, the idea behind Pollard's $p - 1$ also works here. The advantage is that the operations tend to take less time. (It's easier to multiply and add smaller numbers required for elliptic curves than the larger numbers for exponential-based group multiplication.) ECM was originally developed by Lenstra Jr. [7].

As before, we assume that we have a list of all of the primes $\{2, 3, 5, \dots\}$ stored as $\{p_1, p_2, p_3, \dots\}$ less than some bound B.

Elliptic Curve Factorization Method. The elliptic curve will be generated and used to try to find a factor of the integer a. The elliptic curve operations and coordinates will be taken modulo a.

1. Generate A and B as random numbers greater than (or equal to) zero and less than a. Thus, we have an elliptic curve defined by $y^2 = x^3 + Ax + B$ (modulo a).

2. Choose a random point on the elliptic curve, P, that is *not* the point at infinity. For example, choosing a random positive integer x less than a, plugging it into $x^3 + Ax + B$, and solving for the square root will yield a y-value. (I show how to solve for the square root in Chapter 2.)

3. Calculate g, the GCD of the discriminant, $(4a^3 + 27b^2)$, and a. If by some odd chance $g = n$, then generate a new A, B, and P, and try again. If $g \neq 1$, then it divides a, so it is a factor of a, so the algorithm can terminate and return a.

4. Do the following operations for each prime p less than B (each of the p_i values from earlier):

   (a) Let $e = \lceil (\log B)/(\log p) \rceil$. Here, we are taking the prime number and forming an exponent out of it by the logarithm of the bound B and dividing by the logarithm of p. The $\lceil \ \rceil$ operators are called the **ceiling** function, so that you take the integer closest to what is in between them, rounding "up" (taking the opposite action as the floor function).

(b) Set $P = (p^e)P$ — that is, add P to itself p^e times.

Here, we might find a factor, g, of a. How? Recall calculating the inverse of a number (say, x) modulo a. We find a number, x^{-1}, such that $x^{-1}x + kn = 1$. But, this operation only succeeds if the numbers are relatively prime. If we perform the calculation (using one of the Euclidean algorithms), we will have also calculated the GCD of x and a. If the GCD is not 1, then we have a factor of a. In that case, we terminate the algorithm and return g, the GCD.

5. If we have failed to find a factor, g (via the GCD above), then we can either fail or try again with a new curve or point, or both.

Furthermore, g is not guaranteed to be prime, but merely a factor.

3.3.6.1 *Analysis of ECM*

If p is the least prime dividing the integer a to be factored, then the expected time to find the factor is approximately

$$e^{\sqrt{2+\ln p \ln \ln p}}(\ln a)^2$$

The first term in this will typically dominate, giving a number a bit less than e^p.

In the worst-case scenario, when a is the product of two large and similar magnitude primes, then the running time is approximately

$$e^{\sqrt{1+\ln n \ln \ln n}}$$

This is going to be a bit less than e^n, but not so much. In both cases, the average and worst case, these are still exponential running times.

3.4 Subexponential Factoring Methods

The previous factoring methods were all exponential in running time. There are known methods that operate much faster (in subexponential time). However, these algorithms are more complicated, since they all use really nifty, math-heavy tricks to start to chip away at the running time and find factors fast.

Most subexponential factoring algorithms are based on Fermat's difference of squares method, explained above. A few other important principles are also used.

If x, y are integers and a is the composite number we wish to factor, and $x^2 \equiv y^2 \pmod{a}$ but $x \not\equiv \pm y \pmod{a}$, then $\gcd(x - y, a)$ and $\gcd(x + y, a)$ are factors of a.

3.4.1 Continued Fraction Factorization

The continued fraction factorization method is introduced in Reference [10]. The following explanation draws on this paper, as well as the material in References [9] and [15].

First, let's learn some new notation. If we wish to convey "x rounded down to the nearest integer," we can succinctly denote this using the **floor function** $\lfloor x \rfloor$. This means that $\lfloor 5.5 \rfloor = 5$, $\lfloor -1.1 \rfloor = -2$ and $\lfloor 3 \rfloor = 3$, for example. I have avoided using this notation before, but it will be necessary in the following sections.

One more quick definition. A **continued fraction** is a fraction that has an infinite representation. For example:

$$1 + \cfrac{1}{1 + \cfrac{1}{1 + \cfrac{1}{1 + \cdots}}}$$

Furthermore, a continued fraction for any number (say, c) can be constructed noting that $c = \lfloor c \rfloor + c - \lfloor c \rfloor$, or

$$c = \lfloor c \rfloor + \cfrac{1}{\cfrac{1}{c - \lfloor c \rfloor}}$$

Let $c_1 = \cfrac{1}{c - \lfloor c \rfloor}$. We stop whenever $c_i = \lfloor c_i \rfloor$. If not, we continue computing $c_{i+1} = \cfrac{1}{c_i - \lfloor c_i \rfloor}$. After a few steps, c looks like

$$c = \lfloor c \rfloor + \cfrac{1}{\lfloor c_1 \rfloor + \cfrac{1}{\lfloor c_2 \rfloor + \cdots}}$$

Furthermore, with a continued fraction form like the above (written compactly as $[c_0, c_1, \ldots, c_k]$), we can find A_k/B_k, the rational number it represents, by the following method:

1. Let $A_{-1} = 0, B_{-1} = 1, A_0 = c_0, B_0 = 1$.

2. For each i, compute $A_i = c_i A_{i-1} + A_{i-2}$ and $B_i = c_i B_{i-1} + B_{i-2}$.

The above algorithm will eventually terminate if the number being represented is irrational. Otherwise, it continues forever.

Using this method, we can now compute **quadratic residues**, Q_i — remainders when subtracting a squared number. The quadratic residues we are interested in are from $A_i^2 - nB_i^2 = (-1)^i Q_i$, representing the square of the difference between the form A_i/B_i and n. Taking this formula modulo n, we get

$$A_i^2 \equiv (-1)^i Q_i \pmod{n}$$

We will use the quadratic residues to derive a continued fraction sequence for $\sqrt{a}$, where a is the number we wish to factor.

We need an upper-bound on factors we will consider, B. The algorithm for exploiting this works by factoring each Q_i as we calculate it, and if it is B-smooth (contains no prime factors less than B), we record it with the corresponding A_i. After we have collected a large number of these pairs, we look at the exponents of the factors of each Q_i (modulo 2) and find equivalences between them. These will represent a system of equations of the form:

$$x^2 \equiv y^2 \ (\mathrm{mod}\ n)$$

When x is not equal to y, we use the same principle of Fermat's difference of squares to factor n.

The reason this works is that a square is going to have even numbers as exponents of prime factors. If we have two numbers that when multiplied together (adding their exponents) have even numbers in the exponent, we have a perfect square.

3.4.1.1 Analysis of CFRAC

Although the above work is fairly complex and involved, the above method saves an extraordinary amount of time. Using the CFRAC method to factor an integer will yield a running time on the order of $e^{\sqrt{2\ln a \ln \ln a}}$.

For reference, a normal exponential algorithm might be about $e^{\sqrt{\ln a \ln a}}$. For $a = 10,000,000,000$ (10 billion), this means a running time on the order of $10,000,000,000$ operations for an exponential method, and on the order of $170,000$ operations for CFRAC.

3.4.2 Sieving Methods

Two final methods that we shall not delve too deeply into are the **quadratic sieve** (QS) and the **general number field sieve** (GNFS). Both rely on the principle of Fermat's difference of squares and produce factors using this idea.

For QS, the idea is very similar to the continued fraction method in the previous section, using sieve instead of trial division for factorizations. The running time of QS tends to be on the order of about $e^{\sqrt{\ln a \ln \ln a}}$, with a being the integer to be factored. For more information on QS, see References [3] and [13].

A lot of focus has been on the GNFS, since it is the fastest known method for factoring large integers, or in testing the primality of extremely large integers.

The GNFS works in three basic parts. First, the algorithm finds an irreducible polynomial that has a zero modulo n [where n is the modulo base we are working with, so that $\gcd(x - y, n) > 1$, to find a factor]. Next, we find squares of a certain form that will likely yield factors. Then we find the square roots.

The "sieve" in the GNFS comes from the finding of squares in the second step. The special form that the squares come into involves calculating products of the sums of relatively prime integers. These relatively prime integers are calculated using sieving techniques.

For more information on the GNFS, see, for example, References [2] and [8].

3.5 Discrete Logarithms

Many algorithms use large group operations, such as exponentiation and large integer multiplication, to hide data.

For example, we can choose a finite field such as $(\mathbb{Z}_{23}, +, \times)$ and a generator 2. We can easily calculate $2^9 = 6$ in $\mathbb{Z}_{23}$. But, if someone saw a message passed as the integer 6, even with the knowledge that the generator is 2 and the field is over $\mathbb{Z}_{23}$, it is still, in general, a difficult problem to discover the exponent applied to the generator that yielded the given integer.

Solving an equation

$$a^x = b$$

for x in a finite field while knowing a and b is called solving for the **discrete logarithm**. (The standard logarithm is solving for the exponent in $a^x = b$ with real numbers.)

For groups defined by addition of points on elliptic curves, the operation becomes taking a fixed point and adding it to itself some large number of times, or, for P, computing aP in the elliptic curve group over $(\mathbb{Z}_p, +, \times)$ for some prime p.

Examples of such algorithms are the Diffie-Hellman key exchange protocol [4], ElGamal public key encryption [5], and various elliptic curve cryptography methods. To provide a concrete example, the Diffie-Hellman key exchange protocol on a finite field $\mathbb{Z}_p$ works as follows:

1. Two parties, A and B, agree on a finite field $\mathbb{Z}_p$ and a fixed generator g. A generates a secret integer a, and B generates a secret integer b.

2. $A \rightarrow B$: $g^a \in \mathbb{Z}_p$
   B can then compute $(g^a)^b = g^{ab}$ in $\mathbb{Z}_p$.

3. $B \rightarrow A$: $g^b \in \mathbb{Z}_p$
   A can then compute $(g^b)^a = g^{ab}$ in $\mathbb{Z}_p$.

Both parties now share a secret element, g^{ab}. An interceptor listening to their communications will know $\mathbb{Z}_p, g, g^a$, and g^b and will strive to find g^{ab} from this information. The easiest way of accomplishing this is to solve for $a = \log_g(g^a)$ or $b = \log_g(g^b)$, which is computing the discrete logarithm. However, this problem, it turns out, is incredibly difficult.

For the following problems, we will consider the case that we are in a finite field $\mathbb{Z}_p$, where p is a prime number. To make notation consistent, we will consider finding x such that $a^x = b$ in our finite field, where a is a generator and b is the desired result.

Note, however, that the following algorithms are equally applicable on other algebraic structures, such as elliptic curve groups.

3.5.1 Brute-Force Methods

There are, in general, two brute-force methods for computing a discrete logarithm.

If the number of elements in the field is small enough (less than a few billion or so, at least with today's computers), we can **pre-compute** and store all possible values of the generator raised to an exponent. This will give us a lookup table, so that any particular problem will take only as much time as it takes to look up the answer.

Obviously, there are some strong limitations here. With large fields, we can have extremely large tables. At some point, we aren't going to have enough storage space to store these tables.

At the other end of the spectrum is the second method for computing a discrete logarithm. Here, each time we want to solve a discrete logarithm problem, we try each and every exponent of our generator. This method takes the most amount of time during actual computation but has the advantage of no pre-computation.

It's easy to see that there should be a trade-off somewhere, between pre-computing everything or doing all the work every time. However, we need to be a little clever in choosing that trade-off point. Some people have put a lot of cleverness into these trade-off points, discussed below (and similar concepts are discussed in later chapters).

3.5.2 Baby-Step Giant-Step Method

The **baby-step giant-step** algorithm is one of the simplest trade-offs on time versus space, in that we are using some pre-computed values to help us compute the answers we need below.

Baby-Step Giant-Step. For the following algorithm, assume we are working in finite field over $\mathbb{Z}_p$, solving $a^x = b$ in $\mathbb{Z}_p$ for x.

1. Compute $L = \sqrt{p}$, rounded down, using the normal numerical square root operation.

2. Pre-compute the first L powers of a, $\{a^1, a^2, \ldots, a^L\}$, and store them in a lookup table, indexed by the exponents $\{1, 2, 3, \ldots, L\}$.

3. Let $h = \left(a^{-1}\right)^L$, our multiplier.

4. Let $t = b$, our starting point.

5. For each value of j in $\{0, 1, \ldots, L-1\}$, do the following:

   (a) If t is in the lookup table (some index i exists such that $a^i = t$ in the field), then return $i + j \times L$.

   (b) Set $t = t \times h$.

Basically, we are computing $b \times h^j$ in the loop and terminating when it equals some a^i, where $0 \le i < L$, giving us

$$b \times h^j = a^i$$

$$b \times \left((a^{-1})^L\right)^j = a^i$$

$$b \times a^{-Lj} = a^i$$

$$b = a^i \cdot a^{Lj}$$

$$b = a^{Lj+i}$$

Therefore, the discrete logarithm of b is $Lj + i$.

3.5.2.1 *Baby-Step Giant-Step Analysis*

The baby-step giant-step algorithm represents a hybrid of the first two brute-force methods. It has on the order of $\sqrt{p}$ space requirements (for the L powers of a) and about $\sqrt{p} \log(p)$ running time.

Like the previous brute-force methods, this method will find us an answer eventually, and there is no randomness involved. However, the space requirements are fairly large. For example, when p has hundreds or thousands of digits, then $\sqrt{p}$ will have roughly half the same number of digits, which will still be hundreds or thousands of digits! This amount of storage exceeds the capacity of current technology.

3.5.3 Pollard's ρ for Discrete Logarithms

Pollard's ρ method for discrete logarithms [11] relies on a similar principle as Pollard's ρ method for factoring — that is, we are looking for a cycle when stepping through exponents of random elements.

Here, assume that the group we are working with (the field) is the set of integers between 0 and $p - 1$ (written as $\mathbb{Z}_p$) along with normal addition and multiplication.

To perform Pollard's ρ algorithm for discrete logarithms, we partition the set of all integers between 0 and $p - 1$ into three partitions of roughly equal size: P_0, P_1, and P_2. These three sets can be simple, such as either the integers below p divided into three contiguous sets (the first third of numbers less than p, the second third, the third third), or split by the remainder of the number when divided by 3 (so that 2 belongs in P_2, 10 belongs in P_1, and 15 belongs in P_0).

The algorithm expects to solve the problem $a^x = b$ in the group G, thus it takes a and b as arguments.

It relies on three functions to operate: the function f, which takes one argument — an integer modulo p — and returns an integer modulo p; the function g, which takes an integer modulo p and a normal integer and returns an integer modulo $p - 1$; and a function h that takes an integer modulo p and an integer and returns an integer module $p - 1$.

The functions are defined based on the partition they are in. Thus:

$$\text{If } x \text{ is in } G_0 : \begin{cases} f(x) = (bx) \bmod p \\ g(x, n) = (n + 1) \bmod (p - 1) \\ h(x, n) = n \bmod (p - 1) \end{cases}$$

$$\text{If } x \text{ is in } G_1 : \begin{cases} f(x) = (x^2) \bmod p \\ g(x, n) = (2n) \bmod (p - 1) \\ h(x, n) = (2n) \bmod (p - 1) \end{cases}$$

$$\text{If } x \text{ is in } G_2 : \begin{cases} f(x) = (ax) \bmod p \\ g(x, n) = n \bmod (p - 1) \\ h(x, n) = n + 1 \bmod (p - 1) \end{cases}$$

Pollard's ρ for Discrete Logarithms.

1. Set $a_0 = 0$ and $b_0 = 0$, two of our starting helper values.

2. Set $x_0 = 1$, our starting point in G.

3. Let $i = 0$.

4. Repeat the following steps until, at the end, $x_i = x_{2i}$, and thus, we have found that our paths have merged.

   (a) Let $i = i + 1$.

   Now, we calculate the next value for the function traveling slowly:

   (b) Calculate the next x: $x_i = f(x_{i-1})$.

   (c) Calculate the next a: $a_i = g(x_{i-1}, a_{i-1})$.

   (d) Calculate the next b: $b_i = h(x_{i-1}, b_{i-1})$.

   Now, we calculate the next value for the function traveling quickly:

   (e) Calculate the next x: $x_{2i} = f(f(x_{2i-2}))$.

   (f) Calculate the next a: $a_{2i} = g(f(x_{2i-2}), g(x_{2i-2}, a_{2i-2}))$.

   (g) Calculate the next b: $b_{2i} = h(f(x_{2i-2}), h(x_{2i-2}, b_{2i-2}))$.

5. If our b's match, that is, $b_i = b_{2i}$, then the algorithm failed.

6. Set $m = a_i - a_{2i} \bmod (p - 1)$.

7. Set $n = b_{2i} - b_i \bmod (p - 1)$.

8. Solve, for x, the equation $mx \equiv n \pmod{(p - 1)}$. More than likely, this will result in a few possible values of x (usually a fairly small amount). Unfortunately, the only thing to do is to check each one and see if it is the correct answer.

3.5.3.1   *Analysis of Pollard's ρ for Discrete Logarithms*

Pollard's ρ solves the discrete logarithm with running time on the order of $\sqrt{p}$ (the square root of the size of the finite field), with constant space, contrasted to the baby-step giant-step method, which takes a similar amount of time but a large amount of space.

This makes it a great candidate for small discrete logarithm problems, where $\sqrt{p}$ is not too big (more than the number of calculations we are willing to make). The other issue is that this algorithm is not guaranteed to work: The intersection we find may not yield any useful values of x.

3.5.4   Pollard's λ for Discrete Logarithms

Pollard also proposed a generalization of the ρ algorithm for discrete logarithms, called the λ **method** (λ is the Greek letter lambda). Pollard's λ method of finding a discrete logarithm is a neat algorithm — interesting name, an amusing description, and very clever. Here, we want to compute the discrete logarithm for $g^x = h$ in a group G where we have some bound on x, such that $a \leq x < b$.

The following description is derived from References [11] and [15].

This method is sometimes called the **method of two kangaroos** (or hares, or rabbits, depending on the author). The concept is that two kangaroos (representing iterative functions) are going to go for some "hops" around the number field defined by the integer we wish to factor. These two kangaroos (or 'roos, as we like to say) consist of a tame one, controlled by us and represented by **T**, and a wild one that we are trying to catch, **W**.

The tame 'roo, **T**, starts at a random point, $t_0 = g^b$, while **W** starts at $w_0 = h = g^x$. Define $d_0(\mathbf{T}) = b$, the initial "distance" from the "origin" that the tame 'roo is hopping, and let $d_0(\mathbf{W}) = 0$, the initial distance of our wild 'roo from h.

Let $S = \{g^{s_1}, \ldots, g^{s_k}\}$ be a set of jumps, and let G be partitioned into k pieces $G_1, G_2, \ldots, G_k$, with $1 \leq f(g) \leq k$ being a function telling to which partition g belongs. These exponents of g in S should be positive and small compared to $(b - a)$. Most often, we will pick these numbers to be powers of 2 (2^i). These are the hops of both kangaroos.

Now, the two kangaroos are going to hop. **T** goes from t_i to

$$t_{i+1} = t_i g^{s_{f(t_i)}}$$

The tame 'roo will have distance

$$d_{i+1}(\mathbf{T}) = d_i(\mathbf{T}) + s_{f(t_i)}$$

Similarly, **W** goes from w_i to

$$w_{i+1} = w_i g^{s_{f(w_i)}}$$

giving the wild 'roo distance

$$d_{i+1}(\mathbf{W}) = d_i(\mathbf{W}) + s_{f(w_i)}$$

Eventually, $\mathbf{T}$ will come to rest at some position t_m, setting a trap to catch $\mathbf{W}$. If ever $d_n(\mathbf{W}) > d_m(\mathbf{T})$, then the wild kangaroo has hopped too far, and we reset $\mathbf{W}$ to start at $w_0 = hg^z$, for some small integer $z > 0$.

3.5.4.1 Analysis of Pollard's λ

To make this work, we need to set the s_i values so that they are about $0.5\sqrt{b-a}$ on average, and we will have $\mathbf{T}$ set its trap after approximately $0.7\sqrt{b-a}$ hops, giving us that $\mathbf{W}$ will hop about $2.7\sqrt{b-a}$ times before stopping. This method also has on the order of $\ln(b-a)$ space requirements, and on the order of $2.7\sqrt{b-a}$ time requirements.

3.5.5 Index Calculus Method

The **index calculus method** provides a method analogous to quadratic and number field sieves of factoring, shown above. This method is particularly well suited to solving the discrete logarithm on multiplicative groups modulo prime numbers. It was first described as the first subexponential discrete logarithm function by Adleman and Demarrais [1].

In general, this can be a very fast method over multiplicative groups, with on the order of $e^{\sqrt{2\log p \log \log p}}$ setup time and about $e^{\sqrt{\log p \log \log p}}$ running time.

For more information on the index calculus method, please refer to Reference [1].

3.6 Summary

Public key cryptographic systems and key exchange systems often rely on algebraic and number theoretic properties for their security. Two cornerstones of their security are the difficulty of finding factors of large numbers and solving discrete logarithms.

In this chapter, I discussed techniques for attempting to crack these two problems. While factoring and discrete logarithms for large problems are not easy, they represent the best way to perform cryptanalysis on most number theoretic and algebraic cryptosystems.

Exercises

For any of the programming exercises in this chapter, I recommend using a language that supports large number arithmetic. Languages that support such features are C/C++(through gmp), Java, and Python, although most languages will have at least some support for large number arithmetic.

Other languages and environments would also be useful for many of these problems, such as *Mathematica* and MATLAB. However, I find it difficult to recommend these packages for every reader, since they can be very expensive. If you have the ability to experiment with these and other advanced mathematical tools, feel free to use them.

Exercise 1. To get your fingers warmed up, take the Python Challenge, which is available online at www.pythonchallenge.com. This is a set of puzzles, some quite difficult, that require writing programs of various kinds to complete.

Although it is called the "Python" Challenge, there is no reason that any other language could not be used. It just happens that they guarantee that there are usually the appropriate packages available for Python (such as the Python Imaging Library for some of the image manipulation puzzles), along with Python's built-in support for string manipulation, large integer mathematics, and so forth.

Again, I am not trying to condemn or recommend any particular language for any particular purposes. This just happens to be, in my opinion, a good set of programming exercises.

Exercise 2. Implement the standard brute-force factoring algorithm as efficiently as possible in a programming language of your choice. Try only odd numbers (and 2) up to $\sqrt{a}$ (where a is the number you wish to factor).

Exercise 3. Make improvements to your brute-force algorithm. For example, skipping multiples of $3, 5, 7, \ldots$. Discuss the speed improvements in doing so.

Exercise 4. Implement Fermat's difference of squares method in the programming language of your choice. Discuss its performance (running times) with inputs of integers varying in size from small numbers (< 100) up through numbers in the billions and further.

Exercise 5. Implement Pollard's $p - 1$ factorization algorithm.

Exercise 6. Building on the elliptic curve point addition used in the previous chapter, implement elliptic curve factorization (ECF).

Next, provide a chart to compare the performance of Pollard's $p - 1$ and ECF for the same inputs (with the same, or similar, parameters).

Exercise 7. Implement Pollard's ρ algorithm for both factoring and discrete logarithms.

References

[1] Leonard M. Adleman and Jonathan Demarrais. A subexponential algorithm for discrete logarithms over all finite fields. *Mathematics of Computation* **61**(203): 1–15 (1993).

[2] J. A. Buchmann, J. Loho, and J. Zayer. An implementation of the general number field sieve. In *Advances in Cryptology – Crypto '93*, (ed. Douglas R. Stinson), pp. 159–165. Lecture Notes in Computer Science, Vol. 773. (Springer-Verlag, Berlin, 1993).

[3] J. A. Davis and D. B. Holdridge. Factorization using the quadratic sieve algorithm. In *Advances in Cryptology: Proceedings of Crypto '83*, (ed. David Chaum), pp. 103–116 (Plenum, New York, 1984).

[4] Whitfield Diffie and Martin E. Hellman. New directions in cryptography. *IEEE Transactions on Information Theory* IT-22 (6): 644–654 (1976); http://citeseer.ist.psu.edu/diffie76new.html.

[5] T. ElGamal. A public key cryptosystem and a signature scheme based on discrete logarithms. In *Advances in Cryptology: Proceedings of Crypto '84*, (eds. G. R. Blakley and David Chaum), pp. 10–18. Lecture Notes in Computer Science, Vol. 196. (Springer-Verlag, Berlin, 1985).

[6] Donald E. Knuth. *The Art of Computer Programming: Seminumerical Algorithms*, Vol. 2, 3rd ed. (Addison Wesley, Boston, 1998).

[7] H. W. Lenstra, Jr. Factoring integers with elliptic curves. *The Annals of Mathematics, 2nd Ser.* 126(3): 649–673 (1987).

[8] Arien K. Lenstra and Henrik W. Lenstra, Jr., eds. *The Development of the Number Field Sieve*, Vol. 554 of *Lecture Notes in Mathematics*. (Springer-Verlag, Berlin, 1993).

[9] Stephen McMath. *Daniel Shanks' Square Forms Factorization*. (2004); http://web.usna.navy.mil/~wdj/mcmath/SQUFOF.pdf.

[10] Michael A. Morrison and John Brillhart. A method of factoring and the factorization of f_7. *Mathematics of Computation* 29(129): 183–205 (1975).

[11] John M. Pollard. Monte carlo methods for index computation. *Mathematics of Computation* 32(143): 918–924 (1978).

[12] John M. Pollard. Theorems of factorization and primality testing. *Mathematical Proceedings of the Cambridge Philosophical Society* 76: 521–528 (1974).

[13] C. Pomerance. The quadratic sieve factoring algorithm. In *Advances in Cryptology: Proceedings of EuroCrypt '84*, (eds. Thomas Beth, Norbert Cot, and Ingemar Ingemarsson), pp. 169–182. Lecture Notes in Computer Science, Volume 209. (Springer-Verlag, Berlin, 1984).

[14] Daniel Shanks. Five number-theoretic algorithms. *Congressus Numerantium 7* (Utilitas Mathematica, 1973).

[15] Samuel S. Wagstaff. *Cryptanalysis for Number Theoretic Ciphers*. (Chapman & Hall/CRC, Boca Raton, FL, 2003).

# CHAPTER 4

Block Ciphers

So far, we have covered basic mathematics for studying encryption algorithms and even learned how to use several forms of **asymmetric** algorithms (ones that usually have a split key, a **private** and a **public** key). Before progressing further into modern **symmetric** algorithms (ones where both parties share the same key), we need to have an overview of the different forms of block ciphers.

To review, a **block cipher** is one that takes more than one character (or bit) at a time, processes them together (either encryption or decryption), and outputs another block. A **block** usually consists of a contiguous set of bits that is a power of 2 in size; common sizes are 32, 64, 128, and 256 bits. (A block size of 8 or 16 bits would possibly mean that it is not so much a stream cipher, but more just a character-for-character cipher, like we studied earlier.)

The simplest example of a block cipher is the columnar transposition cipher studied above. However, columnar transposition ciphers are based on character transformations and have variable block size, depending on the column size chosen. The ciphers studied from here on out are used in digital computers and thus will normally have bit operations.

Before the 20th century, people normally wanted to send messages consisting of text. This required operations on letters and blocks of letters, since these messages were written, either by hand or perhaps type; thus, the tools and techniques of cryptography were focused on letters and blocks of letters. In the modern age, we are concerned with digital information, such as text files, audio, video, and software, typically transmitted on computers or computer-like devices (e.g., phones, ATMs). The standard way to represent these forms of data is in bits, bytes, and words.

The following section presents a quick review of the basic building blocks of modern cryptography, such as bits and bytes. The rest of the chapter is devoted to more complicated structures of modern ciphers that we need to understand, so that we can break them in further chapters. I also present the inner workings of a few of the most popular targets for modern cryptanalysis (because of their widespread use), such as DES and AES.

This chapter is not an exhaustive study of modern cryptography. There are many good books on cryptography: the building of ciphers, as well as tools and techniques for doing so [11, 16]. Here, we wish to understand the basic structure of most ciphers, especially related to how we can manipulate those structures in later chapters.

4.1   Operations on Bits, Bytes, Words

A **bit**, as seen above but not quite defined, is a binary digit that is either a 0 or a 1. The standard **byte** is composed of 8 contiguous bits, representing values 0 through 255 (assuming we are only concerned with non-negative integers). When writing a byte in terms of its 8 bits, we write them as we do with normal numbers in decimal notation, in **most significant bit** order — as in, left-to-right, the more important, and hence "bigger," bits written first. For example, the byte representing the number 130 written in binary is

10000010

There is such a thing as **least significant bit** order, where the bits are essentially written backwards in a byte (certain communication protocols use this, for example), but I shall not discuss this further.

The next major organization of bits is the **word**, the size of which is dependent on the native size of the CPU's arithmetic register. Normally, this is 32 bits, although 64-bit words have been becoming common for quite some time; less commonly seen are 16-bit and 128-bit words.

We again have two ways of writing down words as combinations of bytes. The **most significant byte** (MSB) writes the "biggest" and most important bytes first, which would be analogous to the most significant bit order first. This is also called **big endian**, since the "big end" is first. For a 32-bit word, values between 0 and 4,294,967,295 ($= 2^{32} - 1$) can be represented (again, assuming we are representing non-negative integers). In big-endian binary, we would write the decimal number 1,048,580 ($= 2^{20} + 2^2 = 1,048,576 + 4$) as

00000000 00010000 00000000 00000100

Equivalently, we can write it in big-endian hexadecimal (base 16) by using a conversion table between binary and hexadecimal (see Table 4-1).

The above number, 1,048,580, written in big-endian hexadecimal ("hex") would be 00 10 00 04.

There is also another way to represent words in bytes: **least significant byte** (LSB) or **little endian** (for "little end" first). Basically, just take the previous way of writing it, and reverse it. The most confusing part is that the bits are still written in most significant bit order.

Table 4-1 Binary to Hexadecimal Conversion Table

BINARY	HEX	BINARY	HEX
0000	0	1000	8
0001	1	1001	9
0010	2	1010	A
0011	3	1011	B
0100	4	1100	C
0101	5	1101	D
0110	6	1110	E
0111	7	1111	F

This would make the above number, 1,048,580, written in little-endian hexadecimal as `04 00 10 00` and in binary as

```
00000100 00000000 00010000 00000000
```

There is no consensus in the computer architecture community on which one of these methods of writing words is "better": They both have their advantages and disadvantages.

I will always be very clear which method is being used in which particular cipher, as different ciphers have adopted different conventions.

4.1.1 Operations

There are a few basic operations that are useful to understand. Before, we studied basic operations on normal text characters, such as by shifting the characters using alphabets. Now, we are concerned with operations on binary data.

The **AND operator** (sometimes written as &, ·, or ×) operates on 2 bits. The result is a 1 if both operands are 1, and 0 otherwise (and hence, only 1 if the first operand "and" the second operand are 1). The reason symbols for multiplication are used for AND is that this operates identically to numerically multiplying the binary operands.

The **OR operator** (sometimes written as | or +) also takes two operands, and produces a 1 if either the first operand "or" the second operand is a 1 (or both), and 0 only if both are 0. Sometimes this can be represented with the plus symbol, since it operates similarly to addition, except that in this case, $1 + 1 = 1$ (or `1 | 1 = 1`), since we only have 1 bit to represent the output.

The **XOR (exclusive-OR, also called EOR) operator**, commonly written as ^ (especially in code) and $\oplus$ (often in text), operates the same as the OR operator, except that it is 0 if both arguments are 1. Hence, it is 1 if either argument is 1, but not both, and 0 if neither is 1.

XOR has many uses. For example, it can be used to flip bits. Given a bit A (either 0 or 1), calculating $A \oplus 1$ will give the result of **flipping** A (producing a result that is opposite of A).

Table 4-2 shows the outputs of the AND, OR, and XOR bitwise operators.

The final basic operation is the bitwise **NOT operator**. This operator takes only a single operand and simply reverses it, so that a 0 becomes a 1 and a 1 becomes a 0. This is typically represented, for a value a, as $\sim a$, $\bar{a}$, or $\neg a$ (in this book, we mostly use the latter). This can be combined with the above binary operators, by taking the inverse of the normal output. The most used of these operators are **NAND** and **NOR**.

All of these operators naturally extend to the byte and word level by simply using the bitwise operation on each corresponding pair of bits in the two bytes or words. For example, let $a = \text{A7}$ and $b = \text{42}$ (both in hexadecimal). Then $a \,\&\, b = \text{02}$, $a \mid b = \text{E7}$, and $a \oplus b = \text{E5}$.

In this book, I will try to show bits numbered from 0 up, with bit 0 being the least significant. When possible, I will try to stick with MSB (big endian) byte order, and most significant bit order as well. One final notation that is handy when specifying cryptographic algorithms is a notation of how to glue together various bits. This **glue** (or **concatenation**) is usually denoted with the $\parallel$ symbol. For example, the simple byte, written in binary as 01101101 would be written as

$$0 \parallel 1 \parallel 1 \parallel 0 \parallel 1 \parallel 1 \parallel 0 \parallel 1$$

We might also specify some temporary value as x and want to specify the individual bits, such as x_0, x_1, and so on. If x is a 4-bit value, we can use the above notation to write

$$x = x_3 \parallel x_2 \parallel x_1 \parallel x_0$$

Because we may be working with large structures with dozens or hundreds of bits, it can sometimes be useful to use the same glue operator to signify

Table 4-2 Bit Operations

A	B	A & B	A | B	A ⊕ B
0	0	0	0	0
0	1	0	1	1
1	0	0	1	1
1	1	1	1	0

concatenating larger structures, too. For example, if y is a 64-bit value and we want to reference 8 of its byte values, we might write them as

$$y = y_7 \parallel y_6 \parallel y_5 \parallel y_4 \parallel y_3 \parallel y_2 \parallel y_1 \parallel y_0$$

In this case, we will let y_0 be the least significant 8 bits, y_1 the next bits, and so forth.

I will try to be clear when specifying the sizes of variables, so that there will be as little confusion as possible. Even I have had some interesting problems when implementing ciphers, only to discover it is because the sizes were not properly specified, so the various pieces did not fit together.

4.1.2   Code

Again, I find it useful to have some code snippets in this chapter so that you can more easily see these algorithms in action.

And again, as in the previous chapter, I will have the examples in Python. This is for several reasons:

- Python has good support for array operations.
- Python code tends to be short.
- Python code tends to be easy to read.
- I already introduced Python, and it would be silly to introduce another language.

I won't have time to introduce every concept used, but I will try not to let something particularly confusing slip through. It is my intention that the examples will provide illumination and not further confusion.

With that little bit of introductory material out of the way, we can start exploring how we build block ciphers using some of the tools that we have developed, as well as a few more additional tools we shall build in the following sections.

4.2   Product Ciphers

One concept has reigned up to this point: We take some chunk of plaintext, subject it to a single process, and after that single process is completed, we have that ciphertext. This is not the case with most real-world ciphers today.

Modern ciphers are designed with the realization that having a single, large, complex operation can be impractical. Moreover, relying on only a single technique, such as a columnar transposition, is putting all of our eggs in one basket, so to speak: All of security is dependent on a single principle.

One of the key concepts in modern cryptography is the **product cipher** — a type of cipher that consists of several operations conducted in sequences and loops, churning the output again and again. The operations used are often those seen so far: substitutions, permutations, arithmetic, and so on. Ideally, the resilience of the resulting ciphertext will be significantly more than the individual strengths of the underlying techniques.

A simple example from Chapter 1 illustrates this concept. Instead of just performing a polyalphabetic cipher (susceptible to Kasiski's method) or a columnar transposition cipher (subject to the sliding window technique with digraph and trigraph analysis), we can combine both techniques — first perform a keyed substitution, letter-by-letter, on the original plaintext, and then run the output of that through the columnar transposition matrix. In this case, the resulting ciphertext would be completely immune to both Kasiski's method and to windowed digraph and trigraph analysis, defeating all of the techniques previously developed.

However, using a small sequence of polyalphabetic and columnar transposition ciphers in sequence does not make a cipher robust enough for modern use. Anyone who can guess which combination of techniques is being used can easily combine several types of analysis at once. There are a fairly limited number of combinations of these simple techniques to be used. And even so, these combinations could be easily broken by modern computing speeds. And finally, because most modern data that need to be encrypted are binary data from computers, and not handwritten or typed messages, these techniques are ill-suited for most current needs.

4.3   Substitutions and Permutations

In Chapter 1 I discussed two useful tools: **substitutions** (as in mono- and polyalphabetic substitution ciphers) and **transpositions** (as in columnar transposition ciphers). It turns out that digital counterparts to these exist and are widely used in modern cryptography.

4.3.1   S-Box

The terminology for a digital substitution is called a **substitution box**, or **S-box**. The term *box* comes from the fact that it is regarded as a simple function: It merely accepts some small input and gives the resulting output, using some simple function or lookup table. When shown graphically, S-boxes are drawn as simple boxes, as in Figure 4-1.

Figure 4-1 Graphical representation of a 4-bit S-box.

S-boxes normally are associated with a **size**, referring to their input and output sizes (which are usually the same, although they can be different). For example, here is a representation of a 3-bit S-box, called simply S:

```
S[0] = 7    S[3] = 4    S[6] = 0
S[1] = 6    S[4] = 3    S[7] = 1
S[2] = 5    S[5] = 2
```

This demonstrates one of the simpler methods of showing an S-box: merely listing the output for every input. As we can see, this S-box, S, almost reverses the numbers (so that 0 outputs 7, 1 outputs 6, etc.), except the last two entries for $S[6]$ and $S[7]$.

We can also specify this S-box by merely writing the outputs only: We assume that the inputs are implicitly numbered between 0 and 7 (since $7 = 2^3 - 1$). In general, they will be numbered between 0 and $2^b - 1$, where b is the input bit size. Using this implicit notation, we have S written as

```
[7, 6, 5, 4, 3, 2, 0, 1]
```

Of course, in the above S-box, I never specified which representation of bits this represents: most significant or least significant. A word of caution: Some ciphers do actually use least significant bit order (such as DES), even though this is fairly uncommon in most other digital computing. This can be very confusing if you are used to looking at ciphers in most significant bit order, and vice versa.

As specified above, S-boxes may have different sizes for inputs and outputs. For example, an S-box may take a 6-bit input, but only produce a 4-bit output. In this case, many of the outputs will be repeated. For the exact opposite case, with, say, a 4-bit input and 6-bit output, there will be several outputs that are not generated.

Sometimes S-boxes are derived from simpler moves. For example, we could have a 4-bit S-box that merely performs, for a 4-bit input x, the operation $4 - x \bmod 16$, and gives the result. The S-box spelled out would be

```
[4, 3, 2, 1, 0, 15, 14, 13, 12, 11, 10, 9, 8, 7, 6, 5]
```

S-boxes have some advantages, as we can see. They can be very random, with little correspondence between any input bits and output bits, and have few discernible patterns.

One primary disadvantage is size: They simply take a lot of space to describe. The 8-bit S-box for Rijndael, shown in Figure 4-2, takes a lot of space and requires implementing code to store the table in memory (although it can also be represented as a mathematical function, but this would require more computation at run time).

Another tool, the **permutation box** (or simply, **P-box**), is similar to an S-box but has a slightly different trade-off: A P-box is usually smaller in size and operates on more bits.

4.3.2   P-Box

A P-box provides similar functionality to transpositions in classical cryptography. The purpose of the permutation box is to permute the bits: shuffle them around but without changing them.

P-boxes operate by mapping each input value to a different output value by a lookup table — each bit is moved to a fixed position in the output. Most P-boxes simply permute the bits: one input to one output. However, in some ciphers (such as DES), there are **expansive** and **selective** permutations as well, where the number of output bits is greater (some bits are copied) or smaller (some bits are discarded), respectively.

P-boxes are normally specified in a similar notation to S-boxes, only instead of representing outputs for a particular input, they specify where a particular bit is mapped to. Assume that we number the bits from 0 to $2^b - 1$, where b is the size of the P-box input, in bits. The output bits will also be numbered from 0 to $2^c - 1$, where c is the size of the P-box output, in bits.

	0	1	2	3	4	5	6	7	8	9	a	b	c	d	e	f
0	63	7c	77	7b	f2	6b	6f	c5	30	01	67	2b	fe	d7	ab	76
1	ca	82	c9	7d	fa	59	47	f0	ad	d4	a2	af	9c	a4	72	c0
2	b7	fd	93	26	36	3f	f7	cc	34	a5	e5	f1	71	d8	31	15
3	04	c7	23	c3	18	96	05	9a	07	12	80	e2	eb	27	b2	75
4	09	83	2c	1a	1b	6e	5a	a0	52	3b	d6	b3	29	e3	2f	84
5	53	d1	00	ed	20	fc	b1	5b	6a	cb	be	39	4a	4c	58	cf
6	d0	ef	aa	fb	43	4d	33	85	45	f9	02	7f	50	3c	9f	a8
7	51	a3	40	8f	92	9d	38	f5	bc	b6	da	21	10	ff	f3	d2
8	cd	0c	13	ec	5f	97	44	17	c4	a7	7e	3d	64	5d	19	73
9	60	81	4f	dc	22	2a	90	88	46	ee	b8	14	de	5e	0b	db
a	e0	32	3a	0a	49	06	24	5c	c2	d3	ac	62	91	95	e4	79
b	e7	c8	37	6d	8d	d5	4e	a9	6c	56	f4	ea	65	7a	ae	08
c	ba	78	25	2e	1c	a6	b4	c6	e8	dd	74	1f	4b	bd	8b	8a
d	70	3e	b5	66	48	03	f6	0e	61	35	57	b9	86	c1	1d	9e
e	e1	f8	98	11	69	d9	8e	94	9b	1e	87	e9	ce	55	28	df
f	8c	a1	89	0d	bf	e6	42	68	41	99	2d	0f	b0	54	bb	16

Figure 4-2 Full listing of the Rijndael's 8-bit S-box.

For example, an 8-bit P-box might be specified as

```
P = [3 5 1 0 4 7 6 2]
```

This stands for `P[0] = 3, P[1] = 5, P[2] = 1,..., P[6] = 6, P[7] = 2`. The operation means to take bit 0 of the input and copy it to bit 3 of the output. Also take bit 1 of the input, and copy it to bit 5 of the output, and so forth. (Note that not all bits necessarily map to other bits — e.g., in this P-box, bits 4 and 6 map to themselves.) The example in Figure 4-3 illustrates this concept graphically.

For the preceding P-box, assume that the bits are numbered in increasing order of significance (0 being the least significant bit, 7 the most). Then, for example, the input of `00` will correspond to `00`. In hexadecimal (using big-endian notation), the input `01` would correspond to `20`, and `33` would correspond to `B8`.

A few things to note about P-boxes: They aren't as random as S-boxes — there is a one-to-one correspondence of bits from the input to the output. P-boxes also take a lot less space to specify than S-boxes: The 8-bit P-box could be written out in very little space. A 16-bit P-box could be written as a list of 16 numbers, but it would require a list of 65,536 numbers to fully specify a 16-bit S-box.

However, technically speaking, P-boxes *are* S-boxes, just with a more compact form. This is because they are simply a mapping of input values to output values and can be represented as a simple lookup table, such as an S-box. The P-box representation is merely a shortcut, albeit a very handy one.

If we look at any of the previously mentioned structures, though, we can see that they should not be used alone. A trivial cipher can be obtained by just using an S-box on an input, or a P-box, or even XORing each input byte with a fixed number. None of these techniques provides adequate security, though: The first two allow anyone with knowledge of the S-box or P-box to immediately decrypt a message, and with a simple XOR, anyone who knows the particular value of one byte in both plaintext and ciphertext could immediately derive the key.

For these reasons, I will use the above concept of a product cipher to combine each of these concepts — bitwise operations, S-boxes, and P-boxes — to create

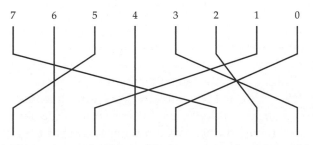

Figure 4-3 A simple graphical representation of an 8-bit P-box. Note that bits 4 and 6 are passed straight through.

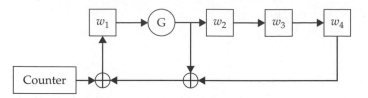

Figure 4-4 Skipjack's Rule A shift register.

a very complicated structure. We won't limit ourselves to just these particular operations and boxes, but the ones explained so far represent the core of what is used in most modern cryptographic algorithms.

4.3.3   Shift Registers

Another tool used in the construction of ciphers is a **shift register**. Look at Figure 4-4, one of two shift registers in Skipjack (called Rule A and Rule B), for an example of how a shift register operates.

Typically, a shift register works by taking the input and splitting it into several portions; thus, in this case, $w = w_1 \parallel w_2 \parallel w_3 \parallel w_4$ is our input. Then, the circuit is iterated several times. In this diagram, G represents a permutation operation. Thus, after one round through the algorithm, w_2 will get the permutation of w_1; w_3 will be the XOR of the old w_2, the counter, and the old w_1; and w_4 will get the old value of w_3; while w_1 gets the old value of w_4. This iteration is repeated many times (in Skipjack, it iterates eight times in two different locations).

Shift registers are meant to mimic the way many circuits and machines were designed to work, by churning the data in steps. These are also designed with parallelism in mind: While one piece of circuitry is performing one part of the computation, another can be computing with a different part of the data, to be used in following steps.

4.4   Substitution–Permutation Network

The first natural extension of the above simple techniques is to merely start combining them. A **substitution–permutation network** (SPN) is just that: It chains the output of one or more S-boxes with one or more P-boxes, or vice versa. The concept is similar to chaining together simple substitution ciphers of text and transposition ciphers: We have one layer substituting values for other values, thereby adding a lot of *confusion* (in that it is a bit harder to see where the output comes from). We then have another layer mixing the output bits from one or more S-boxes and jumbling them together, contributing primarily to *diffusion* (in that input bits influence a lot of output bits).

However, up until this point, we are still going to have trouble with the output being trivially related to the input: Simply knowing the combinations of S-boxes and P-boxes can let us derive one from the other. We need a way of adding a key into the system so that only parties privy to the key will be able to encrypt and decrypt messages.

The most common mechanism for adding keys to the above system is to compute some function of the key to give a set of bits, referred to as the **key schedule**. These bits from the key schedule are then usually integrated into the cipher somehow, normally by XORing them together with intermediate bits in the cipher (such as the input of some S-boxes).

The most common way of forming an SPN is to have many (usually different) S-boxes and P-boxes, with their inputs and outputs chained together. For example, see Figure 4-5. When we chain them together like this, we may XOR in the key schedule bits several times. We call these key schedule bits and not just the key bits because, as I said above, these bits are merely derived *from* the key. Some may be identical to the key, but, for example, we may use different subsets of the key bits at different parts of the network (maybe shifted, or inverted at different parts).

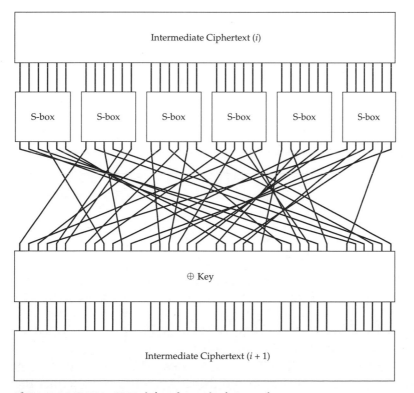

Figure 4-5 EASY1 SPN cipher for a single round.

As Reference [4] points out, SPN ciphers are ideal for demonstrating several cryptanalytic techniques.

4.4.1   EASY1 Cipher

There is a need for a cipher that is easy enough for you to easily implement and see results of various techniques, while still being complicated enough to be useful. For that, we shall create a cipher call EASY1 in this section. We'll use it in later chapters to demonstrate some of the methods of cryptanalysis.

EASY1 is a 36-bit block cipher, with an 18-bit key. EASY1 works by splitting its input into 6-bit segments, running them through S-boxes, concatenating the results back together, permuting them, and then XORing the results with the key. The key is just copied side-by-side to become a 36-bit key (both the "left half" and "right half" of the cipher bits are XORed with the same key).

We will use various numbers of rounds at different times, usually low numbers.

The 6-bit S-boxes in EASY1 are all the same:

```
[16, 42, 28, 3, 26, 0, 31, 46, 27, 14, 49, 62, 37, 56, 23, 6, 40, 48, 53, 8,
 20, 25, 33, 1, 2, 63, 15, 34, 55, 21, 39, 57, 54, 45, 47, 13, 7, 44, 61, 9,
 60, 32, 22, 29, 52, 19, 12, 50, 5, 51, 11, 18, 59, 41, 36, 30, 17, 38, 10, 4,
 58, 43, 35, 24]
```

This is represented in the more compact, array form: The first element is the substitution for 0, the second for 1, and so forth. Hence, an input of 0 is replaced by 16, 1 by 42, and so on. The P-box is a large, 36-bit P-box, represented by

```
[24, 5, 15, 23, 14, 32, 19, 18, 26, 17, 6, 12, 34, 9, 8, 20, 28, 0, 2, 21, 29,
 11, 33, 22, 30, 31, 1, 25, 3, 35, 16, 13, 27, 7, 10, 4]
```

Our goal with EASY1 is that it should be easy to understand and fast to derive keys without the use of cryptanalysis (so answers can be verified).

I'll provide some quick code to perform EASY1.

4.4.1.1   *Python Implementation*

Here, I show a simple EASY1 implementation in Python. For simplicity, I will make the implementation generic so that different values can be easily put in and tested.

Assume that the S-box is input as a simple array in a variable called s, and that the P-box is also stored as an array in s.

We can make generic S-box and P-box functions. The S-box function is simple: Use the argument as an index into the array, which will return the appropriate value. The P-box implementation is a bit trickier, as shown in Listing 4-1.

```python
############################################
# S-box function
############################################

def sbox(x):
  return s[x]


############################################
# P-box function
############################################

def pbox(x):
  # if the texts are more than 32 bits,
  # then we have to use longs
  y = 0l

  # For each bit to be shuffled
  for i in range(len(p)):

   # If the original bit position
   # is a 1, then make the result
   # bit position have a 1

   if (x & (1l << i)) != 0:
    y = y ^ (1l << p[i])

  return y
```

Listing 4-1 Python code for the EASY1 S-box and P-box.

In Listing 4-1, we first have to introduce some cumbersome notation: The "l" (or "L") modifier specifies that the number may grow to become more than 32 bits (which is the size of a normal Python integer). Although it can automatically grow, it gives a lot of warnings if we don't tell Python we are expecting this, by specifying that we want a *long* integer, meaning that it can be much bigger. (The values of the bits of the output that are not copied are all zeros.)

The rest of the code to implement the P-box is not too bad. We have to do an ugly calculation that, for each bit position in the P-box, determines if that input bit is set. If so, then it determines which bit the set bit maps to in the output and sets it as well. All bits not set in this way are set to zero.

The next piece of code (Listing 4-2) is used for splitting apart the pieces to be fed to the S-boxes and then put back together — hence the mux (multiplex, or combine) and demux (demultiplex, or break apart) functions.

```
#########################################
# Takes 36-bit to six 6-bit values
# and vice-versa
#########################################
def demux(x):
  y = []
  for i in range(0,6):
    y.append((x >> (i * 6)) & 0x3f)

  return y


def mux(x):
  y = 0l
  for i in range(0,6):
    y = y ^ (x[i] << (i * 6))

  return y
```

Listing 4-2 Python code for the EASY1 multiplexing and demultiplexing.

The trickiest part of this code is the use of the bit shift operators, which simply take the left-hand side of the expression and shift the bits left (for <<) or right (for >>) by the number on the right. The demux function also uses an AND operation by 0x3F, which is the **bit mask** representing the binary expression 111111 — that is, six 1's, which will drop all the bits to the left, returning only the rightmost six bits.

Finally, we write one last helper function: the code to XOR in the keys. This code is shown in Listing 4-3 — nothing too fancy there.

```
#########################################
# Key mixing
#########################################

def mix(p, k):
  v = []
  key = demux(k)
  for i in range(0,6):
    v.append(p[i] ^ key[i])

  return v
```

Listing 4-3 Python code for EASY1 key XORing.

After all of these helper functions, we can put in the code to do the actual encryption: the round function and a wrapper function (`encrypt`). This code is shown in Listing 4-4.

```
##########################################
# Round function
##########################################

def round(p,k):
  u = []

  # Calculate the S-boxes
  for x in demux(p):
    u.append(sbox(x))

  # Run through the P-box
  v = demux(pbox(mux(u)))

  # XOR in the key
  w = mix(v,k)

  # Glue back together, return
  return mux(w)


##########################################
# Encryption
##########################################

def encrypt(p, rounds):
  x = p
  for i in range(rounds):
    x = round(x, key)

  return x
```

Listing 4-4 Python code for EASY1 encryption.

To complete this code roundup, we have the decryption code (shown in Listing 4-5).

```
##########################################
# Opposite of the round function
##########################################

def unround(c, k):
  x = demux(c)
```

Listing 4-5 Python code for EASY1 decryption.   *(continued)*

```
    u = mix(x, k)
    v = demux(apbox(mux(u)))
    w = []
    for s in v:
     w.append(asbox(s))

    return mux(w)



#############################################
# Decryption function
#############################################

def decrypt(c, k):
  x = c
  for i in range(rounds):
   x = deround(x, key)

  return x
```

Listing 4-5 (*continued*)

SPNs can be used alone (as a complete cipher, such as AES), or, for example, as part of a Feistel structure (see the next section).

4.5   Feistel Structures

One disadvantage to many types of ciphers, including substitution–permutation networks, is that two separate operations are required: encryption and decryption. Most algorithms require separate software routines or hardware to implement the two operations. When writing a cryptographic suite for an ASIC (a fixed, silicon chip), there is often a premium on space available: Implementing two separate functions, one for encryption and one for decryption, will naturally take up about twice as much space.

Luckily, there is a technique that allows both encryption and decryption to be performed with nearly identical pieces of code, which has obvious cost-saving benefits.

This now-common structure for modern ciphers was invented by Horst Feistel and is naturally called the **Feistel structure**. The basic technique is simple: Instead of developing two different algorithms (one for encryption, one for decryption), we develop one simple **round function** that churns half a block of data at a time. The round function is often denoted f and usually takes two inputs: a half-sized block and a **round key**. We then cleverly arrange the inputs and outputs to create encryption and decryption mechanisms for the whole block in the following manners.

For a particular structure, slight variations of the same Feistel structure are common between encryption and decryption rounds — different at least in key choice (this is called the **key schedule**), and sometimes in other parameters, or even the the workings of the structure itself.

Feistel ciphers typically work by taking half of the input at any round and XORing it with the output of the Feistel structure. This is then, in the next round, XORed with the other half, and the two halves are swapped, and the Feistel structure is computed and XORed in again. The two "halves" are not necessarily of equal length (which are called **unbalanced**).

Basic Feistel Encryption Algorithm. The basic Feistel encryption algorithm structure is r rounds long, with the round function f.

1. Split the initial plaintext, P, into two halves: The "left half" (L_0) consists of the most significant bits, and the "right half" (R_0) consists of the least significant bits.

2. For each round, $i = 1, \ldots, r$, do the following:

   (a) Calculate $R_i = L_{i-1} \oplus f(R_{i-1}, K_i)$, that is, the previous left half XORed with the round function (whose arguments are the previous right half and the current round key).

   (b) Calculate $L_i = R_{i-1}$.

This structure will make more sense after looking at Figure 4-6, which shows the encryption in action.

The algorithm then terminates after the appropriate number of rounds, with the output ciphertext, C, obtained by concatenating the two halves after r rounds: L_r and R_r. For example, with three rounds, we would have the following progression:

$$R_0$$
$$L_0$$
$$R_1 = L_0 \oplus f(R_0, K_1)$$
$$L_1 = R_0$$
$$R_2 = L_1 \oplus f(R_1, K_2)$$
$$L_2 = R_1$$
$$R_3 = L_2 \oplus f(R_2, K_3)$$
$$L_3 = R_2$$

Now, the nifty part of the Feistel structure we can see here at the end: If we have the ciphertext, L_3 and R_3, then that means we also have R_2 (since $L_3 = R_2$). The party doing the decrypting will also know the key and thus will then know the appropriate value of the key schedule, K_3, allowing the party to calculate $f(R_2, K_3)$. Now note that

$$R_3 = L_2 \oplus f(R_2, K_3)$$

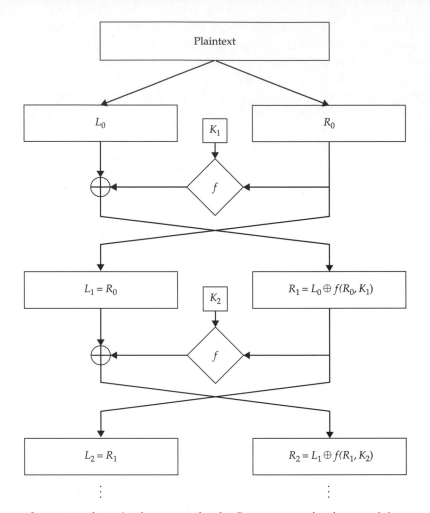

Figure 4-6 The Feistel structure for the first two rounds. The remaining rounds just repeat the structure.

from the above encryption. We can then rewrite this (by exchanging L_2 and R_3 due to the symmetry of XOR) to obtain

$$L_2 = R_3 \oplus f(R_2, K_3)$$

We thus obtain the previous round's intermediate ciphertext, L_2 and R_2. Repeating this again and again will eventually reveal the original plaintext, as shown in the following example:

$$
\begin{aligned}
& L_3 \\
& R_3 \\
& R_2 = L_3 \\
& L_2 = R_3 \oplus f(R_2, K_3)
\end{aligned}
$$

$$R_1 = L_2$$
$$L_1 = R_2 \oplus f(R_1, K_2)$$
$$R_0 = L_1$$
$$L_0 = R_1 \oplus f(R_0, K_1)$$

We can now generalize the decryption operation to work with any number of rounds.

Basic Feistel Decryption Algorithm. Computes a basic Feistel operation of r rounds, with a round function f, and key schedule $(K_1, K_2, \ldots, K_r)$.

1. Split the ciphertext, C, into two halves: The "left half" (L_r) consists of the most significant bits, and the "right half" (R_r) consists of the least significant bits.

2. For each round, $i = r - 1, \ldots, 0$, do the following:

   (a) Set $R_i = L_{i+1}$.

   (b) Set $L_i = R_{i+1} \oplus f(R_i, K_{i+1})$.

As we can see, for decryption, the operations are nearly identical to the encryption algorithm. The primary difference is that the keys (K_i) are submitted in reverse order.

Ciphers that use the above Feistel structure have several notable properties.

- The round function can be relatively simple, as the structure is normally iterated numerous times. Typically 4, 8, 16, and 32 rounds are common.

- Encryption and decryption, for the most part, can use identical structures: The round function does most of the work for both operations. (Encryption and decryption can still differ by more. For example, some ciphers with Feistel structures have different forms for their initial or final rounds, such as initial and final permutations.)

- The round function can be nonlinear and noninvertible. In many ciphers, such as the Caesar cipher, the core function must be invertible: We have to be able to go backwards to decrypt. However, with the Feistel structure, we never need to compute the inverse of the round function, since both encryption and decryption use the normal round function. Normally, the round function is a product cipher of permutations, substitutions, and other functions.

Although using the round function definitely saves time and space, since it operates on half as many bits, there are a few issues to consider. The round function operates on half as many bits; thus, there is less to brute-force with. Furthermore, since the security of the round function *is* the security of the cipher, it must be rock solid.

4.6 DES

The Data Encryption Standard (DES) [8] is based on the Lucifer algorithm, from IBM. DES was the first Feistel-based cipher, and Horst Feistel himself worked on it. For more on the background and history of DES, see References [1] and [16].

DES is a 64-bit cipher in every sense: It operates on 64-bit blocks and has a 64-bit key. However, the key in DES is effectively a 56-bit key; the other 8 bits are used for parity. Although brute-forcing a 56-bit key means evaluating 72,057,594,037,927,936 different keys (about 72 quadrillion, or million billions), which is not a computation to take lightly, it is not outside the realm of possibility. In 1999, a network of computers (`distributed.net` and the Electronic Frontier Foundation's Deep Crack machine) succeeded in brute-forcing a known-plaintext key in less than a day [13].

DES Encryption Algorithm. First, a note on numbering. I will try to be true to the DES specification [8], and in doing so, will have to adopt its backwards numbering scheme. In DES, all bits are numbered from most significant to least significant, 1 to whatever (up to 64). This means that the decimal number 18 (`10010` in binary) has the bit numbers shown in Table 4-3.

This is unlike most other algorithms we will use and see, which number 0, 1, ..., and from least significant to most significant (right-to-left).

DES first takes the 64-bit input block and does an initial permutation, shifting the 64 bits around. (I won't show the details of every box in DES and refer the interested reader instead to Reference [8].)

The DES main round structure then operates identically to the basic Feistel structure shown in the previous section — split the permuted plaintext into L_0 and R_0, and run the following Feistel structure for 16 rounds:

1. Compute $R_{i+1} = L_i \oplus f(R_i, K_{i+1})$.
2. Set $L_{i+1} = R_i$.

After the final round, the ciphertext goes through the inverse of the initial permutation.

The real meat of DES is in the round function and the key schedule. Let's discuss the key schedule first.

Table 4-3 Binary Representation of the Decimal Number 18

Bit Number:	1	2	3	4	5
Value:	1	0	0	1	0

4.6.1   DES Key Schedule

The key schedule produces, from a 64-bit key, a set of 16 keys ($K_1, K_2, \ldots, K_{16}$) using the following method:

1. The key is split into two 28-bit halves (since there are 56 uniquely defined bits), by using a P-box (which throws away bits 8, 16, 24, 32, 40, 48, 56, and 64 of the key, and scrambles the rest). The left half is denoted C_0, and the right half is denoted D_0.

2. For each round, $i = 1, 2, \ldots, 16$, we left rotate the previous round's values for C_i and D_i by 1 (for rounds 1, 2, 9, and 16) or by 2 (for rounds 3–8 and 10–15). The outputs are put through to the next round and also concatenated and put through another selective permutation (which reduces them to 48 bits) for use as the round key K_i. The selective permutation remains the same throughout the algorithm.

We then have 16 48-bit round keys, $K_1, K_2, \ldots, K_{16}$.

4.6.2   DES Round Function

The DES round function consists of four operations, applied in succession:

1. The 32 bits of the input to the round function are put through an expansive permutation to create a 48-bit value (the bits are shuffled around, and some are copied). The selective permutation is represented by the following list:

   [32, 1, 2, 3, 4, 5, 4, 5, 6, 7, 8, 9, 8, 9, 10, 11, 12, 13, 12, 13, 14, 15, 16, 17, 16, 17, 18, 19, 20, 21, 20, 21, 22, 23, 24, 25, 24, 25, 26, 27, 28, 29, 28, 29, 30, 31, 32, 1]

   Here, each entry, numbered 1–48, represents each bit of the output. The value in the entry is which bit in the input to copy. For example, the first bit of the output is copied from bit 32 of the input, the second bit of the output from bit 1 of the input, and so forth, until all 48 bits of the output are copied from the input.

2. The 48 bits are XORed with the round key.

3. The 48 bits are split into eighths (each a 6-bit value), and each of these values is used as the input to a separate S-box, each of whose output is 4 bits. There are eight distinct S-boxes for this step. The outputs are concatenated into a 32-bit number.

4. The 32 bits are put through a P-box, whose output is also 32 bits long. The P-box can be represented by this list:

   [16, 7, 20, 21, 29, 12, 28, 17, 1, 15, 23, 26, 5, 18, 31, 10, 2, 8, 24, 14, 32, 27, 3, 9, 19, 13, 30, 6, 22, 11, 4, 25]

This list is numbered from 1 to 32, where each entry corresponds to a bit of output. The value in the entry represents which bit to copy to the output bit.

The final result from the P-box is then given as the output. Figure 4-7 shows a diagram of DES's round function.

The S-boxes in the third step are the most critical part of the cipher. The rest of DES is fairly straightforward and predictable; thus, a very large part of the security of DES rests in the values of the S-boxes.

4.6.3   Triple DES

An ever-growing flaw with DES is its limited key strength, as already mentioned. Despite this, the algorithm was widely used for decades, and few debilitating weaknesses were found in the algorithm. In order to combat the key weakness but prevent hardware and software manufacturers from having to completely change products that utilize DES, a way to extend the life was proposed in the form of **triple DES** (or, more commonly written, **3DES**).

The 3DES method is fairly similar to how it sounds: We essentially run the cryptographic algorithm three times, each time with a potentially different key. We don't just encrypt three times on one end and decrypt three times on the other end, though. Instead, we encrypt and decrypt plaintext P (and corresponding ciphertext C) with three keys, K_1, K_2, and K_3 (in that order), by computing

$$Encryption: \quad C = \text{Encrypt}_{K_3}(\text{Decrypt}_{K_2}(\text{Encrypt}_{K_1}(P)))$$
$$Decryption: \quad P = \text{Decrypt}_{K_1}(\text{Encrypt}_{K_2}(\text{Decrypt}_{K_3}(C)))$$

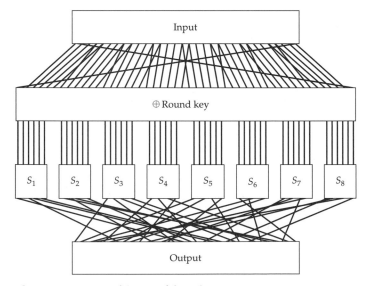

Figure 4-7 DES 32-bit round function.

Hence, 3DES is sometimes referred to as **DES-EDE** (for "Encrypt–Decrypt–Encrypt").

There are a few notes to make here. We have three keys, so wouldn't we have a key of length $56 \times 3 = 168$ bits? The answer is — sometimes, but not usually.

In most implementations of 3DES, there is a 112-bit key; we let K_1 and K_2 be distinct keys, and $K_3 = K_1$. The official specification also allows for two additional modes: using three distinct keys (for a full 168-bit key) and having all three keys be the same. Note that if all three keys are the same, then the first two operations of the encryption cancel each other out, as do the final two of the decryption, which creates the standard DES ciphering scheme. This allows software and hardware made for 3DES to also be easily converted back to the original DES as well (although it will be slower because of the wasted time of encrypting and decrypting with no end result).

4.6.4 DESX

Many different variants of DES have been proposed. An interesting one is meant to make an exhaustive key search (by trying all possible 56-bit keys) much harder, while not increasing the complexity of the original algorithm at all. **DESX** uses the exact same algorithm as DES above but involves extra steps called **whitening**.

Essentially, if we have a DES function using a key k on a plaintext P, we can, for example, write our ciphertext as

$$C = \text{DES}_k(P)$$

To whiten DES, we take two additional keys of 64 bits each, say, k_2 and k_3, and XOR them to the plaintext and ciphertext, respectively:

$$C = k_3 \oplus \text{DES}_k(P \oplus k_2)$$

The XOR operation used is where the "X" in "DESX" comes from.

The security of this is actually more than it appears at first glance: Adding these XORs does not appear to make the cipher less secure and could possibly increase the virtual key to be $56 + 64 + 64 = 184$ bits, instead of the standard 56 bits. In addition, it is trivial to take a normal algorithm that calculates a DES ciphertext and modify it for DESX: Simply XOR the plaintext once before running the algorithm, and XOR the ciphertext afterwards.

This covers the basic workings of DES, although I don't explicitly state the values of the S-boxes and P-boxes. This information is readily available in the specification and in many books.

4.7 FEAL

FEAL (the **Fast Encipherment Algorithm**) is one of the simpler Feistel-based ciphers. Because many cryptanalytic attacks work on FEAL, it demonstrates many weaknesses for us to analyze.

FEAL was created in the 1980's as a fast alternative of DES. There was a feeling that DES was too slow, especially for most personal computers in that era (Intel 8086's, Motorola 68000's, etc.), because of its fairly large number of complicated round functions that must be calculated just to get 64 bits of output. FEAL, like DES, is based on a Feistel structure, but designed to provide a simpler, faster, and still secure variant, replacing the large S-boxes with simple functions. (However, as we see below, it fails miserably in the secure department.)

FEAL Algorithm. The basic encryption and decryption algorithm follows a simple Feistel structure, as seen in Figure 4-8. There are several functions that I will cover, but the overall algorithm is as follows:

1. Calculate a key schedule $(K_0, K_1, \ldots, K_{11})$ in accordance with Section 4.7.4.

2. Break the plaintext, P, into two 32-bit halves: (L_0, R_0).

3. Calculate $L_0 = L_0 \oplus (K_8 \parallel K_9)$.

4. Calculate $R_0 = R_0 \oplus (K_{10} \parallel K_{11}) \oplus L_0$.

5. For $r = 1, \ldots, 8$ (i.e., each of eight rounds):

    (a) $R_r = L_{r-1} \oplus f(R_{r-1}, K_{r-1})$.

    (b) $L_r = R_{r-1}$.

6. Calculate $L_8 = L_8 \oplus R_8 \oplus (K_{14}, K_{15})$.

7. Calculate $R_8 = R_8 \oplus (K_{12}, K_{13})$.

I will break down the different pieces of these and explain each of them in the following sections.

4.7.1 *S-function*

Rather than use a larger, complicated S-box, a simple function is used in FEAL so that it could be implemented in a few standard computer instructions without requiring large lookup tables. The S-box is called the **S-function**, defined as a function of three variables: x, y, and δ. Here, x and y are byte values, while δ is a single bit that changes depending on which round the S-function occurs in.

We define $S(x, y, \delta)$ as

$$S(x, y, \delta) = \text{ROT2}(x + y + \delta) \bmod 256$$

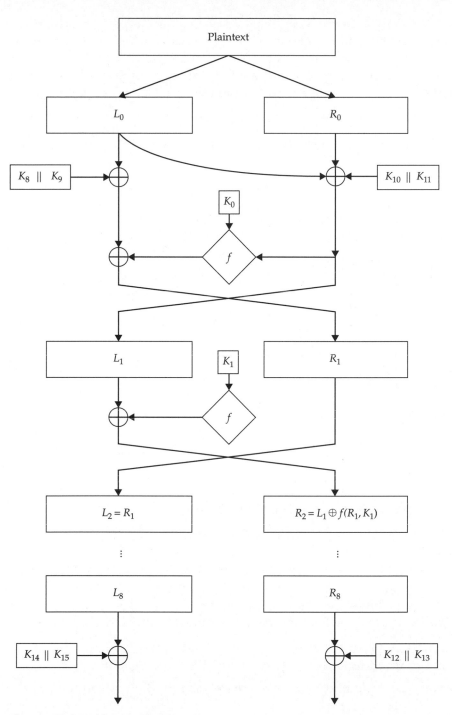

Figure 4-8 FEAL's encryption structure.

The "mod 256" portion indicates that we need to do simple byte arithmetic. The "ROT2" function indicates taking its argument, in this case an 8-bit number, and shifting all of its bits (as seen in its most significant bit form) to the left by two places, with the most significant 2 bits (shifted out on the left) being rotated back in to the least significant bits (on the right). For example:

$$\text{ROT2}(00101011) = 10101100$$

A sample implementation of the *S*-function, including the rotation function, is shown in Listing 4-6.

```
#########################################
# The rot2 function - helper for the S-function
#########################################

def rot2(x):
    r = (x < 2) & 0xff    # Calculate the left shift, removing extra bits
    r = r ^ (x >> 6)       # OR in the leftmost two bits onto the right
    return r



#########################################
# The FEAL S-function
#########################################

def sbox(x, y, delta):
    return rot2((x + y + delta) & 0xff)
```

Listing 4-6 Python code for the FEAL *S*-function.

4.7.2   Key-Generating Function: f_K

The f_K function is a helper function that churns the key to create various subkeys.

Here, the inputs to the key generating function, denoted α and β, are 32-bit quantities, split into four 8-bit quantities. Operations are then done with 8-bit arithmetic, probably since, when FEAL was designed, it was much faster than 32-bit arithmetic, and the 8-bit results are recombined into the 32-bit result.

1. Let the 32-bit result of the key function be referenced by four 8-bit sub-parts, so that $f_K(\alpha, \beta) = f_K^0(\alpha, \beta) \parallel f_K^1(\alpha, \beta) \parallel f_K^2(\alpha, \beta) \parallel f_K^3(\alpha, \beta)$.

2. Let the 32-bit input to f_K, α, be referenced as four 8-bit quantities as well: $\alpha = \alpha^0 \parallel \alpha^1 \parallel \alpha^2 \parallel \alpha^3$.

3. Similarly for β: $\beta = \beta^0 \parallel \beta^1 \parallel \beta^2 \parallel \beta^3$.

4. Calculate $f_K^1 = S(\alpha^0 \oplus \alpha^1, \alpha^2 \oplus \alpha^3 \oplus \beta^0, 1)$.

5. Calculate $f_K^2 = S(\alpha^2 \oplus \alpha^3, f_K^1 \oplus \beta^1, 0)$.

6. Calculate $f_K^0 = S(\alpha^0, f_K^1 \oplus \beta^2, 0)$.

7. Calculate $f_K^3 = S(\alpha^3, f_K^2 \oplus \beta^3, 1)$.

8. Recombine the above three results to obtain f_K.

4.7.3 Round Function: *f*

The *f*-function is the actual round function, acting as the heart of its Feistel structure. It takes as input two 32-bit values (α and β), and produces a 32-bit result.

1. Split the eventual output of the round function into four separately addressable 8-bit parts: $f(\alpha, \beta) = f^0(\alpha, \beta) \| f^1(\alpha, \beta) \| f^2(\alpha, \beta) \| f^3(\alpha, \beta)$. Call the values it returns simply f^0, f^1, f^2, and f^3.

2. Split the 32-bit input, α, into four 8-bit parts: $\alpha = \alpha^0 \| \alpha^1 \| \alpha^2 \| \alpha^3$.

3. Do the same for β: $\beta = \beta^0 \| \beta^1 \| \beta^2 \| \beta^3$.

4. Calculate $f^1 = \alpha^1 \oplus \beta^0 \oplus \alpha^0$.

5. Calculate $f^2 = \alpha^2 \oplus \beta^1 \oplus \alpha^3$.

6. Recalculate $f^1 = S(f^1, f^2, 1)$.

7. Recalculate $f^2 = S(f^2, f^1, 0)$.

8. Calculate $f^0 = S(\alpha^0, f^1, 0)$.

9. Calculate $f^3 = S(\alpha^3, f^2, 1)$.

To implement these nine steps, we first need to define a few helper functions, to split the 32-bit block into four 8-bit parts (demux) and to recombine 8-bit parts into a single 32-bit block (mux). These are very similar to those used in the SPN cipher above, EASY1. In Python, we can use the code in Listing 4-7.

```
#########################################
# Splits a 32-bit block into four 8-bit values
# and vice-versa
#########################################

def demux(x):
    # Create an array of size four to store
    # the result
    y = []

    # Calculate each part in turn
    for i in range(0,4):
```

Listing 4-7 Multiplex and demultiplex routines for FEAL. *(continued)*

```
        # They are numbered left to right, 0 to 3
        # But still in MSB order
        y.append((x >> ((3 - i) * 8)) & 0xff)

    return y

def mux(x):
    # Initialize result to zero
    y = 0

    # The input, x, is an array of 8-bit values
    for c in x:

        # Combine each 8-bit value using OR
        y = (y << 8) ^ c

    return y
```

Listing 4-7 (*continued*)

Now that we have all of the helper functions for FEAL, we can define the
FEAL main round function, as shown in Listing 4-8.

```
##########################################
# Feal round function, f
##########################################

def f(alpha, beta):
    # Split alpha and beta
    a = demux(alpha)
    b = demux(beta)

    # Make the output four 8-bit values
    fs = [0,0,0,0]

    # Calculate each 8-bit value
    fs[1] = a[1] ^ b[0] ^ a[0]
    fs[2] = a[2] ^ b[1] ^ a[3]
    fs[1] = sbox(fs[1], fs[2], 1)
    fs[2] = sbox(fs[2], fs[1], 0)
    fs[0] = sbox(a[0], fs[1], 0)
    fs[3] = sbox(a[3], fs[2], 1)

    # Return the 32-bit result
    return mux(fs)
```

Listing 4-8 The FEAL round function, *f*.

4.7.4 Key Scheduling

The key scheduling algorithm for FEAL is meant to split up a 64-bit key into various derived subparts (based on the f_K key scheduling function), for use in the main round function of FEAL.

1. Let $K = (A_0, B_0)$ and $D_0 = 0$.

2. For eight rounds, $r = 1, \ldots, 8$:

    (a) $D_r = A_{r-1}$.

    (b) $A_r = B_{r-1}$.

    (c) $B_r = f_K(A_{r-1}, B_{r-1} \oplus D_{r-1})$.

    (d) $K_{2(r-1)} = (B_r^0, B_r^1)$.

    (e) $K_{2(r-1)+1} = (B_r^2, B_r^3)$.

In Python, we can implement this fairly easily, as shown in Listing 4-9.

```
##########################################
# FEAL key generating function
##########################################

def fk(alpha, beta):
    # Split alpha and beta
    a = demux(alpha)
    b = demux(beta)

    # Express output as four 8-bit values
    fs = [0,0,0,0]

    # Calculate the four 8-bit values
    fs[1] = sbox(a[0] ^ a[1], a[2] ^ a[3] ^ b[0], 1)
    fs[2] = sbox(a[2] ^ a[3], fs[1] ^ b[1], 0)
    fs[0] = sbox(a[0], fs[1] ^ b[2], 0)
    fs[3] = sbox(a[3], fs[2] ^ b[3], 1)
    return mux(fs)
```

Listing 4-9 FEAL key-generating function, f_K.

Although we will get into more detailed cryptanalysis of FEAL later, there are a few things to note.

It's easy to see that FEAL is almost more complicated than DES: It takes more space to explain and requires more bits and pieces. To give FEAL some credit, most of the operations are indeed very fast: They usually operate on a small number of bits, so that they can be implemented in one machine code instruction.

4.8   Blowfish

Blowfish is another Feistel cipher, created by Bruce Schneier in 1994 [14, 15]. According to Schneier, it was designed to be fast, simple, small, and have a variable key [16]. The following description is based mostly on his description in Reference [16].

Blowfish has a slight variant of the Feistel structure previously used and operates on 64-bit blocks. It uses expansive S-boxes and other simple operations. There are two features that differentiate it from DES:

- Blowfish's S-boxes are key-dependent — the actual substitution values are regenerated whenever the algorithm is rekeyed. It has four dynamic 8-bit to 32-bit S-boxes.

- It has a variable length key, up to 448 bits.

The basic Blowfish algorithm consists of two phases: calculating the key schedule (33,344 bits derived from up to 448 bits of key), and performing the encryption or decryption algorithm.

4.8.1   Blowfish Key Schedule

Schneier refers to the subkeys, generated from the main key, as 18 32-bit keys: $P_1, P_2, \ldots, P_{18}$. The key scheduling algorithm also calculates the S-box, since its values are completely determined by the key itself.

Blowfish Key Scheduling. The P-values and S-box values for the main encryption are calculated based on an input key (of up to a length of 448 bits) and the hexadecimal digits of π.

1. Initialize the P-values (left-to-right) with the hexadecimal digits of π — that is, the digits to the right of the "hexadecimal point." They start off as 24 3f 6a 88 85 a3 08 d3 .... After the P-values are filled, fill the S-boxes, in order with the digits of π. The pre-computed values can be found easily on the Internet.

2. Starting with P_1, calculate $P_1 = P_1 \oplus K_1, P_2 = P_2 \oplus K_2$, and so forth. Here, the K-values represent the originally inputted key values, up to 448 bits. There may be up to 14 K-values, to correspond to the P-values. It is necessary to XOR a K-value with each P-value, so repeat the values as necessary by starting over with K_1, then K_2, and so on, again. For example, with a 128-bit key (representing $K_1, \ldots, K_4$ values), after calculating $P_4 = P_4 \oplus K_4$, then perform $P_5 = P_5 \oplus K_1$, and so on.

3. Encrypt a 64-bit block consisting of all zeros (00 00 00 00 00 00 00 00) using the Blowfish algorithm, with the P-values from the previous step.

4. Replace P_1 and P_2 with the output from the previous step's Blowfish run.

5. Take the output from Step 3 and encrypt it (with the new, modified P-values).

6. Replace P_3 and P_4 with the output from the previous step.

7. Repeat this process (encrypting the previous Blowfish output and replacing the next set of P-values), filling all P-values and then the S-boxes (i.e., the 32-bit outputs of the S-box entry) in order. The order of the S-boxes is defined to be $S_{1,0}, S_{1,1}, \ldots, S_{1,255}, S_{2,0}, S_{2,1}, \ldots, S_{4,255}$.

This will require a total of 521 iterations in order to compute all values.

4.8.2   Blowfish Algorithm

The algorithm is based on the Feistel structure, with a total of 16 rounds. The key to the algorithm, as mentioned above, is that the algorithm is kept very simple: For each round, only three XORs, two additions, and four S-box lookups are required.

Blowfish Encryption Algorithm. The basic cryptographic algorithm operates on a 64-bit input and produces a 64-bit output. The following shows the encryption portion. To obtain the decryption code, simply replace P_i in the following with P_{19-i} (with P_{17} and P_{18} at the end being replaced with P_2 and P_1, respectively):

1. Split the plaintext into two halves: the left half (L_0) and the right half (R_0).

2. For each of 16 rounds ($i = 1, 2, \ldots, 16$):

    (a) Set $L_i = L_{i-1} \oplus P_i$.

    (b) Set $R_i = f(L_i) \oplus R_i$.

    (c) Swap L_i and R_i.

3. Swap L_{16} and R_{16} (undoing the previous swap).

4. Set $R_{17} = R_{16} \oplus P_{17}$.

5. Set $L_{17} = R_{17} \oplus P_{18}$.

The output is the block obtained by recombining L_{17} and R_{17}. This main round procedure is shown in Figure 4-9.

4.8.3   Blowfish Round Function

The core of the algorithm is, as with all Feistel structures, in the round function.

Blowfish Round Function. In this case, the round function (f in the algorithm) works on a 32-bit argument and produces a 32-bit output by the following method:

1. Divide the 32-bit argument into four 8-bit values: a, b, c, and d.

2. Using unsigned arithmetic, calculate $S_{1,a} + S_{2,b}$. Take the result as a 32-bit integer (ignoring any portion that might have extended beyond 32 bits).

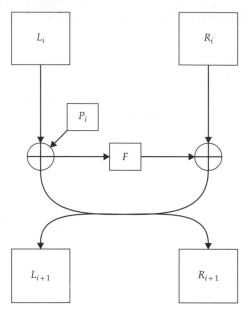

Figure 4-9 The Blowfish algorithm's main encryption loop.

3. Calculate the XOR of the result of Step 2 and the output of $S_{3,c}$.

4. Finally, take the result of Step 3 and add (unsigned, with 32-bit arithmetic, as before) $S_{4,d}$. This will be the result of the round function.

4.8.4   Notes on Blowfish

This round function has a few interesting properties. Notably, which S-boxes are chosen depends on the data themselves: so that the data dictate their own encryption. [This is because the split plaintext (a, b, c, and d) is used to choose the S-boxes.]

The other important note about Blowfish is that it requires 521 encryptions using its own encryption algorithm before it can produce a single block of output. Therefore, encrypting a single block would take very long because of the long setup time. It really only becomes moderately fast to use Blowfish when encrypting at least several hundred blocks (meaning thousands of bits); otherwise, the setup time will dominate the total encryption and decryption times. Luckily, we need to compute the key values and S-boxes only once.

4.9   AES/Rijndael

The **Rijndael algorithm** was chosen by the U.S. Government as the successor to DES [2]. The Rijndael algorithm (and certain parameter settings) was then dubbed the **Advanced Encryption Standard** (**AES**).

Rijndael is a variable-sized block cipher named after its inventors, Vincent Rijmen and Joan Daemen. It is a variant of the SPN concept, with more sophisticated and elegant variants of S-box and P-box operations.

Rijndael itself supports block sizes and key sizes of 128, 160, 192, 224, and 256 bits, although AES supports only 128-bit blocks and keys with bit lengths of 128, 192, and 256. The number of rounds for Rijndael varies depending on the key size and the block size. For AES (block size of 128 bits only), the number of rounds is shown in Table 4-4.

The key is, as for most of the ciphers I have been discussing, broken out into a large key schedule, derived from the original key. This is covered in Section 4.9.3.

Rijndael breaks its blocks into a matrix, called the **state**, with four rows and various numbers of columns (4–8). With block sizes of 128–256, this means that each element of the matrix is an 8-bit value. Figure 4-10 shows an example of this state.

4.9.1   Rijndael Encryption Algorithm

The Rijndael encryption algorithm essentially consists of four basic operations, applied in succession to each other, and looped multiple times:

1. *SubBytes* — Each element of the state is run through an S-box.
2. *ShiftRows* — The elements of each row of the state are cyclically shifted.
3. *MixColumns* — Each column is run through a function to mix up its bits.
4. *AddRoundKey* — A portion of the key schedule is XORed with the state.

The *AddRoundKey* is the only portion of the algorithm dependent on the current round number and the key.

Using the above four pieces, we can specify the Rijndael encryption algorithm.

Table 4-4 The Number of Rounds for Different Values of the Key Length for AES

KEY LENGTH (N_k), IN WORDS	BLOCK SIZE (N_b), IN WORDS	ROUNDS (r)
4	4	10
6	4	12
8	4	14

Here, the values for key length and block size are the number of 32-bit words: Thus "4" corresponds to 128 bits, "6" to 192 bits, and "8" to 256 bits.

$S_{0,0}$	$S_{0,1}$	$S_{0,2}$	$S_{0,3}$
$S_{1,0}$	$S_{1,1}$	$S_{1,2}$	$S_{1,3}$
$S_{2,0}$	$S_{2,1}$	$S_{2,2}$	$S_{2,3}$
$S_{3,0}$	$S_{3,1}$	$S_{3,2}$	$S_{3,3}$

Figure 4-10 A state associated with a 128-bit block size Rijndael, such as in AES. If the state is a 128-bit value, then it it is split into the matrix by breaking it down: $S_{0,0}$ ∥ $S_{0,1}$ ∥ $S_{0,2}$ ∥ $S_{0,3}$ ∥ $S_{1,0}$ ∥ $S_{1,1}$ ∥ $S_{1,2}$ ∥ $S_{1,3}$ ∥ $S_{2,0}$ ∥ $S_{2,1}$ ∥ $S_{2,2}$ ∥ $S_{2,3}$ ∥ $S_{3,0}$ ∥ $S_{3,1}$ ∥ $S_{3,2}$ ∥ $S_{3,3}$.

Rijndael Encryption Algorithm. Assume that there are r rounds (r is dependent on the key size), and that the plaintext has been loaded into the state.

1. Run *AddRoundKey* on the state.
2. Do the following $r - 1$ times.
   (a) Run *SubBytes* on the state.
   (b) Run *ShiftRows* on the state.
   (c) Run *MixColumns* on the state.
   (d) Run *AddRoundKey* on the state.
3. Run *SubBytes* on the state.
4. Run *ShiftRows* on the state.
5. Run *AddRoundKey* on the state.

I'll now describe the four sections in a bit more detail. For a more thorough treatment, see References [2] and [7]. The following examples use the details in the AES for a 128-bit block size.

4.9.1.1   SubBytes

The *SubBytes* operation essentially functions as an 8-bit S-box, applied to each 8-bit value of the state, as shown in Figure 4-11.

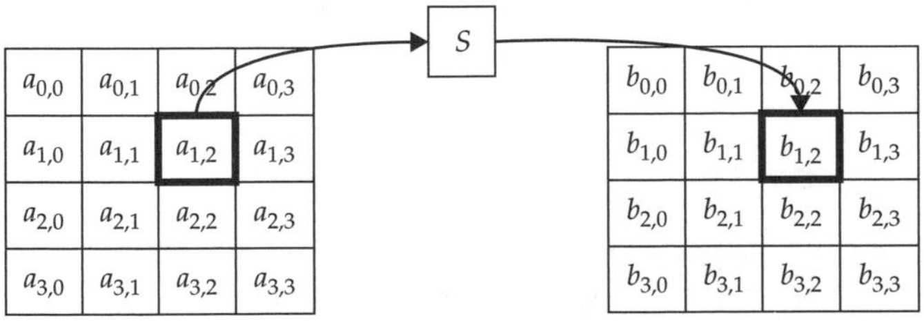

Figure 4-11 The Rijndael *SubBytes* operation.

The S-box can be represented in several ways. The normal S-box implementation, with a fixed lookup table, is shown in Figure 4-2. The way I often show it is, if I define the 8-bit input a to be written as $a_7 \parallel a_6 \parallel \cdots \parallel a_0$ and b to be written similarly, then

$$
\begin{bmatrix} b_7 \\ b_6 \\ b_5 \\ b_4 \\ b_3 \\ b_2 \\ b_1 \\ b_0 \end{bmatrix} = \begin{bmatrix} 1 & 1 & 1 & 1 & 1 & 0 & 0 & 0 \\ 0 & 1 & 1 & 1 & 1 & 1 & 0 & 0 \\ 0 & 0 & 1 & 1 & 1 & 1 & 1 & 0 \\ 0 & 0 & 0 & 1 & 1 & 1 & 1 & 1 \\ 1 & 0 & 0 & 0 & 1 & 1 & 1 & 1 \\ 1 & 1 & 0 & 0 & 0 & 1 & 1 & 1 \\ 1 & 1 & 1 & 0 & 0 & 0 & 1 & 1 \\ 1 & 1 & 1 & 1 & 0 & 0 & 0 & 1 \end{bmatrix} \times \begin{bmatrix} a_7 \\ a_6 \\ a_5 \\ a_4 \\ a_3 \\ a_2 \\ a_1 \\ a_0 \end{bmatrix} \oplus \begin{bmatrix} 0 \\ 1 \\ 1 \\ 0 \\ 0 \\ 0 \\ 1 \\ 1 \end{bmatrix}
$$

where the $\times$ operator means matrix multiplication. If this is confusing, it is fairly easy, and often faster, to just use the lookup-table representation of the S-box.

4.9.1.2 ShiftRows

The *ShiftRows* operation performs a cyclical shift of each row of the state. Each row is shifted by one more value than the previous row (see Figure 4-12):

1. The first row is left intact (no rotation).
2. The second row is rotated once to the left.
3. The third row is rotated twice to the left.
4. The fourth row is rotated three times to the left.

4.9.1.3 MixColumns

The *MixColumns* operation is the most complicated part of the AES algorithm.

Although I won't go into the nitty-gritty of the mathematics of multiplication over GF(2^8)(the finite field of size 2^8, also written as $\mathbb{Z}_{2^8}$),in the case of AES, this essentially means that we will multiply two 8-bit numbers, and take the remainder modulo 283 (which is 100011011 in binary), using **binary XOR long**

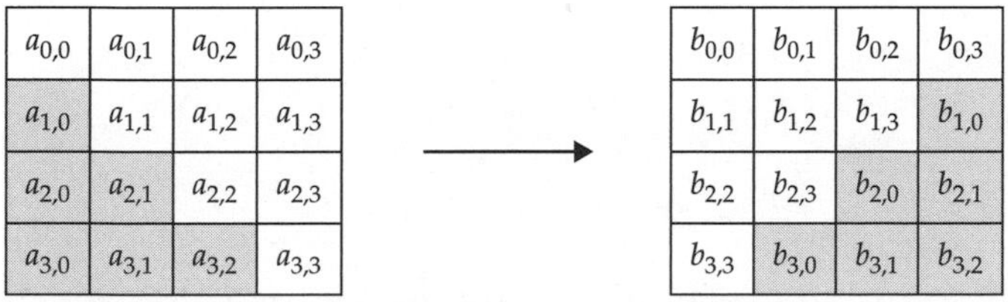

Figure 4-12 The Rijndael *ShiftRows* operation.

division, not normal arithmetic. This is the same as doing normal division, except that instead of successively subtracting, we use binary XOR. Also, while in normal subtraction, we only subtract if we are dividing a smaller number into a larger number at each stage, whereas with XOR, we only divide if they have the same number of binary digits (so either number can be greater). So that we don't confuse this with normal arithmetic multiplication, I will denote the operation as • (as done in the specification [7]).

For example, I will show how to do this with the AES example in Reference [7], calculating $87 \bullet 131$ (or, $01010111 \bullet 10000011$).We first multiply the two numbers as usual, obtaining 11,397, or 1010110111001. We then perform the long division to obtain the remainder when divided by 10011011:

```
                             101000
100011011 |10101101111001
          ⊕100011011
            1000000
            100000011
          ⊕100011011
              11000
              11000001
              11000001
```

For the *MixColumns* operation, we are going to take each column and perform a matrix multiplication, where the multiplication is the • operation shown above. The operation will be

$$\begin{bmatrix} b_{0,c} \\ b_{1,c} \\ b_{2,c} \\ b_{3,c} \end{bmatrix} = \begin{bmatrix} 2 & 3 & 1 & 1 \\ 1 & 2 & 3 & 1 \\ 1 & 1 & 2 & 3 \\ 3 & 1 & 1 & 2 \end{bmatrix} \otimes \begin{bmatrix} a_{0,c} \\ a_{1,c} \\ a_{2,c} \\ a_{3,c} \end{bmatrix}$$

where the $a_{i,c}$ entries on the right are the old column entries, the $b_{i,c}$ entries on the left are new column entries, and the $\otimes$ operator means to perform matrix multiplication with the • operator and XOR instead of addition. We can specify this less abstractly as

$$b_{0,c} = (2 \bullet a_{0,c}) \oplus (3 \bullet a_{1,c}) \oplus a_{2,c} \oplus a_{3,c}$$
$$b_{1,c} = a_{0,c} \oplus (2 \bullet a_{1,c}) \oplus (3 \bullet a_{2,c}) \oplus a_{3,c}$$
$$b_{2,c} = a_{0,c} \oplus a_{1,c} \oplus (2 \bullet a_{2,c}) \oplus (3 \bullet a_{3,c})$$
$$b_{3,c} = (3 \bullet a_{0,c}) \oplus a_{1,c} \oplus a_{2,c} \oplus (2 \bullet a_{3,c})$$

This operation will be performed for each column, that is, for $c = 1, 2, 3$, and 4. The *MixColumns* operation is shown graphically in Figure 4-13.

$$\begin{bmatrix} 2 & 3 & 1 & 1 \\ 1 & 2 & 3 & 1 \\ 1 & 1 & 2 & 3 \\ 3 & 1 & 1 & 2 \end{bmatrix} \oplus$$

$a_{0,0}$	$a_{0,1}$	$a_{0,2}$	$a_{0,3}$
$a_{1,0}$	$a_{1,1}$	$a_{1,2}$	$a_{1,3}$
$a_{2,0}$	$a_{2,1}$	$a_{2,2}$	$a_{2,3}$
$a_{3,0}$	$a_{3,1}$	$a_{3,2}$	$a_{3,3}$

=

$b_{0,0}$	$b_{0,1}$	$b_{0,2}$	$b_{0,3}$
$b_{1,0}$	$b_{1,1}$	$b_{1,2}$	$b_{1,3}$
$b_{2,0}$	$b_{2,1}$	$b_{2,2}$	$b_{2,3}$
$b_{3,0}$	$b_{3,1}$	$b_{3,2}$	$b_{3,3}$

Figure 4-13 The Rijndael *MixColumns* operation.

4.9.1.4 *AddRoundKey*

Finally, the *AddRoundKey* operation takes each 8-bit value of the state and XORs it with an 8-bit value of the key schedule, as shown in Figure 4-14.

4.9.2 Rijndael Decryption Algorithm

Decryption of Rijndael is very similar to encryption: It simply involves doing the operations in reverse (with a reverse key schedule) and using inverse operations for *SubBytes*, *MixColumns*, and *ShiftRows* — these operations are called, surprisingly enough, *InvSubBytes*, *InvMixColumns*, and *InvShiftRows*, respectively.

The use of these inverse functions leads to the following algorithm for decryption:

Rijndael Decryption Algorithm. Assume that there are *r* rounds (*r* is dependent on the key size) and that the ciphertext is loaded into the state.

1. Run *AddRoundKey* on the state.
2. Do the following $r - 1$ times:
   (a) Run *InvSubBytes* on the state.
   (b) Run *InvShiftRows* on the state.
   (c) Run *InvMixColumns* on the state.
   (d) Run *AddRoundKey* on the state.
3. Run *InvSubBytes* on the state.
4. Run *InvShiftRows* on the state.
5. Run *AddRoundKey* on the state.

$a_{0,0}$	$a_{0,1}$	$a_{0,2}$	$a_{0,3}$
$a_{1,0}$	$a_{1,1}$	$a_{1,2}$	$a_{1,3}$
$a_{2,0}$	$a_{2,1}$	$a_{2,2}$	$a_{2,3}$
$a_{3,0}$	$a_{3,1}$	$a_{3,2}$	$a_{3,3}$

$\oplus$

$k_{0,0}$	$k_{0,1}$	$k_{0,2}$	$k_{0,3}$
$k_{1,0}$	$k_{1,1}$	$k_{1,2}$	$k_{1,3}$
$k_{2,0}$	$k_{2,1}$	$k_{2,2}$	$k_{2,3}$
$k_{3,0}$	$k_{3,1}$	$k_{3,2}$	$k_{3,3}$

=

$b_{0,0}$	$b_{0,1}$	$b_{0,2}$	$b_{0,3}$
$b_{1,0}$	$b_{1,1}$	$b_{1,2}$	$b_{1,3}$
$b_{2,0}$	$b_{2,1}$	$b_{2,2}$	$b_{2,3}$
$b_{3,0}$	$b_{3,1}$	$b_{3,2}$	$b_{3,3}$

Figure 4-14 The Rijndael *AddRoundKey* operation.

The most important thing to note is that the keys must be submitted in reverse order.

It is also important to note that the key expansion is changed slightly, as I show in Section 4.9.3.

The inverse operations are fairly easy to derive from the normal ones: We simply construct *InvShiftRows* by shifting in the opposite direction the appropriate number of times. We construct *InvSubBytes* by inverting the S-box used (either with the inverse matrix or the inverse of the table). And finally, the *InvMixColumns* transformation is found by using the following matrix for the multiplication step:

$$\begin{bmatrix} 15 & 11 & 14 & 9 \\ 9 & 15 & 11 & 14 \\ 14 & 9 & 15 & 11 \\ 11 & 14 & 9 & 15 \end{bmatrix}$$

4.9.3   Key Expansion

The key expansion step computes the key schedule for use in either encryption or decryption.

Rijndael computes its sizes in terms of 32-bit words. Therefore, in this case, a 128-bit block cipher would have a block size denoted as N_b of 4. The key size is denoted as N_k in a similar manner, so that, for example, a 192-bit key is denoted with $N_k = 6$. The number of rounds is denoted as r.

Two functions need to be explained in order to describe the key expansion. The *SubWord* function takes a 32-bit argument, splits it into four 8-bit bytes, computes the S-box transformation from *SubBytes* on each 8-bit value, and concatenates them back together. The *RotWord* function takes a 32-bit argument, splits it into four 8-bit bytes, and then rotates left cyclically, replacing each 8-bit value in the word with the 8-bit value that was on the right. Specifically, it computes

$$RotWord(a_3 \parallel a_2 \parallel a_1 \parallel a_0) = a_2 \parallel a_1 \parallel a_0 \parallel a_3$$

Finally, there is a constant matrix that is used, denoted as *Rcon*. The values of *Rcon* can be calculated fairly easily using the finite field multiplication operation •. Essentially, the values are calculated as

$$Rcon(i) = 2^{i-1} \parallel 0 \parallel 0 \parallel 0$$

where each of the four parts is an 8-bit number and a member of Rijndael's finite field. Owing to this fact, 2^{i-1} must be calculated using the • multiplication operator [calculating the previous result times (•) 2], and not normal multiplication. The first few values of 2^{i-1} are straightforward (starting at $i = 1$): 1, 2, 4, 8, 16, 32, 64, 128. When we get to 256, though, we need to start using the finite field modulo. Therefore, the next few values are 27, 54, 108, and so on. Table 4-5 shows the required values.

Table 4-5 Rijndael Table for First Entry of *Rcon* Values

I	RCON[I]
1	1
2	2
3	4
4	8
5	16
6	32
7	64
8	128
9	27
10	54
11	108
12	216

These entries should be sufficient for any implementations of AES.

4.9.4 Notes on Rijndael

Rijndael is a modern cipher. Since it was created in the late 1990's, after many of the standard cryptanalytic techniques that I discuss in this book were known, it was tested against these techniques. The algorithm was tuned so that it was susceptible to none of the techniques, as they were known at the time.

4.10 Block Cipher Modes

Although I have limited the discussion to block ciphers up until this point, I should probably have a few words on some of the different ways they are used, besides just straight block-for-block encryption, which has been the assumed method of using the ciphers. (In the previous discussions, I never had the output of one block's encryption affect a different block's encryption.)

4.10.1 Electronic Code Book

The normal method is normally called **electronic codebook (ECB)**. It simply means that each block of plaintext is used as the normal input to the block cipher, and the output of the cipher becomes the block of ciphertext, just as

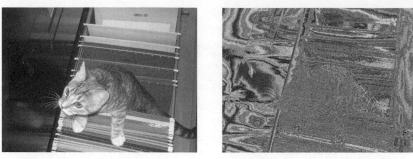

(a) Original image, by Thursday Bram.   (b) Encrypted with AES using ECB.

Figure 4-15 A picture of a cat in a filing cabinet, demonstrating the preserved structure present in ECB.

we would expect. Hence, for each block of plaintext, P, we calculate a block of ciphertext by simply applying

$$C = Encrypt(P)$$

However, there are some issues that can easily arise using a cipher in ECB mode. For example, a lot of the structure of the original data will be preserved, because identical plaintext blocks will always encrypt to identical ciphertext blocks. Figure 4-15 shows how this can occur. In this figure, we encrypt every grayscale (8-bit) pixel (padded with 15 bytes of zeros) with AES in ECB mode, and then take the first byte of the output block as the new grayscale value. (This same method is also used for the CBC example in the next section.)[1]

In general, when identical plaintext blocks always encrypt to identical ciphertext blocks, there is the potential for a problem with **block replay**: Knowing an important plaintext–ciphertext pair, even without knowing the key, someone can repeatedly send the known ciphertext.

For example, assume that we have a very simple automatic teller machine (ATM), which communicates with a bank to verify if a particular individual is authorized to withdraw cash. We would hope that, at the very least, this communication between the ATM and the bank is encrypted. We might naively implement the above scenario in a simple message from the ATM:

ATM: $Encrypt_K$("Name: John Smith, Account: 12345, Amount: $20")

(Assume that the bank sends back a message saying, "OK, funds withdrawn," or "Sorry, insufficient funds.") The above means simply to send the text message, encrypted with the key K. If the encryption scheme merely represented this as an ASCII message and performed an algorithm, such as AES, using the key K, we might think we are safe, since anyone listening in on the transaction will only see something random, such as

```
ATM: CF A2 1E C5 AF 67 2D AC 7A E1 0D 3B 2F ...
```

---

[1]The use of this example (and the CBC that follows) was inspired by the Wikipedia images posted by Lunkwill.

However, someone could do something sinister even with this. For example, someone listening in on this conversation might simply want to replay the above packet, sending it to the bank. Unless additional security measures are in place, the bank will think that the user is making several more ATM withdrawals, which could eventually drain the victim's bank account.

Even though the ATM used strong encryption to communicate with the bank, it was still susceptible to a block replay attack. Luckily, there are methods to help prevent this attack.

4.10.2 Cipher Block Chaining

One of the most fundamental ideas of combatting the block replay problem is to make the output of each block depend on the values of the previous blocks. This will make it so that anyone listening to any block in the middle will not be able to repeat that one block over and over again at a later date.

However, simply chaining together the outputs like this still leaves a flaw: It does not prevent block replay of the *first* block (or the first several blocks, if they are all replayed). A common strategy to fight this is to add an **initialization vector** (the IV, and sometimes called the "salt") to the algorithm. Essentially, this is a random number that is combined with the first block, usually by XORing them together. The IV must also be specified somehow, by sending it to the other party or having a common scheme for picking them.

Using both of these strategies together results in the simple method called **cipher-block chaining (CBC)**. The method I will describe is taken from Reference [9]. It essentially makes each block dependent on the previous block (with the first block dependent also on the initialization vector). Figure 4-16 shows how this eliminates block replay attacks by ensuring that the same plaintext blocks will be encrypted differently.

CBC Encryption. The following describes the basic CBC method, as described in Reference [9]. The method uses a 64-bit block size for plaintext, ciphertext, and the initialization vector (since the reference originally assumes that DES is used, although any cipher can be used in CBC mode). To adapt it for other ciphers, simply change this to the relevant block size, and use the appropriate algorithm.

1. Calculate the first block to send by taking the IV and the first block of plaintext, XORing them, and encrypt the result. Hence,

$$C_0 = Encrypt(P_0 \oplus IV)$$

2. Calculate each successive block by XORing the previous ciphertext block with the next plaintext block, and encrypting the result. Hence, for $i \geq 1$,

$$C_i = Encrypt(P_i \oplus C_{i-1})$$

(a) Original image, by Thursday Bram.   (b) Encrypted with AES using CBC.

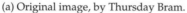

Figure 4-16 A picture of a cat in a filing cabinet. Unlike ECB, CBC obliterates much of the underlying structure.

Decryption in CBC is equally simple.

CBC Decryption. The biggest restriction is that the two users must share the IV or the first block will not be comprehensible to the receiver.

1. Decrypt the first received ciphertext block, and XOR the result with the IV to obtain the first plaintext. Hence,

$$P_0 = IV \oplus Decrypt(C_0)$$

2. For each successive received block, take the received block of ciphertext, run it through decryption, and then XOR it with the previous round's *ciphertext* to obtain the next plaintext. Hence, for $i \geq 1$,

$$P_i = C_{i-1} \oplus Decrypt(C_i)$$

4.10.3   Cipher Feedback

There are other issues facing cryptography in addition to block replay. One is **padding**, or adding additional bits to the end of plaintext so that it is a multiple of the block size. This necessity potentially adds small weakness: We know the last few bits of plaintext if we know the padding scheme. Many ciphers use padding either as all zeros or ones, some other pattern, or perhaps just random bits.

However, the decrypting party needs to know how long the real message is so that any extra padding is thrown away. In some systems, the sending party may not know exactly how long the message is in advance (e.g., it may not have enough buffers to store an entire message of maximum length). In this case, it becomes difficult for the receiving party to know when the message has stopped if padding is used.

In both of these cases, the alternative to using a standard block cipher is to use a **stream cipher** — one that operates a bit at a time rather than a block at a time. We are mostly concerned with block ciphers in this book, but I shall discuss how block ciphers can be turned into stream ciphers, so that they can operate on one bit at a time (and, therefore, not require padding for any length).

Cipher feedback (CFB) mode is one way to turn any block cipher into a stream cipher, where the stream can consist of any number of bits, for example, it could be a bit stream cipher, a byte stream cipher, or a smaller block size cipher. The following construction is taken from Reference [3].

Assume we are implementing an s-bit CFB mode (with output in chunks of s bits). The only requirement is that s is between 1 and the block size.

CFB works by first encrypting input blocks (the first is an IV) with the key. Then, the "top" (most significant) s bits are extracted from this output, and XORed with the next s bits of the plaintext to produce the ciphertext. These bits of the ciphertext are then sent to the receiver.

At this point, the ciphertext bits are then *fed back* into the input block, hence the term **cipher feedback**. The input block is shifted left by s bits, and the *ciphertext bits* are put in on the right (least significant side). The process is then run again with this new input block.

4.10.4 Output Feedback

Output feedback (OFB) mode is very similar to the cipher feedback mode just discussed, and they are often confused.

OFB starts out the same: We have an IV as our initial input block, which we encrypt with the key. Again, we use the most significant bits to XOR against the bits to be output. The result of this XOR is sent out as ciphertext.

Now, the difference is here. Before, we fed back in the ciphertext bits (after XORing with the output).

Instead, we feed back in the *output* bits of the encryption, before XORing with our plaintext (the result of encrypting the input block). These bits are fed into the bottom of the input block by shifting the block to the right and shifting in the new bits — hence the term **output feedback**.

The primary difference between these two modes is that the CFB is dependent on the plaintext to create the **keystream** (the series of bits that are XORed with the plaintext in a stream cipher). With OFB, the keystream is only dependent on the IV and the key itself.

An advantage of using OFB is that if a transmission error occurs, the error will not propagate beyond that corrupted block. None of the following blocks will be damaged by the error; thus, the receiver can recover. With CFB, since the ciphertext is directly put into the input block, the receiving end's incorrect ciphertext value would then be forever sullying the future decrypted bits.

4.10.5   Counter Mode

Ciphers can also be operated in **counter (CTR) mode**, which can also be used to convert them to a stream cipher [3].

A series of counters is used, say, C_0, C_1, and so on. These counters are normally just increments of one another, hence the term **counter**. The first counter, C_0, should normally be a number that is difficult to guess.

The ciphertext for a given set of plaintext bits is then obtained as follows:

1. Encrypt the next counter with the key.
2. Extract the number of bits required, using the most significant bits first. At least one bit will be extracted, and up to all of the bits can be.
3. XOR the selected bits with the plaintext bits.

The result of the last step is then the ciphertext bits. For the next batch of plaintext bits, encrypt the next counter, and so forth.

4.11   Skipjack

Skipjack [17] is a combination of many different cipher techniques, including large permutations and shift registers. It is a very unique block cipher that operates on 64-bit blocks. It uses an unbalanced Feistel network and an 80-bit key.

Skipjack was designed by the U.S. Government to provide a robust encryption algorithm that enabled law enforcement to decrypt messages through an escrowed key. In other words, the algorithm is designed so that a copy of the key is encoded in such a way that law enforcement could, with an appropriate court order, obtain the key. However, the law enforcement and key escrow portions are not what we are mostly concerned about, but the inner workings of the encryption algorithm itself.

Skipjack is a very unique algorithm, differing in many ways from the traditional Feistel structures and SPNs studied above. For example, many of its operations are in the form of shift registers, rather than straight Feistel or SPN structures, although some of the functions used in the shift registers employ these techniques.

4.11.1   Skipjack Encryption Algorithm

Skipjack's encryption algorithm works fairly simply. There are two rules used in different rounds for a total of 32 rounds.

The plaintext is split into four parts (each being a 16-bit value): w_1^0, w_2^0, w_3^0, and w_4^0. For each round, the plaintext is either executed through a loop of Rule A or Rule B.

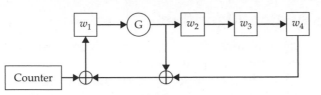

Figure 4-17 Skipjack Rule A.

Both rules rely on a permutation, usually written as G. The exact nature of G depends on the round k (since the key mixing is done in the G permutation), so it can also be written as G^k.

Skipjack Rule A. Rule A follows a simple cyclical structure. Note that the counter is incremented every round.

1. Set the new w_1 value to be the G permutation of the old w_1, XORed with the old w_4 value, as well as the counter.
2. Set the new w_2 value to be the G permutation of the old w_1.
3. Set the new w_3 to be the old w_2.
4. Set the new w_4 to be the old w_3.
5. Increment the counter.

Figure 4-17 shows this process.

Skipjack Rule B. Rule B works similarly to Rule A.

1. Set the new w_1 value to be the old w_4 value.
2. Set the new w_2 value to be the G permutation of the old w_1.
3. Set the new w_3 to be the old w_1 XORed with the counter and XORed with the old w_2 value.
4. Set the new w_4 to be the old w_3.
5. Increment the counter.

Figure 4-18 shows Rule B.

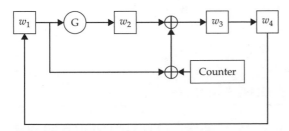

Figure 4-18 Skipjack Rule B.

4.11.2 Skipjack Decryption Algorithm

Decryption of a Skipjack ciphertext is fairly straightforward: Every operation from above is reversible, including the G permutation. The rules are replaced with two new rules: A^{-1} and B^{-1}. The decryption is performed by running Rule B^{-1} eight times, followed by Rule A^{-1} eight times, Rule B^{-1} eight times again, and finally Rule A^{-1} eight times.

Please note that the counter needs to run backwards. The keys are also submitted in reverse order $k = 31, 30, \ldots, 0$. That is, we start knowing the values for $k = 32$ (this corresponds to the ciphertext) and calculate the values for $k = 0$ (this corresponds to the plaintext).

Skipjack Rule A^{-1}. Rule A^{-1} follows a similar structure to Rule A of the encryption.

1. Set the new w_1 value to be the G^{-1} permutation of the old w_2 value.

2. Set the new w_2 value to be the old w_3 value.

3. Set the new w_3 to be the old w_4.

4. Set the new w_4 to be the old w_1, XORed with the old w_2 value as well as the counter.

5. Decrement the counter.

Skipjack Rule B^{-1}. Rule B^{-1} works similarly to Rule B.

1. Set the new w_1 value to be the G^{-1} permutation of the old w_2 value.

2. Set the new w_2 value to be the counter XORed with the old w_3 value, again XORed with the G^{-1} permutation of the old w_2.

3. Set the new w_3 to be the old w_4.

4. Set the new w_4 to be the old w_1.

5. Decrement the counter.

4.11.3 Permutations

The above encryption and decryption relied on functions called the G and G^{-1} permutations. See Figures 4-19 and 4-20 for their structure.

The F-function is simply an 8-bit S-box. I won't show it here, but it can be viewed in the specifications [17].

4.12 Message Digests and Hashes

Often, we might want to verify that we received the correct message and that nothing is missing or corrupted. One way would be to send the entire

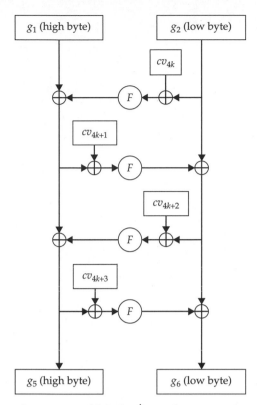

Figure 4-19 Skipjack G^k transform.

message again, but this would double the transmission size, which could be impractical. Naturally, we want this verification message to be as small as possible, while still serving its purpose. This verification message could also be used as a representation of the message itself, if we needed to, for example, prove that we received the message without repeating it in its entirety.

Two constructs that can give us these abilities are message digests and hashes. These calculations provide error detection, smaller representations of data, and sometimes error correction. The representations are called **hashes** or **message digests**, since they essentially "chop" up the input and "digest" them into some form.

For error detection and correction purposes, we often see these calculations in the form of checksums and cyclic redundancy checks. These are not designed for most security purposes (such as providing guarantees that the message was not maliciously altered), but simply to provide robustness against transmission or other benign errors; as such, they are usually based on very simple, fast algorithms meant to catch simple errors (such as a single bit being received incorrectly).

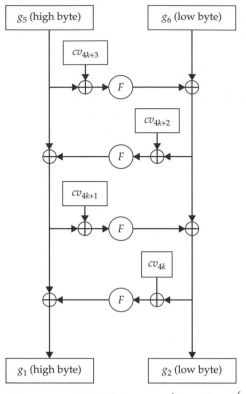

Figure 4-20 Skipjack inverse G^k transform $\left([G^k]^{-1}\right)$.

Hash functions produce hashes from input. These hash functions are designed to provide stronger security than normal checksums: Usually they have complicated, intricate calculations to churn the input to produce output. There are several desirable properties of this in order for the hash to be a secure "representation" of the message:

1. It should not be easy to obtain information about the input from the hash.

2. It should not be easy to find two inputs that have the same hash.

3. It should not be easy to find an input that has a specific hash. Furthermore, it should be even more difficult to find such an input that bears a resemblance to another particular input as well.

   Hash functions designed with these security principles in mind are often called **cryptographic hash functions**.

   One primary use for cryptographic hash functions, which require all of the above security, is in digital signatures. As we learned above, performing public key operations can be very time-consuming (such as when taking exponentials of very large integers). These operations become more difficult and time-consuming as the input size increases: To encrypt a 16,384-bit block with an RSA key would require finding primes larger than 16,384, as well as a key, and then performing thousands of arithmetic operations.

A properly designed cryptographic hash can be a representative of the entire input block because of the above properties; there is neither a way to correlate the input and the hash, nor to find similar blocks with the same hash. Hence, we could encrypt the smaller hash using a public-key mechanism.

If a person uses a private key to encrypt the hash of a message, then anyone with the public key can decrypt and verify the hash (since the hash algorithm must be well known). Furthermore, only the holder of the private key could possibly have created the encrypted (**signed**) hash; thus, we can verify that the message is authentic. This is the essence of a **digital signature**.

In the following sections I discuss checksums and cyclic redundancy checks and then go into the details of the two most popular hash algorithms: MD5 and SHA-1.

4.12.1   Checksums

Checksums are very simple measurements of ciphers. Typically, they are implemented with simple arithmetic or bitwise operators, usually addition or XOR.

For example, to calculate an 8-bit additive checksum of a series of bytes, simply add together the bytes and calculate the result modulo 256. For an XOR-based checksum, simply use the bitwise XOR on each of the bytes, which will return an 8-bit value.

Other checksums use similar methods. The key thing to note here is that they are not made for security. They are designed to check for simple errors, such as transmission or transcription errors. Their simple implementation on processors in very few instructions allows them to be used often in communications protocols.

It is fairly easy to defeat a checksum if it is used for security: Either simply modify the checksum itself, or modify a single portion of the message with the appropriate value to make the checksum come out correctly. For example, with an 8-bit XOR checksum, it is necessary to change just one byte to manipulate the checksum to be whatever is desired. Take the current checksum, XOR it with the desired checksum, and XOR this value with any byte in the message. The new message will now have the desired checksum.

4.12.2   Cyclic Redundancy Checks

A **cyclic redundancy check** (**CRC**) is a bit-centric method of error checking that is more robust than normal checksums against many types of errors, but is a tad more difficult to implement.

A CRC takes the original message and does bitwise (XOR-based) long division of it by a fixed, known polynomial. The remainder after the division is then transmitted, which the receiving end can easily verify by also dividing by the fixed polynomial.

CRCs vary in size, with the remainders having bit sizes between 5 and 32 being the most common.

For example, we can calculate a 5-bit CRC of the binary message 011011011 with the 6-bit divisor 101101:

```
                          111
          101101 |011011011
                 ⊕ 101101
                    11011
                   110111
                  ⊕101101
                    11010
                   110101
                  ⊕101101
                   11000
```

The remainder above is the binary number 11000 (24 in decimal).

4.12.3   MD5

MD5 [12] is a message digest algorithm (so named because it was the fifth in a series). It outputs a 128-bit number from any number of bits as input (including zero).

MD5 works fairly simply. First, the input is padded so that its length is equal to 448 modulo 512 (meaning it is $448 + 512 \times n$ bits long, for any integer n greater than or equal to 0). Then, a 64-bit number representing its length is added to the end of this (or, if the length is more than can be represented in a 64-bit number, then the lower 64 bits of its length). This is appended as the lower-order 32 bits first, and then the upper 32 bits (i.e., in LSB order).

MD5 operates on a 128-bit buffer at a time, split into four 32-bit words, A, B, C, and D. Their initial values are shown in Table 4-6.

Four functions are used in the MD5 computation, one for each major round:

$$f(x,y,z) = (x \& y) \mid ((\neg x) \& z)$$
$$g(x,y,z) = (x \& z) \mid (y \& (\neg z))$$
$$h(x,y,z) = x \oplus y \oplus z$$
$$i(x,y,z) = y \oplus (x \mid (\neg z))$$

Each of the four portions uses one of these functions 16 times, churning through the data in a fairly twisty manner. At each step of the 64 steps, an

Table 4-6 Initial Values of MD5 Buffer, in Hexadecimal

A:	01 23 45 67
B:	89 ab cd ef
C:	fe dc ba 98
D:	76 54 32 10

operation is performed using one of the above functions, followed by a rotation of the bytes:

$$a = b + ((a + F(b,c,d) + X_k + T_i) \lll s)$$

where F represents the f-function (Steps 0–15), the g-function (Steps 16–31), the h-function (Steps 32–47), and the i-function (Steps 48–63). The X_k-value represents the portion of the message block that we are pulling from. The T_i-value actually represents a value of the sine function, defined to be (from $i = 1, \dots, 64$)

$$T_i = (2^{32}) \times \text{abs}(\sin(i))$$

Here, we assume that i is the input to the sine function, in radians. (Recall that 2π radians is the same as 360°.) Finally, we circularly shift left (or rotate left) by different values at each step, represented by the $\lll$ operation.

After this, we rotate the values:

$$a' = d, b' = a, c' = b, d' = c$$

The values with the prime (′) indicate the new values to be assigned.

After the 64 steps are completed, the new values for $a, b, c,$ and d, are added into the working hash buffer (A, B, C, D). Then, the next block is loaded, and the process is run again.

See Figure 4-21 for a graphical representation of this.

Finally, the new values are arithmetically added back into the old values (with 32-bit arithmetic):

$$A = A + a, \quad B = B + b, \quad C = C + c, \quad D = D + d$$

When the last block is processed, the MD5 signature is the final value of (A, B, C, D).

4.12.4 SHA-1

The **Secure Hash Algorithm 1 (SHA-1)** [10] is a hashing algorithm specified by NIST that outputs a 160-bit hash.

The following description is based on References [16] and [18].

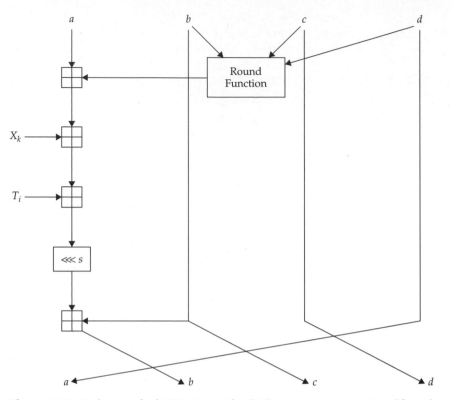

Figure 4-21 Basic round of MD5. Here, the "⊞" operator represents arithmetic addition, modulo 2^{32} (i.e., 32-bit addition).

SHA-1 takes the input as 512-bit blocks and further splits them into 16 32-bit words, labeled m_0 through m_{15}. The words are expanded into 80 such words by the following equation, for $i = 16, \dots, 79$:

$$m_i = (m_{i-3} \oplus m_{i-8} \oplus m_{i-14} \oplus m_{i-16}) \lll 1$$

where the $\lll 1$ operation rotates the bits, circularly, left by 1.

The initial values of $(a_0, b_0, c_0, d_0, e_0)$ and (A, B, C, D, E) are

```
(67452301, efcdab89, 98badcfe, 10325476, c3d2e1f0)
```

The (A, B, C, D, E) values will represent the hash in the end. For now, we will calculate the (a, b, c, d, e) values and eventually add them when finished processing this block.

There are 80 rounds, for $i = 1, \cdots, 80$:

$$a_i = (a_{i-1} \lll 5) + f_i(b_{i-1}, c_{i-1}, d_{i-1}) + e_{i-1} + m_{i-1} + k_i$$
$$b_i = a_{i-1}$$
$$c_i = b_{i-1} \lll 30$$

$$d_i = c_{i-1}$$
$$e_i = d_{i-1}$$

The f_i functions above change depending on the round:

$$i = 0, \ldots, 19: \quad f_i(x, y, z) = (x \& y) \,|\, ((\neg x) \& z)$$
$$i = 20, \ldots, 39: \quad f_i(x, y, z) = x \oplus y \oplus z$$
$$i = 40, \ldots, 59: \quad f_i(x, y, z) = (x \& y) \,|\, (x \& z) \,|\, (y \& z)$$
$$i = 60, \ldots, 79: \quad f_i(x, y, z) = x \oplus y \oplus z$$

The k_i values change depending on the round:

$$i = 0, \ldots, 19: \quad k_i = \texttt{5a 82 79 99}$$
$$i = 20, \ldots, 39: \quad k_i = \texttt{6e d9 eb a1}$$
$$i = 40, \ldots, 59: \quad k_i = \texttt{8f 1b bc dc}$$
$$i = 60, \ldots, 79: \quad k_i = \texttt{ca 62 c1 d6}$$

After we have processed all 80 rounds for the current block, we add the round values (using 32-bit arithmetic) to the ongoing hash values ($A = A + a$, $B = B + b$, $C = C + c$, $D = D + d$, and $E = E + e$) and start processing the next block.

Both SHA-1 and MD5 have other "relatives," such as MD4 (similar to MD5, but with a less thorough, and therefore faster, digesting function). However, I shall not discuss them further.

4.13   Random Number Generators

Although we are primarily focused on block ciphers throughout this book, it can be useful to understand a few principles about random number generators in cryptanalysis.

A **random number generator** is a function that generates a **random** number: one that cannot be predicted. A *true* random number generator, one whose output defies prediction, is difficult to obtain. These are normally based on the measurement of some physical phenomenon, which, based on strong scientific support, has no patterns or other characteristics. For example, measuring components of noise and radioactive decay is popular for these numbers.

For these true random number generators, though, there is little to do, cryptanlytically speaking. If the numbers are truly random, no system could produce meaningful results in most cases. One exception to this rule is found in the following section.

Any method for producing random numbers that aren't true is called a **pseudorandom number generator**.

4.13.1   Bias

Even a true random number generator can have a certain flaw: Certain numbers are generated more often than others. For example, although flipping a coin is a fairly random process, there is a very slight, measurable difference in the output numbers generated by the coin toss. This can be due to any number of factors, such as wind, flipping style, and the relative weight of the two sides of the coin. For example, if a coin is flipped 100 times, it may turn out that on average, we can expect heads to occur about 49 times but tails to occur 51 times (with probabilities 0.49 and 0.51, respectively).

This is an example of **bias**: the characteristic of a process to favor one outcome more often than others, even if that process is truly random.

There are ways to reduce bias, typically by combining several bits to produce one bit, or by combining several sources of randomness with each other. For example, we can simply XOR several bits from different random sources to obtain a new random bit. With the coin example, we will assume that tails is a 0, and heads is a 1. If we take two coin flips, we get a 0 if we have two tails in a row, or two heads in a row, giving us a probability of

$$\left(\frac{51}{100} \times \frac{51}{100}\right) + \left(\frac{49}{100} \times \frac{49}{100}\right) = 0.5002$$

The probability of a 1 is therefore $1 - 0.5002 = 0.4998$. Both probabilities are much closer to 1/2, giving us a bit that has much less bias in its output (since a purely random coin flip would have a probability of 1/2 for both heads and tails).

4.13.2 Linear Congruential Random Number Generator

Of all of the various types of pseudorandom number generators out there, a decent and popular choice is the **linear congruential random number generator** [6]. This is a random number generator that gives a sequence of numbers from numbers of the form

$$X \leftarrow (a \times X + c) \bmod m$$

This gives a sequence of numbers dependent on integers a, c, m, and the **seed**, which is the initial value (X_0) of the series.

This series is called "linear congruential" because it is based on the fact that the next number is linearly related to the next, modulo m.

Knuth [6] gives some guidance to reduce predictability and bias in this series:

1. The seed can be chosen arbitrarily. Three common ways to get a seed include saving it between sessions, generating it from the current date and time, or having the user input it. With all of the other variables the same, using the same seed each time allows experiments with a pseudorandom source to be run with repeatable results.

2. The modulus m should be large, greater than 2^{30}. The word size of the computer, such as 32 or 64 bits, is acceptable, especially with speed concerns. But there must be no roundoff errors possible (meaning integer, and not floating point, arithmetic must be used).

3. If m is the computer word size, such as 2^{32} for a 32-bit computer, then ensure that $a \equiv 5 \pmod 8$. Otherwise, there will be cycles in the output, and certain values will never be hit (because of algebraic properties of linear congruences).

4. Set a to be in the range $m/100$ to $99m/100$, and not have a simple digit pattern (like $12121\ldots$). Furthermore, a should be put through several statistical tests to guarantee that the numbers are acceptable.

5. Choose c so that it shares no common factors with m, essentially, although its choice is far less important than a. Preferably, do not choose $c = 0$.

6. The most significant bits (on the left) are more random than the least significant bits (on the right), and thus these should play a greater role. It's better to use the bits to represent a binary number between 0 and 1, that is, by letting the bits be on the right side after the decimal point (or, better, the ''binary point''). Thus, a pseudorandom number generated of 1100 would represent 0.1100 in binary, or 0.75 in decimal. To obtain an integer (say, between 0 and k), multiply by k and truncate. (The natural inclination is to just take the modulus with the higher end of the range, k. This would lead to more biased results, since the least significant digits would be more influential.)

7. Change a after every $m/1000$ numbers generated, or so, to keep the numbers from going ''stale.''

Further guidance on several of these points, as well as how to implement a linear congruential random number generator without floating point arithmetic, can be found in Reference [6].

4.14 One-Time Pad

I'll end this chapter with an idea important to cryptography and cryptanalysis.

Vernam and Mauborgne proposed that, where you have enough key material as you do material to send, and reliable, secure ways to transfer the key material (or some system), then even a simple Vigenère cipher is completely secure [5, 16]. In such a case, a different key could be used for each block for encryption. This system is usually called a **one-time pad**. (The underlying encryption can be nearly anything, such as a polyalphabetic substitution or simple XOR of the key material with the plaintext.)

The claim of a one-time pad is technically true, but only in the ideal case.

For example, if both parties communicating had a particular book that they would pull key material from, as needed, then they must merely stay synchronized with their material to send messages. The two parties could use the Vigenère Tableau, using letters in words to encrypt the text. It's easy to see that this would completely defeat Kasiski's method, since there are no repetitive patterns of any meaning left.

But, there are three issues: coming up with enough padding material for the one-time pad, synchronizing, and protecting the pad.

Transmitting a lot of information may be very difficult with a one-time pad, because we need one bit of keying material for each bit to be sent. We can't cheat by, say, using a pseudorandom number generator, as above, because there would then be patterns inside the ciphertext that could be exploited. Only a true source of random material that each communicating party can have a copy of will do. In the old days, a large telephone directory or a large book could provide a large set of information to work with (using the letters as keys for a substitution cipher, or deriving bits from the letters for a digital cipher). These aren't truly random, but can be fairly close, depending on how they are used. Today, however, with potentially megabytes, gigabytes, terabytes, petabytes, or even exabytes and beyond needing to be encrypted, the limited amount of information in even these large volumes would be insufficient.

Synchronization is another problem. What happens if a message is lost in transmission when using a one-time pad? Future received messages will then simply start being decrypted as garbage. Sophisticated users of this system could possibly overcome this by using appropriate protocols — for example, once one of the users receives a garbled message, both send the previous message they had sent, starting, say, at the next page whose page number is divisible by 10. This way, they can reset their usage of the key material. However, using even this simple protocol, if it is publicly known, can endanger the cipher, since the adversaries will then know a way to "reset" the cipher to a potentially known pattern.

Finally, protecting the pad is critical: All of the security rests in this one-time pad. The problem is the key distribution problem — how do we transfer this large amount of keying material securely? Furthermore, if we already had this secure channel in place to transmit the very large one-time pad, why can't we just use the same secure channel to send our data? We need a secure channel to establish a secure channel!

While one-time pads are potentially ideal ciphers, their difficulties nearly always make potential users shy away from them and toward different methods, such as using standard ciphers (like DES and AES), with key distribution protocols (like the Diffie-Hellman key distribution protocol).

4.15 Summary

When studying cryptanalysis, we obviously need something to cryptanalyze. The ciphers in this chapter are popular targets for people to attempt to break because of their widespread use.

Furthermore, cryptanalysis of ciphers can also try to attack some of the other characteristics of ciphers, such as message digests and hashes. Since these are often used as representations of messages, such as in digital signatures, the security of the hash function will then affect the security of the digital signature just as the function used to sign it will. Many of the tools and techniques we develop can be used to also analyze these other constructs.

From here, we are going to explore exactly what we do to start breaking these ciphers.

Exercises

Exercise 1. Implement MD5 (using Reference [12]), returning only the most significant 24 bits. Use the birthday paradox to find collisions. Try to find many different collisions on many different runs, and calculate the average time to find a collision. Verify that this agrees with the mathematics of Chapter 2.

Exercise 2. Write an implementation of the EASY1 cipher in your programming language of choice. (This will be useful in later chapters.)

Exercise 3. Write your own implementation of DES in your programming language of choice. Then, discuss your frustration with the conflicting numbering schemes used in this book and how they differ from the DES specification.

Exercise 4. Write an implementation of AES in your programming language of choice. Compare the running time of encryption in AES and DES.

References

[1] William E. Burr. Data Encryption Standard. In *NIST SP 958 – A Century of Excellence in Measurements, Standards, and Technology* (2001); http://nvl.nist.gov/pub/nistpubs/sp958-lide/html/250-253.html.

[2] John Daemen and Vincent Rijmen. *The Design of Rijndael: AES – The Advanced Encryption Standard*, Information Security and Cryptography. (Springer-Verlag, Berlin, 2002).

[3] Morris Dworkin. *Recommendation for Block Cipher Modes of Operation*. (National Institute of Standards and Technology, 2001).

[4] Howard M. Heys. A tutorial on linear and differential cryptanalysis. *Cryptologia* 26 (3): 189–221 (2002).

[5] David Khan. *The Codebreakers*. (Scribner, New York, 1996).

[6] Donald E. Knuth. *The Art of Computer Programming: Seminumerical Algorithms*, Vol. 2, 3rd ed. (Addison Wesley, Boston, 1998).

[7] National Institute of Standards and Technology. *Federal Information Processing Standard 197: Advanced Encryption Standard (AES)*. (2001).

[8] National Institute of Standards and Technology. *Federal Information Processing Standard 46-3: Data Encryption Standard*. (1999).

[9] National Institute of Standards and Technology. *Federal Information Processing Standard 81: DES Modes of Operation*. (1980).

[10] National Institute of Standards and Technology. *Secure Hash Standard*. (Federal Information Processing Standards Publication 180-1, 1995).

[11] Rolf Oppliger. *Contemporary Cryptography*, Computer Security Series. (Artech House, Norwood, MA, 2005).

[12] Ronald L. Rivest. *The MD5 Message-Digest Algorithm*. (Network Working Group, Request for Comments 1321, 1992).

[13] RSA Laboratories. *DES Challenge III*. (RSA Laboratories, 1999); `http://www.rsa.com/rsalabs/node.asp?id=2108`.

[14] Bruce Schneier. The Blowfish Encryption Algorithm. *Dr. Dobb's Journal* 19 (4): 38–40 (1994).

[15] Bruce Schneier. Description of a new variable-length key, 64-bit block cipher (Blowfish). In *Fast Sofware Encryption*, *Combridge Security Workshop Proceedings*, pp. 191–204 (Springer-Verlag, Berlin, 1994).

[16] Bruce Schneier. *Applied Cryptography*, 2nd ed. (John Wiley, New York, 1995).

[17] U.S. Government. *SKIPJACK and KEA Algorithm Specifications*. (1998).

[18] Xiaoyun Wang, Yiqun Yin, and Hongbo Yu. Finding collisions in the full SHA-1. In *Advances in Cryptology – CRYPTO 2005*, (ed. Victor Shoup), pp. 17–36. Lecture Notes in Computer Science, Vol. 3621. (Springer-Verlag, Berlin, 2005).

# CHAPTER 5

General Cryptanalytic Methods

The previous chapters introduced block ciphers and several techniques for attacking them based solely on compromising the underlying mathematics. However, not all ciphers let their security rest solely on the difficulty of computing certain mathematical operations, such as discrete logarithms and factoring; often ciphers are designed with some of the discussed techniques, such as substitution-permutation networks, Feistel structures, and shift registers.

In the following sections, I discuss various general techniques that can be used to attack ciphers of these types.

Here's a quick review of the various forms of attacks possible:

- **Ciphertext-Only Attack** — This method presumes the minimum amount of information for cryptanalysis: that we have intercepted an encrypted communication, and we wish to discover the plaintext and, if possible, the key.

  All modern cryptosystems are designed with at least this attack in mind: if a ciphertext-only attack were not feasible, that would mean that the messages are sent over uncompromisable channels, so there would be no need for the encryption!

- **Known-Plaintext Attack** — A known-plaintext attack dictates that we have obtained a ciphertext and know the associated plaintext with it, and we wish to derive the key. A known-plaintext attack is still often reasonable.

- **Probable Plaintext Attack** — This is a more reasonable, but less useful case of the known-plaintext attack in which certain plaintexts are more likely to be associated with a ciphertext. For example, if we intercepted an encrypted e-mail message, then the first few characters could be fairly easy to guess: the from field, the date and time sent, and so forth. Furthermore, if a message is known to be encoded in a scheme such as

ASCII, then certain bits of the message will be known, and many will appear more often than others.

- **Chosen-Plaintext Attack** — A chosen-plaintext attack is one of the least realistic, but often most powerful. It states that not only can we intercept an encrypted message, but also we have some degree of control over what the plaintext message is for that. Chosen-plaintext attacks often rely on creating plaintexts with certain properties with the hope of affecting some measurable change in the ciphertext to derive information about the key.

- **Chosen-Ciphertext Attack** — An extension to a chosen-plaintext attack is a chosen-ciphertext attack, that is, one in which we can choose ciphertexts to be decrypted with a certain key. This kind of attack is the least realistic, especially when combined with a chosen-plaintext attack (as we do for one of the later methods).

5.1   Brute-Force

Although the majority of the time I will be discussing techniques to find the key in the shortest time possible, we must have a reference point for our work.

Typically, the standard known-ciphertext or known-plaintext attack is simply a **brute-force attack**: so named because no highly developed mathematics or simplifications are necessary — we simply try all possible keys and see which ones give us the correct plaintext–ciphertext pair.

The only real optimization that can be made to brute-force (at least, while still calling it *brute-force*) is to split up the **key space** into chunks and divvy them up between multiple processors or computers. For example, all keys with the first three bits 000 could go to one computer, while 001 would go to another computer, and so on.

For ciphers with small key sizes (say, a 40-bit key or less, depending on how computationally intensive the cryptographic algorithm is), brute-force is not a terrible way to find the key. If we wanted to break a 40-bit key in about a day, this gives us $24 \times 60 \times 60 = 86,400$ seconds to work with, and $2^{40} = 1,099,511,627,776$ keys to try. Therefore, we would like to try about 12,725,829 keys a second. A quick experiment shows that a single fairly fast processor[1] can do at least 4,000,000 AES encryptions a second. Therefore, only about three or so processors could break through a 40-bit key space in a day fairly easily. Considering the growing popularity of multi-core processors, coming up with three or more processors shouldn't pose much of a problem.

[1]This test was run using aesutil, written by Brian Gladman, Markus Lagler, and Tim Tassonis, version 1.07 on a pair of dual-core 2.66 GHz Intel Xeon 5150 processors under Mac OS X 10.4.

Furthermore, Moore's Law of transistor growth says that we can break a key with length increased by an additional bit every two years (since computing power doubles every other year, and an additional bit doubles the amount of work to be done) [8]. This means DES's 56-bit key will be breakable on a desktop PC in a day around the year 2043.

Brute-Force has one key advantage — it is *always guaranteed* to find the correct key after some length of time; this is not always true of other cryptanalytic techniques, especially those based on statistical methods to find keys. Another advantage is ease of implementation, which gains several additional benefits, such as ease of optimization.

5.2   Time–Space Trade-offs

In computer science, there is almost always a trade-off that must be made between running time and space requirements. Generally, it is possible to take less time to do certain computational tasks at the cost of increasing the space requirements. For example, to solve a discrete logarithm problem faster, it is conceivable to build vast tables of the powers of generators in various finite fields. However, there are an infinite number of finite fields and a potentially large number of generators; the particular field and generator used for a given problem may not even be known until a message is actually sent. Both of these prevent the discrete logarithm from benefitting from such a time–space trade-off.

A similar argument could easily be applied to most cryptographic systems: The key, plaintext, and even ciphertext may be unknown until a message is sent, rendering pre-computation useless. However, there are a few tricks that can be used to perform pre-computation for any key-based cryptographic algorithm.

The following sections show some of these techniques to trade space for time.

5.2.1   Meet-in-the-Middle Attack

A lingering question we have yet to answer is, why use 3DES? Why not just use two DES keys back to back (i.e., 2DES)? In other words, just calculate, for two keys, K and L

$$C = Encrypt_L(Encrypt_K(P)).$$

The reason this isn't as secure as we might wish to believe is due to Diffie and Hellman's **meet-in-the-middle attack** [6]. Although we would naturally assume that by encrypting a plaintext with one DES key and then immediately with another, we would have a theoretical security of using a $56 + 56 = 112$-bit key.

However, we can actually trade space for time very well in this particular case, using the birthday paradox, by "meeting in the middle." To explain this, let's break out the cipher into two steps:

1. $D = Encrypt_K(P)$.

2. $C = Encrypt_L(D)$.

The intermediate ciphertext, D, is what we are going to use to break the cipher.

The essence of the attack is to keep a large store of encrypts of the plaintext and decrypts of the ciphertext (using only a *single* encryption and decryption, and not two). We then, for a new key (J) that we want to try, will use it to encrypt the plaintext and decrypt the ciphertext (again, using only the single encryption and decryption).

We then compare the results of the encryption with the table of previously decrypted blocks, and decryption with the table of previously encrypted blocks we have stored. If we get a match with either result, then we have found the two keys. For example, if the decryption with J matched some encryption for a key I, then we know that

$$Encrypt_I(P) = D = Decrypt_J(K),$$

and therefore,

$$C = Encrypt_J(Encrypt_I(P)).$$

Thus, we have found $J = L$ and $I = K$ — our two keys. The technique works vice versa if we found an encryption with J that matched a decryption for I.

How long will it take for this time–space trade-off to work? To brute-force and calculate for all possible keys (which are pairs of keys of size n, for a total size of $2n$) would take 2^{2n} time. However, since we are storing every value and checking it against the table, looking for a repeat, then we can use the birthday paradox to find that it is only going to take about the square root of that time, or 2^n. However, we have to do twice as much work as normal brute-force, since we have to perform an encryption and decryption each time, which gives us 2^{n+1}. In other words, it takes only about twice as long as normal brute-forcing of a single n-bit key (instead of exponentially longer).

Of course, the trade-off comes at the cost of storage. We must store the entire table in order to accomplish this, which grows by two entries each time. We can expect success after about 2^n attempts, each time storing two items, giving us a total of about 2^{n+1} space (times the size of the key).

This attack is a good reason why 3DES uses a process of three encryptions and decryptions, even when using two keys. The order of the keys' use in 3DES is geared so that no meet-in-the-middle attack is possible. Since the intermediate ciphertexts depend on alternating keys, there is no way to coordinate them to induce the above attack.

5.2.2   Hellman Time–Space Trade-off

Another attack, usually simply called the **Hellman time–space trade-off**, is a chosen (or very probable) plaintext attack, but a relatively simple one: We choose a single plaintext to encrypt with a variety of keys [7]. This means that we should be certain that whatever ciphertext we wish to test will correspond to the chosen or probable plaintext.

We start with some large number of keys (say, M keys of the form K_i). We also have the chosen plaintext, P. Then, we construct a list of ciphertexts, corresponding to encrypting the plaintext with each key, K_i:

$$C_i^0 = Encrypt(P, K_i).$$

(Here, we have to adjust the notation slightly so that the second argument of the encryption function is the key.)

Now, we perform the following computation: Take each C_i^0 calculated from before, and compute

$$C_i^1 = Encrypt(P, Reduce(C_i^0)).$$

In other words, we are encrypting the plaintext again, but this time *using the output of the previous encryption as the key*. If the block size of the output is larger than the key (e.g., DES has a block size of 64, but a key size of 56, or AES with a block size of 128 and a key size of 256), then we will have to run the output C_i^0 through a reduction function, *Reduce*.

The reduction function need not be complicated; something simple, such as removing the first few bits, will suffice. If the block size and key size are the same, then the reduction function is unnecessary.

We then iterate the above procedure, using the new ciphertexts as keys. We will stop after some number of times (say, S), each time computing (for a round j)

$$C_i^j = Encrypt(P, Reduce(C_i^{j-1})).$$

This process generates the following flow of ciphertexts:

$$
\begin{array}{ccccccccc}
C_0^0 & \to & C_0^1 & \to & C_0^2 & \to & \cdots & \to & C_0^S \\
C_1^0 & \to & C_1^1 & \to & C_1^2 & \to & \cdots & \to & C_1^S \\
C_2^0 & \to & C_2^1 & \to & C_2^2 & \to & \cdots & \to & C_2^S \\
\vdots & & \vdots & & \vdots & & \ddots & & \vdots \\
C_M^0 & \to & C_M^1 & \to & C_M^2 & \to & \cdots & \to & C_M^S
\end{array}
$$

For the attack, we will only actually store the starting points (C_i^0 values) and final entries (C_i^S values), creating two lists of ciphertexts.

Now, the properties of this list allow us to easily ascertain the key used some portion of the time. For example, assume that we intercept the ciphertext A of the known plaintext used to generate our table. If $A = C_i^S$ for some i, then we know that $A = E(P, \mathcal{R}(C_i^{S-1}))$, and thus the key used is C_i^{S-1}!

However, we do not want to store too much — this just increases our storage requirements, which we always want to minimize. Depending on how small our final generated list is, we will seldom have a match after one step. In this case, we iterate using the same idea as above. Let $A_0 = A$ be our original ciphertext; compute $A_1 = E(P, \mathcal{R}(A_0))$. If A_1 matches any of the C_i^S, then $A_1 = E(P, \mathcal{R}(A_0)) = E(P, \mathcal{R}(C_i^{S-1}))$, meaning that $A_0 = E(P, \mathcal{R}(C_i^{S-2}))$; thus, the key used in the original encryption matches the reduction of C_i^{S-2}.

The process repeats, continuing until the A_j value equals a C_i^S value yielding the position to find the key, or we give up after S times. We would then have run past the left end of the table, where we started generating.

If we learn that $A_j = C_i^S$, then we know that $A_0 = C_i^{S-j} = E(P, C_i^{S-j-1})$; thus, we know that the encryption key is possibly C_i^{S-j-1}. However, it is not guaranteed to be that value; a reduction operator can produce false positives. Also, we do not know the value of C_i^{S-j-1}, since we threw away all but the final values of our above tables. This means that in order to get our potential key, we must start at C_i^0 and regenerate the chain up to that point.

Since we take an average of $S/2$ operations to find the collision and $S/2$ operations to find the key, we take S operations in total.

5.2.3 Time–Space Trade-off Success

The success of this method in general relies on two values: S and M, the size of the table and the number of iterations to perform, respectively. Obviously, if S and M are small, fewer keys will be covered in the intermediate values of the ciphertext chains. For example, if $S = M = 2^{25}$, then a total of 2^{50} keys are pre-computed in the chains. If our key is a 64-bit value, then we have a $2^{50}/2^{64} = 2^{-14} \approx 6.25$ percent chance of finding a random key.

Clearly, then, we wish to have sizes that will yield good results. The optimal result is a guarantee (or as much of one as we can obtain) that the key will be found using the above algorithm. This requirement essentially means that $S \times M = 2^{keysize}$. Hellman suggests in his original paper that the values be chosen so that if a key size is k (i.e., 2^k total keys), then S will be $2^{2k/3}$ and M will be $2^{k/3}$ [7]. This indicates final memory requirements of $2^{k/3}$. To compute the final time requirements for looking up a given key, we have a ciphertext list size of $2^{k/3}$. Assuming that we can perform a lookup of a ciphertext in this list in inconsequential time, and an encryption/reduction combination requires one computation step, then we can estimate that on average it will take $S/2$ to find a value. With the above value of S, this means $2^{2k/3-1}$.

There are two consequences of using these values: The entire keyspace must be pre-computed, but the final result allows us to perform a brute-force in two-thirds the time it would normally take. For example, using DES (56-bit key, 64-bit block size), this would result in memory requirements of $2^{56/3} \times 56$

bits or about 2.9 MB. The average lookup time would be $2^{56/3}$ or $2^{37.33}$ operations (about 173 billion).

5.2.4 Flaws

One fundamental flaw of our system is the possibility of chain collision and convergence. Basically, if two chains "collide," where two of the intermediate values of two different chains are equal at some point, they will converge and become the same chain after that point, owing to the deterministic nature of the chain iteration function. This means significant redundant computations and storage.

Furthermore, the larger the table, the more likely we are to converge. At some point, the probability of a convergence is so great that having a larger table actually will only decrease performance without providing any additional benefits.

Another problem is *false positives* from the reduction function. In the above example with a 64-bit block size and 60-bit key, there are 16 ciphertexts corresponding to the same key. This means we only have a 6.25 percent chance of getting the correct key on the first try. Each false positive requires an additional $\approx S/2$ operations to check the solution.

Finally, we also have the problem of loops. Our particular chain, through the reduction function, might find itself in an infinite loop between some set of values. This would be equivalent to a self-convergence.

5.2.5 Multi-Table Trade-off

There is a remedy for at least some of the collisions in the above scenario, as well as to address the problem of the large monolithic table. We can reduce the possibility of collisions by having multiple, smaller tables, each using a different reduction function. This way, converging chains between tables would all but be eliminated (they might collide, but it is nearly impossible for them to converge). This also increases the complexity of the search, and possibly the memory requirements.

Generally, the recommendation has been to have each table length be equal to the number of tables, so that both values are S. This would be equivalent to having a larger table of size S^2, but with a larger probability of success.

The **multi-table approach** is a universally adopted measure to improve the time–space trade-off, since it takes the same amount of space and drastically increases the success rate.

However, there is a potential problem here: We now have S reduction functions to calculate. This gives us a slightly higher running time of S^2 (S for the normal lookup, and S for the number of tables we have to do it on).

However, in this case, since our S is the square root of the original S, the time requirement is actually the same as before, averting the potential problem.

5.2.6   Rivest's Distinguished Endpoints

Ronald Rivest suggests an optimization on the above system to reduce the size of the stored values [5]. That is, if we stop iterating a chain of the above whenever we get a ciphertext that has some feature we are looking for (e.g., the first 5 bits are all zero) and some minimum of iterations has been performed, then we will save quite a few bits of storage. For example, if we have a 64-bit block size and agree to stop whenever the first 4 bits of the ciphertext are zero, then we shrink the final size of our table by $4/64 = 6.25$ percent.

Other than the obvious advantage, there is an additional benefit: This method also gives some hope of detecting collisions. If the computations stop at some predetermined characteristic, two chains that collided have a chance of stopping at the same point, depending on when they collided and converged. What to do when collisions are detected is another matter, but often it will be redoing the computation on a fresh, new starting ciphertext.

However, there are some disadvantages to the **distinguished endpoint method**. Waiting for a distinguished point to occur can be dangerous: It could occur very far from where the optimal endpoint is. If it occurs well before the endpoint is reached, then many keys in the space will be left untouched in our computation. If it occurs well after, then we are wasting time to compute it. The table was constructed to optimally hit keys; thus, any extra keys will most likely be repeats. Also, additional computations increase the likelihood of collisions.

However, despite these drawbacks, the space-saving feature and collision detection properties have managed to make Rivest's method integrated into almost every implementation of the Hellman time–space trade-off.

5.3   Rainbow Tables

Rainbow tables [10] were designed to counteract several of the fundamental drawbacks to the standard Hellman time–space trade-off. Particularly, rainbow tables are constructed to avoid collisions and to slightly increase the probability of success using the time–space trade-off.

Rainbow tables achieve this success by slightly changing the way the functions generate the next key in the list. Specifically, instead of using the same reduction function for every single iteration, rainbow tables use a *different reduction function each time.*

This gives us a **rainbow chain** that looks like

$$C_0^0 \xrightarrow{r_0} C_0^1 \xrightarrow{r_1} C_0^2 \xrightarrow{r_2} \cdots \xrightarrow{r_{s-1}} C_0^S.$$

Similar to the original time–memory trade-off, we will construct these chains into a larger table, or size S. However, there is no need to do so for multiple tables, since we have no need of more reduction functions. We can also do away with distinguished endpoints, giving us a better bound on the time required for the key recovery (and a slightly higher success rate).

Recovering a key is an identical process to the standard time–memory trade-off, only taking into account that different reduction functions are used in each step. Another difference is that, since we have only one reduction function to compute each time, we will have less to do than a multi-table approach. In this case, to search for a key, we have to apply reduction functions in successive order: once, then twice, then three times, and so on, giving us a total of $S(S-1)/2$ times to find the appropriate entry, and then $S/2$ operations to recover the key (working from the starting point). Adding these two values together gives us $S^2/2$ operations, which is half of the standard table method.

5.3.1 Advantages of Rainbow Tables

Rainbow tables give us a few advantages:

1. Collisions have less impact. If two chains collide, meaning they have the same value at some point, there will not be an issue if they collide at different parts in the chain. In this case, they will not merge, since different reduction functions will be used. A merge can still occur if two chains have a collision on the exact same iteration (and will therefore use the same reduction functions).

2. Distinguished endpoints are not necessary to detect collisions and merges. If a true merge happens, then they will always stop at the same point at the end (since they would have had to have collided at the same iteration, and therefore would be in lock-step the whole way), and one chain could be removed.

3. There is a significant amount of speedup (approximately twice as fast).

A final note made in Reference [10] is that multiple rainbow tables can be used. The advantage of having multiple tables is a higher success rate, at the higher cost of maintaining multiple tables (both in computation time and storage space). One table, for example, might give an 80 percent coverage of the keys, whereas several tables could provide up to 99 percent coverage.

5.3.2   Microsoft LAN Manager Password Hash

One popular example of the use of rainbow tables is in breaking the cryptosystem used by Microsoft LAN Manager. Although LAN Manager has not been actively used in years, the cryptosystem it uses is still in use for compatibility reasons. The LAN Manager used the following cryptosystem to **hash** a password for later verification against user input.

The first step is to split the user's password into either one or two 7-byte chunks (i.e., 56 bits). It also only allows letters and digits for the password (and converts all of the letters to uppercase). The next step in the hashing is to use these chunks to create two DES keys, which are then used to encrypt the ASCII string ''KGS!@#$%''. This string is represented in hexadecimal as the 8 bytes:

$$4b\ 47\ 53\ 21\ 40\ 23\ 24\ 25$$

Assuming that we have the final hash, we wish to find a password that gives this hash. With 26 letters and 10 numbers, we have 36 different characters possible in the password. With seven positions, we then have $36^7 = 78,364,164,096$ different possible ciphertexts corresponding to the original plaintext. With each ciphertext occupying 64 bits, it would require 626,913,312,768 bytes (about 583 GB[2]) to store a table of every possible password. Only in the past couple of years has this kind of storage been available. Even so, it may not be practical to store quite so much. We also would not want to perform 36^7 encryptions for every key.

Luckily, we could use rainbow tables that will allow us to easily break this in far less time and space. Oechslin even used this problem as one of the first demonstrations of rainbow tables [10]. The rainbow table attack demonstrated used five tables, each having 35,000,000 rows (chains) with 4,666 columns (elements in the chain). Using such a table, the passwords were cracked in a matter of seconds.

5.4   Slide Attacks

A generally held belief among cryptographers is that merely increasing the number of rounds of even a weak cipher will increase the strength of the cipher. Although this may be true against certain attacks, such as those that rely on probabilities of each individual round (where the number of rounds can dictate how effective the attack is), it cannot be taken for granted.

One attack in particular can work on any number of rounds, since it takes advantage of the key schedule. This attack is called the **slide attack** [2] (name chosen by Bruce Schneier). It can be used as either a known-plaintext or chosen-plaintext attack.

---

[2]Despite what many hard drive manufacturers like to advertise, a gigabyte (GB) is $2^{30} = 1,073,741,824$ bytes.

The basic attack, as described in Reference [2], requires two properties. First, the attack requires that the cryptographic algorithm have a **weak** round function — "weak" is used to mean that, if given two blocks, A and B, and a found function, F, it is computationally "easy" to tell if $B = F(A)$, regardless of the key used. Although this requirement seems strong, many ciphers are built around weak round functions.

The second requirement is less reasonable. The attack works only with fairly weak key-scheduling algorithms, such as using the same key every round, or alternating between two keys every round.

Although these requirements may not be practical for most ciphers, slide attacks have been used successfully on several ciphers, including variants of Blowfish and DES (some of which were meant to strengthen their security) [1,2].

At this point, we will also assume that each round function is identical. (For most ciphers, this will not be quite true, since each round will depend on a different portion of the key schedule.) Hence, we will refer to them both as F.

The known-plaintext strategy is to collect a large number of known plaintexts and their corresponding ciphertexts. The goal is to find two plaintext–ciphertext pairs, say, (P,C) and (Q,D), such that $Q = F(P)$. As we can see from Figure 5-1, if $Q = F(P)$, then we also know that $D = F(C)$, since they are only off by 1.

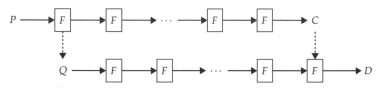

Figure 5-1 A slid pair for a very simple cipher.

When these two pairs of plaintext–ciphertext pairs have this property, we call them a **slid pair**.

The useful thing about a slid pair is that, if the round function is very weak (like we assume), then we can find the key very easily from a slid pair, since we have two simple relationships:

$$Q = F(P), \quad D = F(C).$$

Both the plaintext pair (P, Q) and the ciphertext pair (C, D) give us information that we can use to derive the key.

Let's move to a practical example of this. Consider the FEAL cipher, with the round function:

$$f^1 = S(\alpha^1 \oplus \beta^0 \oplus \alpha^0, \alpha^2 \oplus \beta^1 \oplus \alpha^3, 1).$$
$$f^2 = S(\alpha^2 \oplus \beta^1 \oplus \alpha^3, f^1, 0).$$
$$f^3 = S(\alpha^0, f^1, 0).$$
$$f^4 = S(\alpha^3, f^2, 1).$$

If we want to check for a slid pair, the only unknown variables would be the β's.

This means that for the second step, we get

$$f^2 = S(\alpha^2 \oplus \beta^1 \oplus \alpha^3, f^1, 0).$$

And if we already know the value of f^2, α^2, α^3, f^1, then we can easily calculate β^1 by reversing the S-box and plugging in the appropriate values.

Similarly, we can use the first step to derive β^0, since we will know all of the other parts.

Once we know the two β values, we can calculate $F(A)$ and check to see if it matches up with B. If everything matches up, then we have, in all likelihood, found a slid pair. We then perform the same derivations as above on the ciphertexts to determine more of the key schedule.

With some luck, finding the slid pair will reveal enough bits of the key to allow brute-forcing the remaining bits. For example, several bits of the output of the round might be independently modified by portions of the key material, sometimes by direct XOR, allowing the key bits to be easily derived.

5.4.1   Slide Attacks on Feistel Ciphers

Finding a slid pair with a Feistel cipher is not difficult. After one round of encryption on a Feistel cipher, the output will have half of the bits the same as the input (the old left half becomes the new right half).

With a known-plaintext attack, we can simply look at the slid pair's plaintexts and ciphertexts to check if $F(P) = Q$ and $F(C) = D$. Finding the slid pair is a simple matter of sorting tables of plaintexts and ciphertexts so that matches can be quickly found.

There is the possibility of a false alarm here, but it is not too significant; on average, we can expect one false alarm for every real slid pair.

This known-plaintext attack requires about $2^{n/2}$ plaintext–ciphertext pairs (half of the size of the cipher, which is also the size of the Feistel structure), and about the same amount of work.

For a chosen-plaintext attack, we do a very similar attack. First, we choose a random $n/2$ bit value, x, for one of the halves, and then we select $2^{n/4}$ random values for y to form the plaintext (x, y) (where x is the left half, y is the right half).

For our second plaintext, we again use a fixed x and generate a value z that is completely random. We generate another $2^{n/4}$ of these values and store the plaintext (z, x) (this time, the right half is x, and the left half is z).

We also calculate the encryptions of both plaintexts to form the pairs and store these pairs in a large table. With this many pairs, we expect to find about one slid pair.

An individual Feistel round is usually fairly weak; thus, when a slid pair is found using either method, we can usually expect to get the entire key, or most of it, fairly easily.

5.4.2   Advanced Slide Attacks

One issue with standard slide attacks is that ciphers with two or more rounds of self-similarity tend to make the attack less practical. **Self-similiarity** means that the cipher switches between two or more round functions or keys (or both) every round. To combat a two-round, self-similar cipher with a standard slide attack, we would have to slide two rounds instead of one, which makes the attack more difficult.

There are a few tricks that can be used to combat these problems [1]. The first is called the **complementation slide attack**. We perform a complementation slide attack by, instead of sliding by two rounds, as we suggested before, sliding by one.

The change comes in that we will now have to look for a different type of slid pair. Previously, we looked for a slid pair so that $F(P) = Q$, but now we want one so that $F(P) \oplus Q = \Delta$ where Δ is not zero.

In these cases, if we find multiple slid pairs, we will always have the same Δ. Therefore, identifying slid pairs is still fairly easy.

To derive the key, we can analyze the value of Δ. Typically, Δ will be equal to something along the lines of the XOR of the two round subkeys, giving us a lot of information that can be used to break them (such as by doing an exhaustive search against half of the bits to derive the rest).

Another property of two-round self-similarity is that the decryption process looks nearly identical to the encryption process: They just start one round off from each other, since they do the rounds in reverse order. We can use this property in a method called **sliding with a twist** [1].

The twist is that we will look at the second plaintext–ciphertext pair of the slid pair backwards to look for the slid pair. The two-round self-similarity will then give us $F(P) = D$ and $F(C) = Q$, and allow us to derive a key very similarly to above.

Consider the above case, only with four-round self-similarity (four distinct rounds, perhaps with different keys used each time). The above complementation attack could be used by sliding two rounds to achieve the similarity, but this would again be decreasing our effectiveness.

Both methods can be combined, creating a **complementation slide with a twist** [1]. These two methods combined will allow us to develop a better attack against that four-round self-similar version.

Essentially, we are looking for a fixed difference, and we are using the second part of the slid pair in reverse order. This will line up the keys submitted to the Feistel round function as follows (the top is the encryption, the bottom is the decryption, slid once):

$$K_0 \quad K_1 \quad K_2 \quad K_3 \quad K_0 \quad K_1 \quad K_2 \quad K_3 \quad K_0 \quad \ldots$$
$$K_3 \quad K_2 \quad K_1 \quad K_0 \quad K_3 \quad K_2 \quad K_1 \quad K_0 \quad \ldots$$

With this slid pair then, all of the differences cancel out except for the $K_1 \oplus K_3$ pairs. We then can look for a Δ of $K_1 \oplus K_3$ and use it to derive the key.

5.5   Cryptanalysis of Hash Functions

One goal of hash functions is to generate a digest of a source that cannot easily give information about that source (and ensure the one-wayness of the hash function). The other goal is to ensure that when an attacker knows the source text and its corresponding hash, he or she cannot easily produce another text that produces the same hash, especially for texts that are similar to the original source text.

Hence, the main goal of **cryptanalysis of hash functions** is to either obtain information about the original source text, or to produce a duplicate hash. A pair of messages with hashes is called a **collision**. There are three types of attacks to obtain collisions that we will be concerned with. In increasing order of difficulty, they are:

1. Finding two messages that produce the same hash, with no necessary link to any other particular item. This is the ''easiest'' of the goals, since there are no constraints on the output digest. This is a standard **collision attack**.

2. Finding another message that generates a target hash. The target hash would probably belong to some important item. This is called a **pre-image attack**. (This term is taken from mathematical terminology, where the hash would be called the *image* of the message, and the message is called the *pre-image* of the hash.)

3. Finding another message that generates a target hash, with the original item being a plausible alternative to some target original item. This is an extension of the **pre-image attack**.

   For example, if a Word document contains some instructions and a hash is calculated, someone might be interested in swapping it with a Word document with different instructions, but have it produce the same hash. This is the hardest collision to produce.

The simplest method on the first and simplest kind of collision is to simply keep choosing random data, calculating the hash, and storing both. The birthday paradox says that we only need to wait and store about $\sqrt{n}$ entries (for a hash size of n) before we can expect to find a collision, and hence any better method should have run time or storage less than $\sqrt{n}$.

For the other methods, we do not have the birthday paradox to help us out; thus, the standard brute-force would require a run time or storage of n. Therefore, any technique having a run time or storage less than n would be an improvement.

As shown above, checksums and CRCs are not very appropriate for digital signatures and other security purposes. The current standard is to use the more sophisticated hashing algorithms, like MD5 and SHA-1 for these purposes.

The intricate churning used in them makes it very difficult to map anything in the message digest to say anything about the original message. Hence, for both MD5 and SHA-1, it is still a difficult task to find collisions or any other kinds of weaknesses in these algorithms. The upper limit on time is governed by the birthday paradox; thus, for example, the 160-bit hash of SHA-1 would require a store of 2^{80} message digests before a better-than-50-percent chance of finding a collision. Therefore, any method to find collisions should ideally work in less time than this.

Of course, because of the popularity of the two algorithms, there is a lot of attention given to them by cryptanalysts.

Going into the full analysis of hash functions is beyond the scope of this book. Many of the principles used in Chapter 7 are applied to the hash algorithms, including tracing difference paths through the hash to generate collisions

To date, the two best collision attacks against SHA-1 [13] can generate collisions in less than 2^{69} operations (with an improvement to 2^{63}), and a recent (2006) attack produced a collision with approximately 2^{35} time [4] (with the expected run time at the time the paper was written, in 2006, of 18 hours). Both attacks are better than the 2^{80} operations needed for the birthday attack.

For MD5, the current best collision attack known can produce a collision in less than a minute on a modest 2006-era PC [9].

In light of the ever-raging battle between hash algorithm maker and hash algorithm breaker, we wish to emphasize the following point.

Principle of Multi-Hash Security: Computing cycles and storage space are getting cheaper. Using multiple hashing functions can exponentially increase the security. Therefore, when possible, store several hashes and redundancy checks of data.

This principle takes advantage of one feature that is not present if one simply increases the length of the returned hash function: Using different hash functions with different design philosophies means that, with any luck, vulnerabilities found in one hash function (such as the ability to generate texts with the same hash) won't work on more than one hash at a time; hence, only one of the hashes used will be compromised. If a hash is simply extended to more bits, it's possible that the underlying structure is still weak, and the hash can still be compromised.

5.6   Cryptanalysis of Random Number Generators

A primary reason for cryptanalyzing random number generators is to try to determine information about a key used in a standard cipher.

For example, in a classroom experiment that I led, students in the class all had accounts to trade goods in a virtual economy. During various discussions, the students cleverly asked me how the account numbers (10 decimal digits) and RSA keys (hundreds of decimal digits) were generated. I told them that I had just used the standard Java random number generator, and informed them of a rough guess of the time at which they were generated.

The standard Java method at the time[3] was to use a linear congruential random number generator seeded with the current time in milliseconds to generate numbers. Considering that they had a good guess at the time, they could try various values for the system clock at the time and try to find the seed by seeing if their own account numbers appeared in the output.

Assuming a class size of 100 students, with about 14 digits per account number (there was also a 4-digit password generated), and 3,600,000 milliseconds per hour, there are

$$100 \times 14 \times 3,600,000 = 5,040,000,000$$

digits to generate and check to account for all of the possible seeds that could occur in 1 hour.

With a few processors, it is very possible to chew through a few hours of the possible random numbers in just a few days at most.

This example illustrates one of the methods for breaking linear congruential random number generators: guessing the seed. Finding out the way in which the seed is generated and attempting to re-create it will work on this as well as on any other types of ciphers that rely on a seed.

Another method is to use mathematical properties to determine the values of a, c, m, for the standard linear congruential method:

$$X \leftarrow (a \times X + c) \bmod m.$$

For example, if three consecutively generated values of X can be discovered (say, A, B, C), then it is fairly straightforward to solve the system of equations:

$$C \equiv (a \times B + c) \bmod m.$$
$$B \equiv (a \times A + c) \bmod m.$$

Here, we have two equations and two unknowns (assuming m is known). If we subtract the second equation from the first (i.e., subtract the sides from the corresponding size), we obtain the relation

$$(C - B) \equiv (a \times (B - A)) \bmod m.$$

---

[3]Unfortunately for the students, I was using a beta version of Java 1.5, which used the current time in *nanoseconds* for the seed. In addition, the seed is added to an integer that is updated for every time the Java random number generator is used, so that even knowing the time would not provide sufficient information to find the account numbers.

If we knew that m was a prime, then we could multiply $(C - B)$ by the inverse of $(B - A)$ (modulo m), and obtain a. We can then compute $C = B - a \times A$ and check to make sure that $c = C - a \times B$.

If m is not prime, or if we do not know m at all, then there are other fast methods to find all of the parameters (see References [3] and [11]).

5.7 Summary

The methods described in this chapter, for the most part, are not successful with only one cipher or type of cipher. I don't delve into the depths of how each cipher works, for example, to use rainbow tables. The techniques are nearly identical for any cipher.

Random number generators can also play an important part in cryptanalysis; thus, a brief example was given to show sample cryptanalysis of this. For more on cryptographic uses of random number generators, see Reference [12].

In the next two chapters, I am going to discuss several methods that do rely heavily on the internal structure of individual ciphers. While the general principles of the attacks are the same, every attack will have to be uniquely constructed to fit the properties of the cipher.

Exercises

Exercise 1. Can the meet-in-the-middle attack be extended to a normal cryptoscheme? For example, could we use this to reduce the amount of computation required to brute-force DES down from 2^{56} by trading space in a similar way? Why or why not?

Exercise 2. Write an implementation of a rainbow table attack against the Microsoft LAN Manager password-hashing scheme.

Exercise 3. Since the round functions of the Easy1 cipher are identical, attempt to mount a slide attack on, say, a 20-round version of this cipher.

References

[1] Alex Biryukov and David Wagner. Advanced slide attacks. In *Advances in Cryptology – EUROCRYPT 2000*, (ed. Bart Preneel), pp. 589–606. Lecture Notes in Computer Science, Vol. 1807. (Springer-Verlag, Berlin, 2000).

[2] Alex Biryukov and David Wagner. Slide attacks. In *Fast Software Encryption '99*, (ed. Lars R. Knudsen), pp. 245–259. Lecture Notes in Computer Science, Vol. 1636. (Springer-Verlag, Berlin, 1999).

[3] Jane Boyar. Inferring sequences produced by pseudo-random number generators. *Journal of the ACM* **36**(1): 129–141 (1989).

[4] Christophe De Cannière and Christian Rechberger. Finding SHA-1 characteristics: General results and applications. In *Advances in Cryptology – ASIACRYPT 2006*, (eds. Xuejia Lai and Kefei Chen), pp. 1–20. Lecture Notes in Computer Science, Vol. 4284. (Springer-Verlag, Berlin, 2007).

[5] Dorothy Elizabeth Robling Denning. *Cryptography and Data Security*. (Addison-Wesley, Boston, 1982).

[6] Whitfield Diffie and Martin E. Hellman. Exhaustive cryptanalysis of the NBS data encryption standard. *IEEE Computer* **10**(6): 74–84 (1977).

[7] Martin E. Hellman. A cryptanalytic time–memory trade-off. *IEEE Transactions on Information Theory* **26**(4): 401–406 (1980).

[8] Intel Corporation and Gordon E. Moore. *Moore's Law*; http://www.intel.com/technology/mooreslaw/.

[9] Vlastimil Klima. *Tunnels in Hash Functions: MD5 Collisions Within a Minute*. Cryptology ePrint Archive, Report 2006/105. (2006); http://eprint.iacr.org/2006/105.

[10] Philippe Oechslin. Making a faster cryptanalytic time-memory trade-off. In *Advances in Cryptology – CRYPTO 2003*, (ed. D. Boneh), pp. 617–630. Lecture Notes in Computer Science, Vol. 2729. (Springer-Verlag, Boston, 2003).

[11] J.A. Reeds. "Cracking" a random number generator. *Cryptologia* **1**(1): 20–26 (1977).

[12] Bruce Schneier. *Applied Cryptography*, 2nd ed. (John Wiley, New York, 1995).

[13] Xiaoyun Wang, Yiqun Yin, and Hongbo Yu. Finding collisions in the full SHA-1. In *Advances in Cryptology – CRYPTO 2005*, (ed. Victor Shoup), pp. 17–36. Lecture Notes in Computer Science, Vol. 3621. (Springer-Verlag, Berlin, 2005).

# CHAPTER 6

Linear Cryptanalysis

The previous chapters introduced some general methods of analyzing block ciphers. The methods were "general" in that there was not a lot of analysis of a specific cipher; the attacks work equally well on many different classes of ciphers. Any errors exploited weren't so much inherent to the ciphers: Detailed analysis of the ciphers was not what yielded these attacks.

While there are many cryptanalytic strategies that might rely on deep analysis of a cipher, I wish to focus on a few different classes of these ciphers. In this chapter, I'll discuss a very important class of newer cryptanalysis methods — linear cryptanalysis.

Linear cryptanalysis is a known-plaintext attack first detailed by Mitsuru Matsui and Atsuhiro Yamagishi in the early 1990s against FEAL and DES [4,5]. This formal method attempts to relate the inputs and outputs of algorithm components together so that solving a system of *linear* equations will yield information about the bits of the key used to encrypt them.

Linear cryptanalysis is also a statistical attack: It is not guaranteed to work in every single case. However, it does work most of the time, which I'll define more precisely below.

Previous methods did not rely on deficiencies of the cryptographic algorithm, at least in the same way. The methods in this and the next chapter are designed to take advantage of weaknesses in some of the cipher structures.

Ideally, a cipher would have nearly perfect diffusion and confusion; that is, there would be no easy way to make predictions about the output based on the input without knowing the key. However, no cipher can have truly *perfect* diffusion; there will also be some imperfections in the structures. The nature of these weaknesses and how to exploit them yield the different attacks.

This chapter explains and demonstrates the method of linear cryptanalysis. We also look at how effective the method is against many ciphers. Finally, I show several extensions and alterations of the method used to increase its effectiveness.

6.1   Overview

Linear cryptanalysis was first explained and demonstrated in References [4] and [5]. It is a known-plaintext attack, meaning that we will have some set of plaintexts and associated ciphertexts, all encrypted with the same key, which is what we wish to discover. Another good source on linear cryptanalysis (and differential) is Howard Heys [1], which provides a nice development framework for learning this technique through simpler ciphers first (which is how I'll approach the subject).

So far, we know well what the term *cryptanalysis* means. The "linear" in *linear cryptanalysis* stems from the fact that we want to manipulate and solve **linear binary equations**. For linear binary equations, this means the equations looks like

$$A \oplus B \oplus C \oplus \cdots \oplus Y = Z$$

Because of the commutativity of the XOR operator, this equation is the same as

$$A \oplus B \oplus C \oplus \cdots \oplus Y \oplus Z = 0$$

(obtained by taking the previous equation and XORing Z to both sides).

These binary equations will be built to relate the inputs and outputs of various portions of the ciphers. For example, we might wish to have an equation of two input bits of a round input — X_0 and X_2 — with three output bits of a round — Y_1, Y_2, and Y_4 — which would look like

$$X_0 \oplus X_2 \oplus Y_1 \oplus Y_2 \oplus Y_4$$

This equation will most likely not be true all the time, but some of the time. We will generate many such equations, and eventually, we will use these relations to build up a linear "approximation" of the entire cipher, where the final input bits and output bits will consist of the key, plaintext, and ciphertext. The more accurate the approximation, the less work we will have to do to figure out the key.

One quick note: The equations don't quite work out if we have an expression equal to 1 (instead of 0), such as

$$A \oplus B \oplus C = 1$$

Technically speaking, this is not a linear equation, but an **affine** equation (since it uses a nonzero constant).

Sometimes people refer to these equations as "parity" equations, since **parity** is the sum of all of the bits of a number, and we are interested in the parities for the left-hand side and the right-hand side to match.

The linear cryptanalysis method models the cipher as a linear equation, similar to the ones above, using bits of the plaintext, ciphertext, and key as the variables in the equation. For most ciphers, the ciphertext is sufficiently random-looking, with regard to the plaintext, so that any arbitrary linear expression should be true about half the time. For example, when we examine any one of the ciphertext bits, we should see that the bit is 0 half of the time and 1 the other half of the time.

Linear cryptanalysis attempts to find expressions that aren't quite as random: The probability of getting a 0 or 1 isn't *quite* 1/2. As we find expressions with probabilities farther from 1/2, the success rate of determining the key from these expressions goes up.

6.2   Matsui's Algorithms

Matsui proposes two algorithms for linear cryptanalysis, although only one is regularly used.

Assume that we have some equation involving bits of plaintext, ciphertext, and a key, such as

$$P_0 \oplus P_2 \oplus \cdots \oplus C_1 \oplus C_2 \oplus \cdots = K_1 \oplus K_3 \oplus \cdots$$

(although we haven't discussed how to obtain such a representation).

Assuming the bits have good diffusion and confusion characteristics, this equation is true fairly randomly and unpredictably, that is, happening about half of the time. When the events have probability different from 1/2, we say that this difference is a **bias**. If p is the probability that the above is true, then $|p - 1/2|$ is the bias — that is, the difference between p and 1/2, ignoring the sign of the result (the absolute value).

Assuming a known-plaintext attack, we would know several values of the P and C bits, and we would be looking for the K bits. Matsui's "Algorithm 1" uses the above equation, along with its bias, to get us a single bit of information about the key itself.

This algorithm, and the next, both use the **principle of maximum likelihood**: If it's the most probable (or one of the most probable) causes, then assume it is the correct cause.

Matsui's Algorithm 1. Assume that we have a linear expression of the form:

$$P_{i_1} \oplus P_{i_2} \oplus \cdots \oplus C_{j_1} \oplus C_{j_2} \oplus \cdots = K_{k_1} \oplus K_{k_2} \oplus \cdots$$

Also, we must know the probability, p, of this equation holding true.

1. Collect many valid plaintext–ciphertext pairs for a particular key (the amount of which to be determined by the probability of the equation, specified below).

2. For each plaintext–ciphertext pair, calculate the left side of the above linear expression. Let T be the number of times the left side is equal to 0.

3. If T is more than half of the pairs **and** p is greater than 1/2, then we guess that the right side (the K bits XORed) is 0.

4. If T is less than half of the pairs **and** p is less than $1/2$, then we also guess 0 for the XOR of the K bits.

5. Otherwise, guess that the XOR of the K bits must be 1.

These last three steps are there because we are assuming that our bias and probability are accurate, meaning that if p is less than $1/2$, we expect that the equation is usually false, and if p is greater than $1/2$, then the equation is usually true, which would require the above scenarios to work out, for example, since if we expect it to be false and the left side is 0, then the right side must be 1 so that the whole equation is false, and so forth.

This algorithm doesn't offer a whole lot: We get a small amount of information for some collection of plaintext–ciphertext pairs. If we had a large collection of plaintext–ciphertext pairs as well as several such equations with large biases, then we might be able to construct a set of equations of key bits, which could possibly be used to derive the key bits themselves.

This isn't always practical. For most good ciphers, the biases for the full cipher will usually be very small (in that any linear expression will usually be true close to half the time). Luckily, Matsui issued another algorithm for extracting key bits, which relies on, potentially, only a single number of linear expressions, but a large number of plaintext–ciphertext pairs.

The idea is to have another equation, similar to the one above. However, instead of counting how many times the left-hand side is true, we will try *every* value of the K bits and count how many times the overall equation is true.

Matsui's Algorithm 2. Assume we have a linear expression of the form:

$$P_{i_1} \oplus P_{i_2} \oplus \cdots \oplus C_{j_1} \oplus C_{j_2} \oplus \cdots = K_{k_1} \oplus K_{k_2} \oplus \cdots$$

Also, we must know the probability of this equation holding true, p.

1. Collect a large number of plaintext–ciphertext pairs for a single key that we wish to obtain (again, depending on the probability of the equation).

2. For each candidate set of key bits, calculate a T-value, representing the number of times that the linear equation holds true with the plaintext–ciphertext pairs.

3. Select the candidate keys that are the farthest "away" from half the number of pairs. Thus, if N is the number of pairs, calculate $T - (N/2)$ for each candidate, with the end result being some set of key candidates with $|T - (N/2)|$ (the absolute value of the difference) being maximized.

The point here is we are trying all values of key bits, trying to find the most likely candidate set of them. For example, if we had a 64-bit key and we managed to find an expression involving 32 bits of the key that required, say, 2^{20} operations per key, then we would have $O(2^{20} \times 2^{32}) = O(2^{52})$ operations to derive 32 bits of key. We could then just simply brute-force the other 32 bits [in $O(2^{32})$ time], which would be much easier than the previous $O(2^{52})$ operations. Essentially, we would then have derived the key in less than $O(2^{53})$ operations.

The following sections help us to find these linear expressions, as well as estimations on the number of plaintext–ciphertext pairs and the amount of time and space that this approach will take.

6.3   Linear Expressions for S-Boxes

The first step to constructing a full linear equation to use with Matsui's algorithms is learning how to calculate simple linear expressions and how to determine their biases.

It's easiest to first look at an example. Consider the following 3-bit S-box

```
[3, 7, 2, 4, 1, 5, 0, 6]
```

(i.e., substitute 3 for 0, 7 for 1, 2 for 2, 4 for 3, etc.).

Finding linear expressions of S-boxes requires us to find equations involving the input bits and output bits, such as $X_0 \oplus X_2 = Y_1 \oplus Y_2$. We can run this linear equation against all possible input values (0–7) of the example S-box, counting it true 2 out of 8 times [for $S(3) = 4$ and $S(7) = 6$], giving us a probability of $1/4 = 0.25$. The bias, usually abbreviated ϵ, is then $\epsilon = (2 - 4)/8 = -1/4$. Figure 6-1 shows a small S-box with a linear expression drawn over it.

Keeping in mind the idea behind Matsui's Algorithm 2, we try every possible set of input bits and output bits and measure the bias. We are interested most in linear expressions with the largest amount of bias (regardless of sign).

Since we have three possible input bits and three possible output bits that we may either keep or omit in each linear expression, we then have to look through $2^3 \times 2^3 = 2^{3+3} = 2^6 = 64$ different expressions. Furthermore, we have to try all possible values of the input–output value pairs which is 2^3 (since we have 3 input bits and the output is completely determined by them). This gives us $2^6 \times 2^3 = 2^9 = 512$ operations in total on the S-box.

Generalizing this, with an n-bit S-box (n-bit input, n-bit output), we have to perform several operations equal to 2^{3n}.

Figure 6-1 Graphical representation of the expression $X_2 = Y_1 \oplus Y_2$ on a 3-bit S-box.

Using our previous idea (from Chapter 5) that 2^{40} is not too taxing an amount of work, we find n such that

$$2^{3n} = 2^{40}$$

This gives us $n = 13$, which would mean we could reasonably analyze all of the relationships in a 13-bit S-box. The industry standard seems to be to use 8-bit S-boxes or less, so we are all right for now.

Now that we understand calculating biases for linear expressions, we can then choose every possible linear expression. As such, we will be left with a large listing of biases, as shown in Table 6-1.

A few things to note: The highest value is (positive) 1/2, and the smallest is −1/2, which are both good values (they mean that the equation is always true or always false, respectively). However, the valid linear expression $0 = 0$, while always true (with bias 1/2), is meaningless; of course, it is always true, but it yields no information.

In general, we want to focus on the values that have a high bias and that involve the least possible number of bits. Involving fewer bits in the input and the output helps us to manage the eventual linear cryptanalysis, which is composed of many of the linear expressions built on each other.

However, the syntax shown in Table 6-1 is a bit cumbersome. It's good to see exactly which bits affect which bits, along with the associated bias, but it isn't very easy to parse.

A notation used by Matsui is very helpful in this case. The representation of the input and output bits will be a pair of numbers (usually written in hexadecimal). A bit being present in the linear expression would be translated to a 1 (in the binary representation) of the number, and a bit not being present translates to a 0.

Table 6-1 A Few of the Linear Expressions from a Simple 3-Bit S-Sox

EQUATION	BIAS (ϵ)
$0 = 0$	1/2
$X_0 = Y_0$	0
$X_0 = Y_1$	0
$X_0 = Y_0 \oplus Y_1$	0
$X_0 = Y_2$	1/2
$X_1 = Y_0$	−1/2
$X_2 = Y_1 \oplus Y_2$	−1/4
$\vdots$	

Table 6-2 Complete Set of Biases for All Possible Linear Expressions on the Sample 3-Bit S-Box

		0	1	2	3	4	5	6	7
					Y				
	0	4	0	0	0	0	0	0	0
	1	0	0	0	0	4	0	0	0
	2	0	−4	0	0	0	0	0	0
	3	0	0	0	0	0	−4	0	0
X	4	0	0	−2	2	0	0	−2	−2
	5	0	0	−2	−2	0	0	−2	2
	6	0	0	−2	2	0	0	2	2
	7	0	0	2	2	0	0	−2	2

The entries with the largest biases (in magnitude) are bold. Ignore the upper-left entry, which represents 0 = 0.

For example, if the input side is $X_0 \oplus X_2 \oplus X_3 \oplus X_6$, we would use the binary number 01001101, or 4D in hexadecimal. For no particular reason, we usually write the linear expression starting with subscript 0, then 1, and so forth, while we translate this to mean bit 0, bit 1, and so forth, which are normally represented in most significant bit order in the final number.

Therefore, for the last row in Table 6-1, we have the expression $X_2 = Y_1 \oplus Y_2$. This would correspond to the number pair (3,5).

The above compact form of representing the equations can allow us to more easily analyze S-boxes by constructing tables, with the row number representing the input bits, the column number representing the output bits, and the entry in the table corresponding to the bias. For example, Table 6-2 shows the complete set of linear expressions of the previous 3-bit S-box.

Large tables are good for seeing the characteristics of an S-box, although ordered listings of individual entries spelled out (as above) are still useful for building larger linear expressions. For example, a graphical representation of AES's S-box is shown in Figure 6-2, where there would be too much information for a large table, and a listing of top entries would be more useful.

In S-box analysis tables, we are looking for entries with large biases, either negative or positive. If all of the entries are small, then the S-box does not have a very linear structure, and it may make linear cryptanalysis on the cipher difficult.

Figure 6-2 Linear correlation between the input and output of AES's S-box (with darker values meaning higher correlation, since the table would be too large to show individual numbers). This shows a great deal of diffusion between the input and input, since the color is spread all over.

Notice that when we are analyzing these potential linear expressions, we don't have to worry about key bits, or collecting plaintext–ciphertext pairs, as we will for the full technique. This analysis is nonrandom and fairly straightforward. Granted, we do have to try every possible input possible for the S-boxes, but usually this is a fairly small number (in the grand scheme of things).

6.4   Matsui's Piling-up Lemma

Now that we have linear expressions for S-boxes, how do we combine them to perform linear cryptanalysis, and what kinds of results will we get? The simple answer is that we trace the output bits of one S-box to be the input values of other S-boxes, repeating until we have an expression relating only plaintext bits, ciphertext bits, and key bits.

But what happens when they combine? With more rounds, the biases of the overall expression are going to change, but how? Our natural inclination is that the biases will be multiplicative — meaning that an expression's bias of $1/4$, when combined with another linear expression of bias $1/3$ (lining up their inputs and outputs appropriately) would be $1/4 \times 1/3 = 1/12$. This is approximately what happens, but not quite.

Matsui shows that the linear expressions "pile up" in a different sort of way [4].

Piling-up Lemma. Assume that we have n independent linear expressions, say, $X_1, X_2, \ldots, X_n$, with associated biases $\epsilon_1, \epsilon_2, \ldots, \epsilon_n$. We also need to assume that they are random, as we have no real preconceptions of their values, and binary, in that they output 0 or 1. Then, the bias of an aggregate binary, linear expression,

$$X_1 \oplus X_2 \oplus \cdots \oplus X_n$$

is the expression

$$\epsilon_{1,2,\ldots,n} = 2^{n-1} \left(\epsilon_1 \times \epsilon_2 \times \cdots \times \epsilon_n \right)$$

(where $\epsilon_{1,2,\ldots,n}$ is the new bias). Remember that this bias is relative to $1/2$, meaning that the probability of it happening is $1/2$ plus the bias.

Matsui's piling-up lemma can be easily proven by mathematical induction, with the assumption that each linear expression is independent. It isn't necessary to go into the full proof here — I refer the interested reader to Reference [4].

Since the underlying expressions will not have probabilities of 100 percent or 0 percent, we cannot construct completely exact and precise linear expressions. Instead, we try to construct expressions that are true as often (or as seldom) as possible; hence, we often call these expressions approximations. Matsui's piling-up lemma provides us with a means of determining how good our approximation is (if it has a very large bias, either positive or negative).

6.5 EASY1 Cipher

Now let's return our attention to the slimmed-down, simple cipher called EASY1 introduced above.

Every portion of the cipher will use the same S-box, although linear cryptanalysis works quite well regardless of the variety and number of S-boxes used. We keep it to one S-box to make the analysis a little easier. To reiterate, our S-box is represented as

```
[16, 42, 28, 3, 26, 0, 31, 46, 27, 14, 49, 62, 37, 56, 23, 6, 40, 48, 53, 8,
20, 25, 33, 1, 2, 63, 15, 34, 55, 21, 39, 57, 54, 45, 47, 13, 7, 44, 61, 9, 60,
32, 22, 29, 52, 19, 12, 50, 5, 51, 11, 18, 59, 41, 36, 30, 17, 38, 10, 4, 58,
43, 35, 24]
```

Furthermore, a permutation will take place in between rounds to accomplish more diffusion. Here is the permutation used throughout the cipher:

```
[24, 5, 15, 23, 14, 32, 19, 18, 26, 17, 6, 12, 34, 9, 8, 20, 28, 0, 2, 21, 29,
11, 33, 22, 30, 31, 1, 25, 3, 35, 16, 13, 27, 7, 10, 4]
```

Recall also that six 6-bit S-boxes feed into the 36-bit P-box, which is then XORed with an 18-bit key (the 36-bit wide full key used in the cipher is derived from repeating the 18-bit key, concatenating it to itself to get 36 bits).

Table 6-3 A Small Part of the Complete 64×64 Linear Expression Bias Table for the EASY1 S-Box

	0	1	2	3	4	5	6	7	8	9	a	b	c	d
0	20	0	0	0	0	0	0	0	0	0	0	0	0	0
1	0	-4	-2	6	-6	2	-4	-8	4	-4	6	-6	-6	-2
2	0	2	2	4	4	2	-2	4	2	0	4	2	-6	4
3	0	6	0	-6	2	0	-2	0	2	0	-2	0	-4	2
4	0	4	-2	-2	0	4	-2	6	0	4	2	-6	8	-4
5	0	0	4	-4	6	-6	6	2	-4	0	0	-c	-2	6
6	0	2	0	-2	0	-2	8	2	2	0	-2	0	6	0
7	0	-2	6	4	2	0	-4	2	2	0	-8	-2	4	2
8	0	-2	6	0	2	0	0	2	-4	2	2	4	2	0
9	0	2	0	2	-4	2	0	6	0	6	4	-6	-4	-2
a	0	4	0	0	2	2	2	-2	2	2	-6	6	-4	0
b	0	0	-6	2	0	0	6	6	2	-6	0	0	-2	-2
c	0	-2	0	6	2	8	-6	8	4	-6	-8	-2	-6	0
d	0	2	2	0	-8	-2	6	0	0	-2	2	4	0	a
e	0	0	2	-6	-2	2	0	4	2	-2	8	4	0	-8
f	0	4	4	-4	0	4	8	0	2	6	-2	-2	-2	-6

This requires the input to be first split six ways, fed into the S-boxes, and then rebuilt and run through the P-box, and then finally XORed with the key. Repeat this for every round.

Note that the individual S-boxes are relatively small (as far as number of input and output bits): We can enumerate all possible linear expressions and test for large biases. Once we have discovered some expressions with large biases, we can start to chain rounds together, discovering linear expressions that operate between multiple rounds. Obviously, the more rounds we have to "stitch" together in this manner, the lower the bias is going to be, and therefore the tougher our job is going to be.

Since more rounds generally lower the overall bias, it makes no sense (from the point of view of the communicating parties) to use a 1-round variant of the cipher. Even without linear cryptanalysis, we can use the known S-box and P-box values and simply rewrite the known-plaintext problem to be a simple XOR equation. We can do this because the plaintext can be processed up until the key XOR, and the ciphertext is merely the result of this XOR, giving us a trivially solvable equation (XORing the processed plaintext, and the ciphertext will then reveal the key). For this reason, we'll need to analyze at least a 2-round variant.

But first thing's first: the bias table. Since this is a 64×64 table, I can't show all of it. Instead, Table 6-3 shows a small portion of the linear expression values.

Normally, we simply pick the entries with the highest bias out of the full bias table, as shown in Table 6.4, because of the unwieldy nature of the full table.

Table 6-4 The Linear Expressions of EASY1's S-Box That Have the Highest Bias

EXPRESSION	BIAS
$X_0 = Y_1 \oplus Y_2 \oplus Y_3 \oplus Y_4$	-12
$X_0 \oplus X_1 \oplus X_2 = Y_0 \oplus Y_4 \oplus Y_5$	12
$X_0 \oplus X_1 \oplus X_2 \oplus X_3 \oplus X_4 \oplus X_5 = Y_0 \oplus Y_3 \oplus Y_4 \oplus Y_5$	-12
$X_0 \oplus X_1 \oplus X_2 \oplus X_3 \oplus X_5 = Y_0$	-12
$X_0 \oplus X_1 \oplus X_2 \oplus X_4 = Y_4$	-12
$X_0 \oplus X_1 \oplus X_2 \oplus X_5 = Y_1 \oplus Y_2 \oplus Y_4 \oplus Y_5$	-12
$X_0 \oplus X_1 \oplus X_4 \oplus X_5 = Y_2 \oplus Y_4$	-12
$X_0 \oplus X_1 \oplus X_5 = Y_0 \oplus Y_1 \oplus Y_3 \oplus Y_4$	-12
$X_0 \oplus X_2 = Y_0 \oplus Y_1 \oplus Y_3$	-12
$X_0 \oplus X_2 \oplus X_3 = Y_1 \oplus Y_3 \oplus Y_4 \oplus Y_5$	12
$X_0 \oplus X_2 \oplus X_3 \oplus X_4 = Y_0 \oplus Y_2 \oplus Y_5$	12
$X_0 \oplus X_2 \oplus X_3 \oplus X_4 \oplus X_5 = Y_0 \oplus Y_1 \oplus Y_5$	12
$X_0 \oplus X_3 \oplus X_5 = Y_1 \oplus Y_3 \oplus Y_4$	-12
$X_0 \oplus X_5 = Y_4 \oplus Y_5$	-12
$X_1 \oplus X_2 \oplus X_3 = Y_0 \oplus Y_1 \oplus Y_2 \oplus Y_3 \oplus Y_5$	12
$X_1 \oplus X_3 \oplus X_4 = Y_1 \oplus Y_2 \oplus Y_3$	12
$X_2 \oplus X_5 = Y_1 \oplus Y_3 \oplus Y_4$	-12
$X_3 = Y_0 \oplus Y_4 \oplus Y_5$	-12
$X_0 \oplus X_1 \oplus X_2 \oplus X_3 \oplus X_4 = Y_3$	14
$X_3 = Y_0 \oplus Y_1 \oplus Y_2 \oplus Y_4 \oplus Y_5$	16

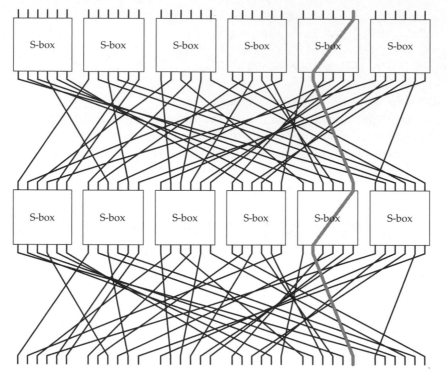

Figure 6-3 A simple linear expression for two rounds of EASY1 (ignore the influence of the key bits at this point).

Let's consider a simple example of using the piling-up lemma on the EASY1 cipher.

Although not shown in the Table 6-4 diagram, one of the equations is $X_0 = Y_4$, which has a bias of -4. If you look at the diagram of the EASY1 cipher in Figure 6-3, there is one fairly easy pattern to follow using this bias: In the second from the right S-box (second least significant), we have bit 4 of the S-box's output being mapped to bit 0 of the same S-box's input for the next round.

Using the piling-up lemma, we can make the following deductions.

Take $\epsilon_1 = -4/32 \approx -0.125$, which is the bias for the S-box expression $X_0 \oplus Y_4 = 0$. The same bias will apply for the next round's bias (ϵ_2).

Since Y_4 is mapped to X_0 in the next round, let's differentiate the rounds with superscripts. Thus, the first round's equation is $X_0^0 \oplus Y_4^0 = 0$, whereas the second round's equation is $X_0^1 \oplus Y_4^1 = 0$.

We can then combine the two equations, knowing that $Y_4^0 = X_0^1$, by XORing the two equations together (where the common terms XOR and cancel each other out), obtaining

$$X_0^0 \oplus Y_4^1 = 0$$

The bias for this is obtained using the piling-up lemma. We know that $\epsilon_1 = \epsilon_2 = -4/32$; thus, the combined bias (say, $\epsilon_{1,2}$) is obtained from

$$\epsilon_{1,2} = 2^{-(2-1)} \left(\frac{-4}{32} \times \frac{-4}{32} \right) = \frac{1}{128} = 2^{-7}$$

Figure 6-3 shows a representation of this expression.

Matsui claims that, in theory, to get a decent guess at the key bits, we will need to have on the order of $8\epsilon^{-2}$ plaintext–ciphertext pairs. In the case above, with a bias of 2^{-7}, we would need about $8(2^{-7})^{-2} = 2^{17} = 131,072$ plaintext–ciphertext pairs. This large number of pairs shows us that this expression is not very good — since there are only 2^{18} keys possible, we are doing almost the same amount of work as brute-force. Furthermore, this is only for a two-round variant of the cipher: More likely, we will have more rounds, and therefore the bias for our expression will keep getting worse.

6.6   Linear Expressions and Key Recovery

The previous attack is only for a two-round variant of the cipher and does not go into how the key is derived from a linear expression. Let's try building a slightly more complicated linear expression to represent a slightly larger cipher. We are going to use the two linear expressions in Table 6-5 to attack a three-round EASY1 cipher.

We simply chain together the two linear expressions. The combined bias for the two of them is therefore

$$\epsilon = 2^1 \left(\frac{14}{64} \times \frac{10}{64} \right) = \frac{35}{512} \approx 0.0684$$

We can then calculate the approximate number of pairs required:

$$8\epsilon^{-2} = 8 \times \frac{512^2}{35^2} \approx 1,712$$

Comparing this with the previous required number of plaintext–ciphertext pairs (131,072), we can see the value of having linear expressions with higher biases.

Table 6-5 Two Linear Expressions Used to Perform Linear Cryptanalysis on the EASY1 Cipher

EXPRESSION	BIAS
$X_0 \oplus X_1 \oplus X_2 \oplus X_3 \oplus X_4 = Y_3$	14
$X_5 = Y_1 \oplus Y_2$	10

Up until this point, we haven't really seen how the bits of the key fit into this analysis. Now I'll show how to use the expressions to find the key bits.

The first question one might ask is, how do key bits affect these linear expressions for a cipher? In short, they don't. This is the beauty of the linear cryptanalytic method. For example, if we have a simple cryptographic function that operates on a plaintext (P) to produce a ciphertext (C), then we can use two keys (K_1 and K_2), as well as an S-box function (S), to obtain

$$C = K_2 \oplus S(P \oplus K_1)$$

Assume that we have a linear expression for the S-box, say, $X_0 = Y_1 \oplus Y_3$. It turns out that this linear expression will be true for the entire cryptographic function as well with the same bias as the original expression (or it will be false with the same bias, if the key bits all XOR to 1 instead of 0). To show this, we rewrite the above equation as

$$X_0 \oplus Y_1 \oplus Y_3 = 0$$

We can then XOR in the appropriate key bits that the linear expression "runs through," obtaining something along the lines of

$$K_{1,0} \oplus X_0 = Y_1 \oplus Y_3 \oplus K_{2,1} \oplus K_{2,3}$$

or, rewriting it:

$$X_0 \oplus Y_1 \oplus Y_3 = K_{1,0} \oplus K_{2,1} \oplus K_{2,3}$$

The only thing changed is the right-hand side; instead of a 0, we have some key bits. Furthermore, the key bits aren't going to change (since we are doing a known-plaintext attack against a single key); they are always going to XOR to a 0 or a 1. In the case of a 1, the sign of the bias just flip flops; and won't change much in the expression.

The basic linear cryptanalytic method is to use a linear expression for only as much of the encryption algorithm as is necessary. We chain together the linear expressions for the individual S-boxes into rounds, and the rounds together to the point that we need.

The critical part comes when we run into key bits. As shown above, we will acquire key bits on the right-hand side of the equation, but since those bits don't change, we ignore them. However, one of the times that we do run into key bits, we will, instead of simply tacking them onto the end of our ever-growing linear expression, stop right there and brute-force the relevant key bits. Depending on where we stop, we will have a different number of key bits that will affect the linear expression. Essentially, whichever key bits give us the largest measured bias for a large number of plaintext–ciphertext pairs will be the key bits that, most likely, are correct.

This is best illustrated with a simple example, as shown in Figure 6-4. For the three-round variant, we brute-force six of the bits that affect the output of the third round, and we figure out which key gives us the correct bias. For each subkey (representing the values of the desired key bits concatenated), in the order of 0 to 63, we can construct a list of how many plaintext–ciphertext pairs matched the linear expression on the previous page.

39	28	18	3	1	4	4	30
23	**121**	9	27	33	46	11	8
1	16	17	21	12	36	30	4
10	27	1	12	4	15	2	23
20	13	12	2	18	32	24	10
10	39	28	27	23	9	5	29
9	26	22	11	22	27	67	33
32	1	12	7	0	13	5	32

This table actually gives the difference of each count from half of the total number of plaintexts (equivalent to the bias). In this test case, we had 1,800 plaintext–ciphertext pairs (slightly more than required). The one with the highest bias (usually fairly close to the expected value) is normally the key. The difference for entry number 9 above, which is the highest value, is $121/1800 \approx 0.0672$. This is fairly close to the expected value of approximately 0.0684.

6.7   Linear Cryptanalysis of DES

Performing linear cryptanalysis on the EASY1 cipher is pretty straightforward: Simply trace the bits forward. The analysis is not quite as easy when integrating more complicated structures, such as Feistel structures.

No Feistel structure will be quite the same, but we can adapt the same technique as before to trace our way through the cipher. I'll show how this is done for DES, as outlined in Reference [4]. Note that for this, and other techniques working with DES, we ignore the initial and final permutations, as they do nothing to thwart cryptanalysis of the algorithm.

First, note that the following linear expression holds for the round function of DES (with input X, round key K, and round function value F):

$$X_{15} \oplus F_7 \oplus F_{18} \oplus F_{24} \oplus F_{29} = K_{22}$$

This equation is true with a probability of $12/64 = 0.1875$ (bias -0.3125).

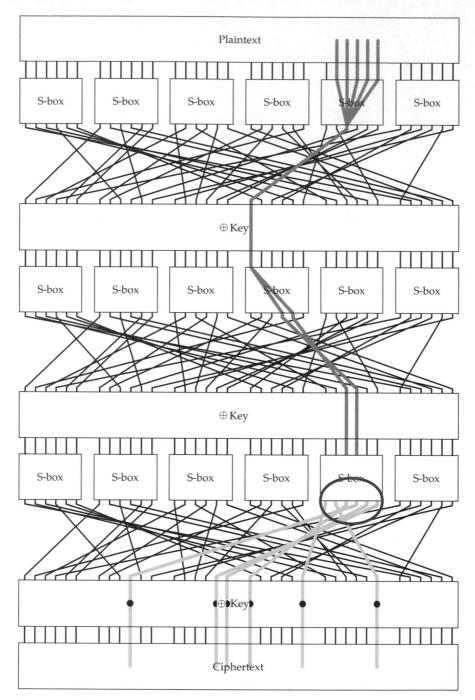

Figure 6-4 Linear cryptanalysis of a three-round variant of EASY1.

When we are doing analysis on larger ciphers (such as the 64-bit DES), it is necessary to introduce a more compact way of specifying the bits to be used. Instead of writing $F_7 \oplus F_18 \oplus F_{24} \oplus F_{29}$, we would rather use brackets to denote which bits we are extracting and XORing, so that instead we could write $F_{[7,18,24,29]}$. This lets us write the previous equation as

$$X_{[15]} \oplus F_{[7,18,24,29]} = K_{[22]}$$

Now that we have a round function equation, we can extend this into an equation for the entire round, by XORing it with the appropriate bits in the other half in the round.

For example, in the first round of DES, we have $L_1 = R_0$ and $R_1 = L_0 \oplus f(R_0, K_1)$. Obviously, there isn't much to do for L_1, since it is just a copy of R_0, but by using the linear equation above, we can get a linear equation for the entire round. Denote the output of the round function for the first round as F_2 (and the other rounds will, naturally, be F_2, etc.), with the corresponding keys K_1, and so on, as well. Therefore, we have the following linear expression:

$$L_{0\,[15]} \oplus F_{1\,[7,18,24,29]} \oplus R_{1\,[7,17,24,29]} = K_{1\,[22]}$$

This equation holds because the input to the function is the plaintext (L_0) and the linear expression output of the function must match up with the appropriate portion of the round values.

We can do a very similar calculation to obtain a linear expression for the third round. It turns out that, since we are using the same equation to derive it, the R_1 portion drops out, leaving us with known values and the key bits on the right-hand side. If we were analyzing a three-round variant of DES, we would then use Matsui's Algorithm 1 to start deriving information about the key bits at this point (which I omit since it will not add much to our discussion).

However, we are more concerned with breaking the full cipher. In essence, we simply obtain an expression for the cipher, being one round short of the full cipher (as done above with EASY1). We engineer it so that the final round of calculation depends on only a subset of all of the bits involved in the final round key.

Matsui gives us the following 15-round linear expression to attack the full 16 rounds of DES:

$$L_{0[7,18,24]} \oplus R_{0[12,16]} \oplus L_{16[15]} \oplus R_{16[7,18,24,29]} \oplus F_{16,[15]} = K_{[\ldots]}$$

Here, we omit all of the key bits on the right-hand side for Matsui's Algorithm 2 (since we don't use them to derive any key information). Also, note that F_{16} depends on the 48-bit subkey K_{16}. However, only 6 bits of the subkey are used to calculate bit 15, so we can brute-force those bits.

We do get one advantage (among the increased complexity) in attacking a Feistel structure: There is very little difference between using the above 15-round approximation and deriving six key bits on the last round and doing a very similar calculation for a 15-round approximation, but *working backwards*, and using the approximation for the last 15 rounds rather than the first. This way, we can also, independently, brute-force the bits of K_1, and we double our key bits.

Matsui claims that this method allows us to derive 14 key bits of a 56-bit DES key, by using 2^{47} known plaintexts [4]. Note that this isn't an awfully big improvement over brute-force guessing of the entire key; we still have to brute-force a 6-bit key (twice); our running time would be on the order of 2^{54}.

After the calculation of the 14 key bits is done, it's not relatively time-consuming to take one of the plaintexts and brute-force the other 42 key bits until the correct ciphertext comes out. This technique is definitely better than the normal time of 2^{56} required to brute-force the DES key.

Matsui later came to improve even further on this method [3]. By backing off a little and using a 14-round linear approximation, it is possible to require even fewer known plaintexts with even more accuracy than before. Using his improved method, DES is breakable with an 85 percent success rate using 2^{43} known plaintexts and a running time of about 2^{43}.

6.8   Multiple Linear Approximations

There are two clear ways to make linear cryptanalysis more powerful: collecting more plaintext–ciphertext pairs, or using more linear expressions with the same plaintext–ciphertext pairs. The technique of **multiple linear approximations** focuses on this second technique, introduced in Reference [2].

This concept can be used with Matsui's Algorithm 1 or Algorithm 2, using the idea that rather than requiring more plaintext–ciphertext pairs, we should attempt to use several linear approximations at each step. This, in turn, makes the linear expressions have a lower variance, which can either make the results more accurate or allow us to use fewer plaintext–ciphertext pairs with the same accuracy.

In normal linear cryptanalysis, we are looking at equations of the form

$$P_0 \oplus P_2 \oplus \cdots \oplus C_1 \oplus C_2 \oplus \cdots = K_1 \oplus K_3 \oplus \cdots$$

We will then collect many plaintext–ciphertext pairs, and attempt to brute-force keys as was done previously: by taking each potential key and calculating the left-hand side of the equation's value.

Our first instinct in using multiple linear approximations might tell us to just perform this whole process again, with an entirely new linear approximation for the cipher. However, it is better to try to obtain a linear approximation that *has the same right-hand side* as the other approximation, that is, intersects exactly the same key bits. If both linear expressions are affected by the exact same key bits, then the two linear approximations will match up better and can be "combined."

When combining two linear approximations, we use a weighted sum to add together the counts acquired from the plaintext–ciphertext pairs. If the two linear expressions have different right-hand sides, then we might inadvertently have our overall biases reversed (since one's right-hand side might evaluate to be 0 and the other to be 1), which would make them not line up properly.

The weights multiplied against each count are simply the ratio of the bias of the expression to the sum of the biases for all of the expressions being measured, that is,

$$T = \sum_{i=0}^{m} T_i \times \left(\frac{\epsilon_i}{\sum_{j=0}^{m} \epsilon_j} \right)$$

This gives the total count (T) for each individual count (T_i) multiplied by its weight.

Multiple linear approximations make a lot of sense in one way: The bulk of our work is in looping through every single key and every single plaintext–ciphertext pair. We only have one line that actually computes the linear expression's value, and it is not the most computationally intensive portion. It would be very easy to tack on another computation right there, and not even come close to doubling the time requirement of running the algorithm.

Overall, multiple linear expressions don't save us much time. They do, however, increase the effectiveness of using the same number of plaintext–ciphertext pairs by increasing the success rate of using them, and lowering the false-positive rate. The primary difficulty in using this method is, of course, coming up with several good linear expressions involving the same key bits.

6.9   Finding Linear Expressions

Throughout this chapter, I have glossed over finding good linear expressions. It should come as no surprise that finding good linear expressions with high biases is a fairly difficult task, even more so to find the "best" such expression.

Matsui developed an algorithm to perform these searches [3].

Matsui Linear Expression Search. Here, we are looking for the best linear expression, B, using induction, building from one good guess and working our way up to the best expression for a given cipher. We must assume that we already have a pretty good expression (perhaps developed by hand), which I write as $\hat{B}$. The "closer" to B that $\hat{B}$ is, the more efficient the search. The search is split into rounds, with each one giving a linear expression for one more round of the cipher (until all n rounds).

Round 1:

1. For each possible set of output bits in the first round, which Matsui calls a **mask**, set O_1 to be the mask, and do the following:

   (a) Set p'_1 to be the maximum probability for any linear expression that outputs O_1.

   (b) If the best expression starting with p'_1 is less than the probability of $\hat{B}$, then we skip back to Step 1 (and try the next value of O_1). This is because there is no way, using p'_1, to obtain an expression better than $\hat{B}$.

   (c) Go to Round 2.

2. If no key was found, return $\hat{B}$.

Round 2:

1. For each possible value of the input bit mask (I_2) and output bit mask (O_2):

   (a) Let p'_2 be the probability of the input bits leading to the output bits (i.e., the probability of the linear expression $I_2 \oplus O_2 = 0$).

   (b) If the expression starting with p'_1 and p'_2 can't do better than $\hat{B}$, try the next value for I_2 and O_2.

   (c) Otherwise, go to Round 3.

2. If none of the input and output masks work, return to Round 1.

Rounds 3, 4, . . . , (n − 1):

1. Let the round number be i.

2. For each possible value of the input bits, I_i:

   (a) Set $O_i = O_{i-2} \oplus I_{i-1}$ (because of the Feistel structure).

   (b) Set p'_i to be the probability for the linear expression of I_i yielding O_i.

(c) If the linear expression involving $p'_1, p'_2, \ldots, p'_i$ is not better than $\hat{B}$, then try the next value of I_i.

(d) Otherwise, call the next round $(i + 1)$.

3. Return to the previous round.

Round n:

1. Set $O_n = O_{n-2} \oplus I_{n-1}$.

2. Set p'_n to be the maximum probability possible for any input giving O_n.

3. If the expression using $p'_1, p'_2, \ldots, p'_n$ is better than $\hat{B}$, then set $\hat{B}$ to be this new expression.

4. Return to the previous round.

Although Matsui's algorithm works pretty well for finding linear expressions of DES, it has two deficiencies:

1. Several expressions explored will be equivalent to other expressions already searched, because of symmetry in the cipher.

2. Several expressions explored are not truly valid candidates.

To combat these differences, Ohta et al. [6] invented another search algorithm aiming to eliminate these problems. Their algorithm is mostly successful in doing this; however, it comes at the cost of increased complexity and sometimes can require more computing time (such as for DES keys). For more information on their method and analysis of Matsui's method, see Reference [6].

6.10 Linear Cryptanalysis Code

The following pieces of Python code can be used to implement linear cryptanalysis. They are currently tuned to break the EASY1 cipher, although they can be easily adapted to any other ciphers.

All of the code in this chapter relies on the Python code for EASY1 to be already loaded beforehand (from Chapter 4), that is, the encryption and decryption functions.

First, I define a few extra helper functions in Listing 6-1. They are used to help us process the ciphertext to an appropriate level so that we can calculate a linear expression. There are three functions defined: calculating an inverse (or reverse) S-box given the original definition of the S-box, calculating the reverse

P-box given the original definition of the P-box, and a function to obtain the value of a given bit from a number.

```
#########################################
# Calculate the reverse S-Box
#########################################
s2 = []

for i in range(0,len(s)):
    s2.append(0)
for i in range(0,len(s)):
    s2[s[i]] = i

def asbox(x):
    return s2[x]


#########################################
# Reverse P-box
#########################################
def apbox(x):
 y = 01
 for i in range(len(p)):
  if (x & (11 << p[i])) != 0:
   y = y ^ (11 << i)
 return y


#########################################
# Extract a bit from the argument
#########################################
def grab(x, pos):
 return (x >> (pos)) & 1
```

Listing 6-1 A few helper functions for performing linear cryptanalysis on the EASY1 cipher. We assume that the S-box and P-box functions are already set up, as specified in Chapter 4.

Next, we need code to generate the known plaintext–ciphertext pairs that that we will use to evaluate the linear expressions. Listing 6-2 generates the known plaintext–ciphertext pairs for the EASY1 cipher. First, it defines the simple encryption function using the key (in binary, 0100 1001 0010 0100 1001 0010 0100 1001 0010). It then generates 1,800 random plaintexts and stores them, along with the resultant ciphertexts (after encrypting with the three rounds of the EASY1 cipher).

Finally, we get to the Python code for doing the actual cryptanalysis in Listing 6-3. In this code, we set all of the counts to zero, and then, for each possible subkey, take every plaintext–ciphertext pair and see if the linear expression is true, and if so, increment the count of the key.

To calculate the linear expression, we first have to process the ciphertext. First, we undo the last permutation. Then, we XOR in the current subkey guess. Finally, we run the process backwards through the last layer of S-boxes. We now have all of the bits necessary to calculate the linear cryptanalysis expression. Throughout the process, we keep track of the best key (with the highest or lowest count).

```python
# Set the number of known plaintext--ciphertext pairs
# 1800 is sufficient for our simple expression
numplaintexts = 1800

# Here we set a simple key
key = mux([0x12, 0x12, 0x12, 0x12, 0x12, 0x12])

# The encryption function, with no key schedule
def encrypt(p, rounds):
 x = p
 for i in range(rounds):
  x = round(x, key)
 return x

# Import the random package
import random

# Use a fixed seed, so that we get reproducibility
random.seed(12345)

# Create lists for the plaintext and ciphertext
plaintext = []
ciphertext = []

# Generate the texts
for i in range(0,numplaintexts):
 # Generate a random plaintext
 r = long(random.randint(0,2**36))
 plaintext.append(r)

 # Also store the corresponding ciphertext
 c = encrypt(r,3)
 ciphertext.append(c)
```

Listing 6-2 Python code for generating known plaintext–ciphertext pairs for use in EASY1 linear cryptanalysis.

```
# Best deviation so far
maxdev = -1

# Best deviation's index
maxk = -1

# Which S-box we are working with
koffset = 6

# Initialize all of the counts to zero
count = [0 for i in range(ssize)]

# Brute force the subkeys
for k1 in range(ssize):
 # Calculate target partial subkey
 k = k1 << koffset

 # For each plaintext-ciphertext pair
 for j in range(0,len(plaintext)):

  # Get the pair
  pt = plaintext[j]
  ct = ciphertext[j]

  # Undo the last mixing layer with
  # target partial subkey
  v = apbox(ct)
  v = demux(v)
  v = mix(v, k)

  # Go backwards through last S-box
  u = mux([asbox(v[0]),asbox(v[1]),\
  asbox(v[2]),asbox(v[3]),asbox(v[4]),\
  asbox(v[5])])

  # If the linear expression holds, increment
  # the appropriate count
  if grab(pt, 6) ^ grab(pt, 7) ^ grab(pt, 8) ^ \
  grab(pt, 9) ^ grab(pt, 10) ^ grab(u, 8) ^ \
  grab(u, 9) == 0:
   count[k1] = count[k1] + 1

 # If this was the best so far, then mark it
 if abs(count[k1] - len(plaintext)/2) >= maxdev:
  maxdev = abs(count[k1] - len(plaintext)/2)
  maxk = k

 # Uncomment the following lines if you want to see your progress
```

Listing 6-3 Python code for performing linear cryptanalysis on the EASY1 cipher.

(continued)

```
  # print k1,
  # print count[k1]
```

Listing 6-3 (*continued*)

Just so that we have a nice, easy-to-read display of what happened in the linear cryptanalysis, we can print out the following summary, showing us the relevant candidate keys, as well as the proper keys. Simply add the code in Listing 6-4 to the end of the above algorithm. In the code, we define a simple function to print out its argument binary. We then print out the key derived from the linear cryptanalysis code, and also show the actual relevant subkey.

```
  # Prints out its argument in binary
  def binary(x):
   if x != 0:
    y = binary(x >> 1) + str(x & 1)
    if y == "":
     return "0"
    else:
     return y
   else:
    return ""

  print "guess:",
  print (binary(maxk >> koffset)).rjust(6, '0'),
  print maxk >> koffset,
  print "⎵deviation:⎵",
  print maxdev/float(len(plaintext))

  print "real:⎵",
  print (binary((apbox(key) >> koffset) & 0x3f)).rjust(6, '0'),
  print (apbox(key) >> koffset) & 0x3f
```

Listing 6-4 Python code for printing out the results of the previous linear cryptanalysis of EASY1. Note that the rjust function takes the string it is applied to and pads it up to the given length (the first argument) by inserting the pad character (the second argument) on the left until it is the correct length.

6.11   Summary

In this chapter, we explored a powerful technique for deriving keys in many ciphers. This technique is the first attack against DES to operate in less time than an exhaustive search. The downside is that a large number of known plaintext–ciphertext pairs must be collected, and that because the attack is probabilistic, it isn't guaranteed to work for every key.

Nearly every attack we cover in the rest of the book will have a similar structure to linear cryptanalysis: We typically generate some kind of expression for each individual cryptographic element (such as an S-box) and build the expression to encompass rounds and eventually the entire cipher. The nature of these expressions changes depending on the attack, although several are based on linear expressions. As such, understanding the basic linear cryptanalytic attack is extremely helpful in comprehending the attacks of the next chapter.

Exercises

Exercise 1. Write an S-box linear analyzer that will generate tables of linear biases. Verify the tables presented in this book.

Exercise 2. Try using your program from the previous exercise to analyze the S-box in AES. What are your results?

Exercise 3. Write and test your own implementation of the linear cryptanalytic method against the EASY1 cipher.

Exercise 4. Generate a new cipher, similar to EASY1, by generating a random new array for the S-box and P-box. Perform linear cryptanalysis on it, for three rounds.

Exercise 5. Use the same S-box and P-box from the previous exercise, but extend this cipher to be a Feistel cipher with the S-box, P-box, and key mixing for the round function. Extend the number of rounds to eight, and then attempt to perform a linear cryptanalytic attack.

Exercise 6. Write a program to find the best linear expression possible for your random Feistel cipher in the previous exercise.

References

[1] Howard M. Heys. A tutorial on linear and differential cryptanalysis. *Cryptologia* 26(3): 189–221 (2002).

[2] B. S. Kaliski and M. J. B. Robshaw. Linear cryptanalysis using multiple approximations. In *Advances in Cryptology – Crypto '94*, (ed. Yvo Desmedt), pp. 26–39. Lecture Notes in Computer Science, Vol. 839. (Springer-Verlag, Berlin, 1994).

[3] M. Matsui. The first experimental crypt analysis of the Data Encryption Standard. In *Advances in Cryptology – Crypto '94*, (ed. Yvo Desmedt), pp. 1–11. Lecture Notes in Computer Science, Vol. 839. (Springer-Verlag, Berlin, 1994).

[4] M. Matsui. Linear cryptanalysis method for DES cipher. In *Advances in Cryptology – EuroCrypt '93*, (ed. Tor Helleseth), pp. 386–397. Lecture Notes in Computer Science, Vol. 765. (Springer-Verlag, Berlin, 1993).

[5] M. Matsui and A. Yamagishi. A new method for known plaintext attack of FEAL cipher. In *Advances in Cryptology – EuroCrypt '92*, (ed. Rainer A. Rueppel), pp. 81–91. Lecture Notes in Computer Science, Vol. 658. (Springer-Verlag, Berlin, 1992).

[6] K. Ohta, S. Moriai, and K. Aoki. Improving the search algorithm for the best linear expression. In *Advances in Cryptology – Crypto '95*, (ed. Don Coppersmith), pp. 157–170. Lecture Notes in Computer Science, Vol. 963. (Springer-Verlag, Berlin, 1995).

Differential Cryptanalysis

In the previous chapter, I introduced the concept of linear cryptanalysis, based on exploiting linear relationships between bits in the ciphers. In this chapter, we explore the use of differential relationships between various bits in the cipher.

Although the concept of exploiting differences is not necessarily new, the way it is approached for sophisticated ciphers, such as DES, was not well understood until fairly recently.

The standard differential cryptanalysis method is a chosen-plaintext attack (whereas linear cryptanalysis is a known-plaintext attack, thus is considered more feasible in the real world). Differential cryptanalysis was first made public in 1990 by Eli Biham and Adi Shamir Biham and Shamir [2]. In the years following, it has proven to be one of the most important discoveries in cryptanalysis.

In this chapter, we explore the technique of differential cryptanalysis. I then show how this method can be used on several different ciphers. Finally, I show some of the more advanced techniques that have evolved from differential cryptanalysis.

7.1   Overview

Although differential cryptanalysis predates linear cryptanalysis, both attacks are structured in a similar fashion — a simple model of individual cipher components and a predictive model of the entire cipher. Instead of analyzing linear relationships between input and output bits of S-boxes, as in linear cryptanalysis, **differential cryptanalysis** focuses on finding a relationship between the changes that occur in the output bits as a result of changing some of the input bits.

Like linear cryptanalysis, differential cryptanalysis is a *probabilistic attack*: In this case, we will be measuring how changes in the plaintext affect the output, but since we do not know the key, the measurements will be random, but guided, in nature. How close the measurements are to what we desire will tell us information about the key.

7.2 Notation

First, a few definitions and conventions. There are a few conventions used in cryptanalysis literature, and I'll use these as much as possible, but the notation used can sometimes sacrifice conciseness for clarity.

The fundamental concept here is that of **measured differences in values**. We use the term **differential** to mean the XOR difference between two particular values, that is, the XOR of the two values. Differentials are often denoted as Ω values, such as Ω_A and Ω_B.

A **characteristic** is composed of two differentials, say Ω_A and Ω_B, written as

$$(\Omega_A \Rightarrow \Omega_B)$$

The idea is that a characteristic is showing that the differential, Ω_A, in an input gives rise to another differential, Ω_B, in an output. Most of the time, this characteristic is not a certainty; it will be true only some of the time. Hence, we are often concerned with the **probability** that a differential Ω_A in the input will result in a differential Ω_B in the output.

As a quick example, assume that we are using a simple XOR cipher that encrypts data by XORing each byte with an 8-bit key (which is the same throughout). Hence, a message representing the text `"hello"` in hexadecimal ASCII would be

```
68 65 6c 6c 6f
```

If we XORed this with the constant hex key `47`, we would get

```
2f 22 2b 2b 28
```

We can try to use a differential of, say, `ff` (all ones) in the original plaintext, and then XOR again with the key to obtain a new ciphertext:

```
d0 dd d4 d4 d7
```

Finally, we compare the two ciphertexts by XORing them, obtaining the differential:

```
ff ff ff ff ff
```

Note that this is the exact differential we used on the plaintext! This should give us a clue that the cipher is not very strong. We can then write the characteristic for this as

```
(ffffffffff ⇒ ffffffffff)
```

We consider input and output here to refer to either the input and output of a S-box, some number of rounds of a cipher, or the total cipher itself. Most importantly, we will take characteristics of an S-box to create characteristics for various rounds, which are then stitched together to create a characteristic for the entire cipher — this is how a standard differential attack is realized.

7.3   S-Box Differentials

Now we are ready to start analyzing the components of a cipher. Since most ciphers utilize S-boxes (or something analogous, such as the *SubBytes* operation in AES) at their heart, it is natural to start there. Thus, the first step of differential cryptanalysis is to compute the characteristics of inputs and the outputs of the S-boxes, which we will then stitch together to form a characteristic for the complete cipher.

For the following, assume that we have an S-box whose input is X and output is Y. If we have two particular inputs, X_1 and X_2, let

$$\Omega_X = X_1 \oplus X_2$$

Here, Ω_X is the differential for the two plaintexts. Similarly, for the two corresponding outputs of the above plaintexts, Y_1 and Y_2, respectively, let

$$\Omega_Y = Y_1 \oplus Y_2$$

To construct the differential relation, we consider all possible values of Ω_X, and we want to measure how this affects Ω_Y. So, for each possible value of X_1 and Ω_X (and, therefore, X_2), we measure Y_1 and Y_2 to obtain Ω_Y and record this value in a table. Table 7-1 shows some the results of performing this analysis on the EASY1 cipher, with each entry being the number of times Ω_X gave rise to Ω_Y. (The entry in Table 7-1 corresponding to $0 \Rightarrow 0$ is the hexadecimal value 40, meaning that it is always true. This is because no difference in the input will always, of course, give no difference in the output.)

However, more often it is useful to collect characteristics with the highest probabilities in a list format. By searching through the complete table of the differential analysis of the EASY1 cipher's S-box, we would note that the two largest entries are 6 and 8, representing probabilities of 6/64 and 8/64, respectively. Tables 7-2 and 7-3 give listings of all of the characteristics with these probabilities.

In general, entries with fewer bits set in the Ω_X and Ω_Y that have higher occurrence counts are desirable.

However, there is the issue of round keys. Specifically, in EASY1, as well as many other ciphers, there is a layer of key mixing after the input bits are used in the S-box. In linear cryptanalysis, these were kept track of and taken care of at the end of the linear expression. However, in differential cryptanalysis,

Table 7-1 Top-Left Portion of the EASY1 Table of Characteristic Probabilities

		0	1	2	3	4	5	6	7	8	9	a	b	c	d	e	f
	0	40	0	0	0	0	0	0	0	0	0	0	0	0	0	0	0
	1	0	0	0	0	0	0	0	0	0	0	0	2	0	2	2	2
	2	0	0	0	0	0	2	0	0	0	0	0	0	2	2	2	0
	3	0	0	2	0	0	2	2	0	2	0	0	0	0	2	4	0
	4	0	2	0	2	2	0	0	0	2	2	2	0	2	2	0	0
	5	0	0	0	0	0	2	0	0	4	0	0	0	0	0	0	0
	6	0	0	0	2	2	0	6	0	2	2	0	2	2	0	2	2
	7	0	0	0	2	0	4	0	0	0	4	2	0	0	0	2	0
Ω_Y	**8**	0	4	2	0	0	0	4	2	2	0	2	2	2	2	0	2
	9	0	2	0	0	0	2	0	2	0	0	0	0	0	0	0	4
	a	0	0	0	0	0	0	2	2	0	2	0	2	0	4	0	2
	b	0	2	0	2	0	0	0	0	0	0	8	2	0	0	0	4
	c	0	2	2	0	0	2	0	0	0	0	2	2	2	0	2	2
	d	0	2	0	2	0	0	0	2	0	2	0	0	2	0	2	2
	e	0	2	2	0	2	0	0	2	0	2	0	0	0	0	0	2
	f	0	0	2	2	2	0	0	0	0	0	0	0	0	0	0	2

The column headers are under Ω_X.

Note that this is only a sample of the complete table.

we are not accumulating a massive linear expression; therefore, we need to address the key influence.

In our EASY1 cipher, denote W to be the corresponding input into the S-box after the key has been mixed in, or $W = X \oplus K$, and let Y be the output of the S-box. We will naturally now rework our above analysis to be on Ω_W instead of Ω_X. Then, we have inputs to the S-box, W_1 and W_2, with $\Omega_W = W_1 \oplus W_2$. We substitute in the appropriate values in this equation, to obtain

$$\Omega_W = W_1 \oplus W_2 = (X_1 \oplus K) \oplus (X_2 \oplus K) = X_1 \oplus X_2 = \Omega_X$$

Therefore, having the key bits mixed in does not affect our analysis at all and can be safely ignored in this cipher. Normally, this is the case with most ciphers. (However, there are some ciphers that provide more trouble, such as Blowfish, where the S-boxes themselves are determined by the key.)

Table 7-2 S-Box Characteristics of EASY1 with a Probability of 6/64

(000110 ⇒ 000110)	(000110 ⇒ 100001)
(000110 ⇒ 110000)	(000111 ⇒ 101001)
(001001 ⇒ 011000)	(001001 ⇒ 100010)
(001001 ⇒ 110010)	(001010 ⇒ 110111)
(001100 ⇒ 101110)	(001101 ⇒ 010100)
(001110 ⇒ 110001)	(010001 ⇒ 010100)
(010010 ⇒ 000001)	(010011 ⇒ 001000)
(011011 ⇒ 100101)	(011100 ⇒ 001100)
(011100 ⇒ 111111)	(011101 ⇒ 111001)
(011110 ⇒ 010101)	(011111 ⇒ 100110)
(100000 ⇒ 100111)	(100010 ⇒ 001101)
(100011 ⇒ 000110)	(100101 ⇒ 000001)
(101000 ⇒ 001100)	(101011 ⇒ 001100)
(101011 ⇒ 111100)	(101100 ⇒ 101011)
(101101 ⇒ 000011)	(110010 ⇒ 101101)
(110011 ⇒ 011111)	(110011 ⇒ 101111)
(111000 ⇒ 100000)	(111001 ⇒ 001001)
(111001 ⇒ 001101)	(111011 ⇒ 010100)
(111011 ⇒ 111110)	(111100 ⇒ 011100)
(111100 ⇒ 100000)	(111101 ⇒ 000100)

Table 7-3 S-Box Characteristics of EASY1 with a Probability of 8/64

(001011 ⇒ 001010)
(010000 ⇒ 011001)
(011001 ⇒ 010110)
(110101 ⇒ 101001)

7.4   Combining S-Box Characteristics

Note that characteristics are not estimates, as the expressions in linear cryptanalysis are, but actual occurrences in the S-boxes themselves that have known probabilities. Hence, we do not need the Piling-up Lemma to combine S-box equations but can merely chain them together, multiplying the probabilities directly using normal rules of probability.

We have a graphical representation of this process of combining S-box characteristics in Figure 7-1. In this diagram, we are using two different relationships (in binary):

$$(001001 \Rightarrow 011000)$$

$$(010010 \Rightarrow 000001)$$

Both of these characteristics have a probability of 6/64. The first round uses the first characteristic, which has only two output bits affected by the two input bits. These output bits then feed into the second S-box of the second round after permutation.

Each charactistic is expected to be independent of the others; thus, we can multiply the probability of each to obtain a probability for each occurring at the same time:

$$\frac{6}{64} \times \frac{6}{64} \approx 0.008789$$

Note that other S-boxes have no input difference and, therefore, no output difference.

We now have built a characteristic for the entire three-round cipher, starting with two input bits and affecting one intermediate output bit some of the time. We can use this model to derive six of the 18 key bits by selecting a set of plaintext pairs, with their difference being the input differential used to develop the model. Measuring the resulting change in the ciphertext pairs will enable us to find a portion of the key. When the ciphertext pairs yield the expected differential, they form what is called a **right pair** of plaintext–ciphertexts. (Obviously, plaintext–ciphertext pairs that do not exhibit the desired differentials are called **wrong pairs**.)

An important addition to the idea of building up characteristics is the idea of an **iterative characteristic** — one whose input differential is the same as its output differential at some point. These are particularly useful because they can be chained together very easily to create the larger characteristics required for analyzing ciphers with many rounds. I'll show some examples of these when we explore the differential cryptanalysis of DES in Section 7.7.2, although it can apply to any kind of cipher.

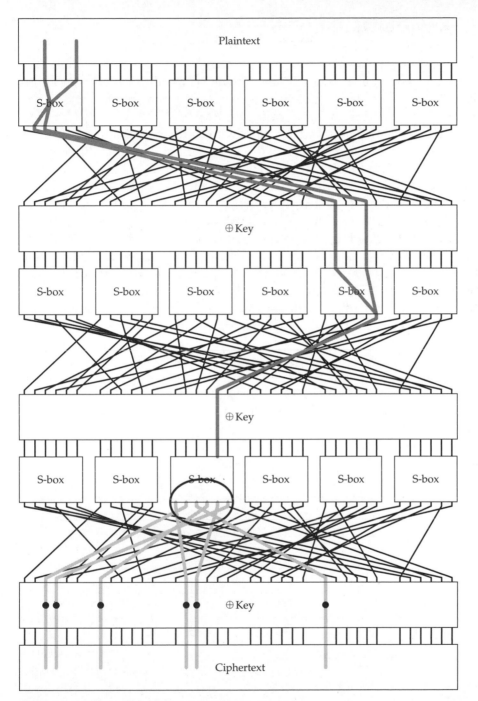

Figure 7-1 Differential attack on the EASY1 cipher.

7.5 Key Derivation

Just as in linear cryptanalysis, we desire to have some number of plaintext–ciphertext pairs to determine the key. However, because differential cryptanalysis is a chosen-plaintext technique, we need to be able to pick certain plaintexts to make the technique work.

Specifically, we pick plaintexts in pairs with differences that are necessary for the characteristic we are testing. In our EASY1 cipher, this difference is $\Omega_P =$ 02 80 00 00 00 (bits 30 and 32). We obtain the ciphertexts for both plaintexts and measure the difference in the output. However, in this case, we did not construct the differential characteristic equation to relate the plaintext and the ciphertext: We relate the plaintext to the inputs to the last set of S-boxes. We then brute-force the relevant bits of the key, mix the key bits with the ciphertext, reverse the mixed bits through the S-boxes, and then attempt to perform a match on the output differential. We increment a counter for each key whenever any plaintext/ciphertext pair matches our expected differential.

In general, we expect the correct key to exhibit the probability that we found during analysis. When running the analysis, we obtain Table 7-4 of count values in a sample run.

From Table 7-4, we can note that the largest count is 87, corresponding to the entry for subkey 33 (100001). The key used to generate the ciphertext was 555555555, and we can confirm that the bits of subkey 33 match up correctly with the bits of the key (by looking at how the subkey is mapped to the real key through the permutation, as shown in Figure 7-1).

Table 7-4 Results From Differential Cryptanalysis of the EASY1 Cipher

11	28	7	11	14	25	16	10
21	21	15	13	16	16	24	9
15	8	30	19	14	17	29	13
17	33	13	12	15	21	12	13
12	**87**	19	16	10	19	15	17
12	7	15	23	19	21	20	18
17	11	8	5	17	9	24	21
9	12	14	15	18	6	17	13

Note how entry 33 (since we start counting at 0), whose value is 87, stands out among the rest.

In total, this technique required approximately $2^6 \times 1000 \approx 2^{16}$ operations to work. Brute-forcing the remaining bits will take about 2^{12} operations, which is not as great as the 2^{16} already done. Together, these operations take less time than brute-forcing the 18-bit key (which would take 2^{18} operations).

If a full 36-bit key were used, we would have 2^{30} operations left after the key derivation to brute-force the remaining 30 bits. The 2^{30} operations in this case would take much longer than the 2^{16} operations to derive the 6 bits using differential cryptanalysis; thus, the overall key derivation would still require approximately 2^{30} operations (less than the 2^{36} required for brute-forcing a 36-bit key).

7.6   Differential Cryptanalysis Code

The code for implementing differential cryptanalysis, in general, is extremely straightforward. Typically, we do the analysis part offline, where we determine which characteristics to use.

First, we need to perform a simple differential analysis of an S-box. Assume that we have the S-box implemented as a lookup table (in the array s). Listing 7-1 gives us the code to do this, by taking every possible input value for the S-box, calculating the output value, and then measuring, for each input differential possible, the resultant output differential. A table is kept of how many times certain differentials give rise to other differentials.

```
# The number of bits in the S-box
sbits = 6

# Calculate the maximum value / differential
ssize = 2**6

# Generate the matrix of differences, starting
# at all zeros
count = []
for i in range(ssize):
  count.append([0 for j in range(ssize)])

# Take every possible value for the first plaintext
for x1 in range(0, ssize):
  # Calculate the corresponding ciphertext
  y1 = s[x1]

  # Now, for each possible differential
```

Listing 7-1 Python code for performing a differential analysis of an S-box, loaded into the s matrix. *(continued)*

```
for dx in range(0, ssize):
  # Calculate the other plaintext and ciphertext
  x2 = x1 ^ dx
  y2 = s[x2]

  # Calculate the output differential
  dy = y1 ^ y2

  # Increment the count of the characteristic
  # in the table corresponding to the two
  # differentials
  count[dx][dy] = count[dx][dy] + 1
```

Listing 7-1 (*continued*)

Next, we show how to generate large numbers of plaintexts and ciphertexts, with the plaintexts having a known differential (see Listing 7-2). This is simply a matter of taking a random plaintext, XORing it with the necessary difference for the differential attack to produce another plaintext, and calculating the relevant ciphertexts to both plaintexts, and storing them. This process is repeated as many times as necessary.

Finally, we perform the differential attack, as shown in Listing 7-3. To perform the differential cryptanalysis, we go through each possible subkey (in this case, there are 64 such subkeys, since it is a 6-bit value). For each of these, we process all of the pairs of ciphertexts (by undoing the last permutation, XORing the subkey in, and going backwards through the appropriate S-box). We then calculate the differential of these processed ciphertexts, and if the differential corresponds to the characteristic we are concerned with, we increment the count of the subkey.

```
# Import the random library
import random

# Seed it with a fixed value (for repeatability)
random.seed(12345)

# Set the number of rounds in the encryption function
rounds = 3

# Set the number of bits in a plaintext or ciphertext
bits = 36

# Set the plaintext differential
pdiff = 0x280000000L
```

Listing 7-2 Creating chosen plaintext–ciphertext pairs with a fixed differential.

(continued)

```
# Set the number of pairs to generate
numpairs = 1000

# Store the plaintexts and ciphertexts
plaintext1 = []
plaintext2 = []
ciphertext1 = []
ciphertext2 = []

for i in range(0, numpairs):
    # Create a random plaintext
    r = random.randint(0, 2**bits)

    # Create a paired plaintext with a fixed differential
    r2 = r ^ pdiff

    # Save them
    plaintext1.append(r)
    plaintext2.append(r2)

    # Create the associated ciphertexts
    # Assume that the encryption algorithm has already
    # been defined
    c = encrypt(r,rounds)
    c2 = encrypt(r2,rounds)
    ciphertext1.append(c)
    ciphertext2.append(c2)
```

Listing 7-2 (*continued*)

```
keys = 64 # number of keys we need to analyze
count = [0 for i in range(keys)]  # count for each key
maxcount = -1 # best count found so far
maxkey = -1   # key for the best differential
cdiff = 2 # the ciphertext differential we are looking for

# Brute force the subkeys
for k1 in range(0,keys):
  # Adjust the key to match up with the correct S-box
  k = k1 << 18

  # For each p/c pair
  for j in range(numpairs):
    c1 = ciphertext1[j]
    c2 = ciphertext2[j]
```

Listing 7-3 Performing differential cryptanalysis on the EASY1 cipher.   (*continued*)

```
    # Calculate whatever needs to be done using
    # key bits, storing the results as u1 and u2
    v = mix(demux(apbox(c)), k)
    u = asbox(v[3])

    v2 = mix(demux(apbox(c2)), k)
    u2 = asbox(v2[3])

    # If the differential holds, increment count
    if u1 ^ u2 == cdiff: count[k1] = count[k1] + 1

# If this was the best key so far, then save it
# Otherwise, ignore it for now
if count[k1]  >= maxcount:
 maxcount = count[k1]
 maxkey = k1
```

Listing 7-3 (*continued*)

7.7   Differential Cryptanalysis of Feistel Ciphers

The sections above introduce the basic concept of differential cryptanalysis on this fairly simple product cipher. However, the concept extends over to Feistel ciphers, the ciphers we are usually most concerned with, quite gracefully.

The first steps are nearly identical: We identify S-box characteristics, and we start tracing those through the cipher. However, the exact way we trace them through the cipher differs somewhat.

Since we have the interaction of the left and right halves, we often have a more difficult task of choosing appropriate characteristics. We often want the differentials to mostly cancel each other out, so that we can control the effects on the next round.

Usually, this is through the use of iterative characteristics. These iterative characteristics will start with a differential. After several rounds through the cipher, they give the same output differential as the input. This enables us to repeat them several times, making analysis very easy. We will see examples of these in the next two sections.

Finally, the last part is key derivation. After the differentials have been traced all the way to the second-to-last round, as before, we then have to ensure that this final differential only modifies the bits of the round function that are affected by some subset of the key bits.

At this point, just as before, we take the two values of the ciphertext and run them through the previous round function. We will be brute-forcing the appropriate key portions of the round functions. The key value that gives us the highest number of the expected characteristics will be our guess.

In the next sections, I'll show how to use these ideas on FEAL and DES.

7.7.1   Differential Cryptanalysis of FEAL

In this section, we will see how the differential cryptanalysis method can be applied to the FEAL block cipher I introduced in Section 4.7. This technique was first presented in Reference [3].

To review, FEAL has a simple DES-like Feistel structure, with an S-box that uses a combination of integer addition, the XOR operation, and bitshifting.

Note, however, that the S-boxes are slightly more complicated than they appear at first glance. They take a 16-bit input and give an 8-bit output. To combat this, consider the middle 16 bits of the f-function, denoted by the equations

$$f^1 = S(f^1, f^2, 1)$$
$$f^2 = S(f^2, f^1, 0)$$

These can be regarded together as one S-box with a 16-bit input and 16-bit output, since their inputs are the same. The distribution table for this "super" S-box has some very interesting properties. Notably, most of the entries (98%) are 0. Furthermore, three of the entries hold with a probability of 1, for example:

$$(\Omega_P = (L \parallel 80\,80\,80\,80)) \Rightarrow (\Omega_T = (L \oplus 02\,00\,00\,02) \parallel 80\,80\,80\,80)$$

Some interesting characteristics include **iterative characteristics**, those in which the input and output XOR differentials are the same. These allow us to construct longer expressions with less complicated analysis. For example, in FEAL, the following is a four-round iterative characteristic that holds with probability 2^{-8}:

$$(\Omega_P = 80\,60\,80\,00\ \ 80\,60\,80\,00) \Rightarrow (\Omega_T = 80\,60\,80\,00\ \ 80\,60\,80\,00)$$

7.7.2   Differential Cryptanalysis of DES

At the time when differential cryptanalysis was developed, DES was in widespread use and was often the target of many new techniques. The use of differential cryptanalysis against DES was first presented in Reference [2], as one of the first uses of differential cryptanalysis, and with surprising results (see Table 7-5).

Table 7-5 Differential Cryptanalysis Attack Against DES: Complexities for Different Numbers of Rounds [2]

ROUNDS	COMPLEXITY OF ATTACK
4	2^4
6	2^8
8	2^{16}
9	2^{26}
10	2^{35}
11	2^{36}
12	2^{43}
13	2^{44}
14	2^{51}
15	2^{52}
16 (full DES)	2^{58}

To start off, I'll show how to break the three-round DES, and then extrapolate the process further.

For our plaintext differential, we will always have the right (least significant) 32 bits be all zeros, with the left (most significant) being a particular pattern.

Recall from Chapter 4 that DES's main round function looks as follows:

1. $R_{i+1} = L_i \oplus f(R_i, K_{i+1})$.
2. $L_{i+1} = R_i$.

Expanding this out to three rounds (values in bold are known values):

1. $\mathbf{R_0} = 0$.
2. $\mathbf{L_0}$ (arbitrary, random).
3. $R_1 = \mathbf{L_0} \oplus f(0, K_1)$.
4. $\mathbf{L_1} = \mathbf{R_0} = 0$.
5. $\mathbf{R_2} = \mathbf{L_1} \oplus f(R_1, K_2) = f(R_1, K_2)$.
6. $L_2 = R_1$.
7. $\mathbf{R_3} = L_2 \oplus f(\mathbf{R_2}, K_3) = R_1 \oplus f(\mathbf{R_2}, K_3)$.
8. $\mathbf{L_3} = \mathbf{R_2} = f(R_1, K_2)$.

Now, if we have a second plaintext-ciphertext pair (say, L'_0, R'_0, L'_3, R'_3), with the new plaintext having a known differential to the previous plaintext (Ω), then we have the following derivation:

1. $\mathbf{R'_0} = 0$ ($= \mathbf{R_0}$).
2. $\mathbf{L'_0} = \mathbf{L_0} \oplus \Omega$ (arbitrary, random).
3. $R'_1 = \mathbf{L'_0} \oplus f(0, K_1) = \underline{R_1 \oplus \Omega}$.
4. $\mathbf{L'_1} = \mathbf{R'_0} = 0$.
5. $\mathbf{R'_2} = \mathbf{L'_1} \oplus f(R'_1, K_2) = f(\underline{R_1 \oplus \Omega}, K_2)$.
6. $L'_2 = R'_1$.
7. $\mathbf{R'_3} = L'_2 \oplus f(\mathbf{R'_2}, K_3) = R'_1 \oplus f(\mathbf{R'_2}, K_3)$.
8. $\mathbf{L'_3} = \mathbf{R'_2} = f(\underline{R_1 \oplus \Omega}, K_2)$.

Here, we have underlined where the differential propagates.

From the last steps of the two previous lists, since we know the values of L_3 and L'_3, we can calculate Δ, the difference in the ciphertexts. We also can perform a differential analysis of the S-boxes of DES, so that the effect of the differential Ω would be known, and we can choose Ω to exploit this for each S-box (since DES has several distinct S-boxes).

Once we know some good characteristics of the round function, we can then set up the three-round cipher to use the plaintext differential on the left to create differences in the plaintext. After measuring enough of these, we will be able to make good guesses at the key bits.

In general, we can easily see that if the right-half XOR is 0, and the left half has an arbitrary differential (say, L), we can construct a characteristic for a round of DES.

First, as shown above, if the input to the round function (f) is the same (with a zero XOR), then the output is the same. The new left half in both cases is the old right half (which is the same, since there is a zero XOR). The new right half is the XOR of the round function value (which is the same) and the old left half, which has a differential of Ω_L. The characteristic can be written as

$$((\Omega_L \parallel 0) \Rightarrow (0 \parallel \Omega_L))$$

Furthermore, there is no guessing in this; thus, this characteristic has a probability of 1.

Let's construct another good characteristic. Again, assuming a constant differential for the left half (Ω_L), if we consider the right half having the differential 60 00 00 00, then the input to the round function will also have that same XOR. Using S-box analysis, we can show that the output differential of the round function 00 80 82 00 occurs with probability 14/64.

This differential would then be XORed with the previous differential (Ω_L), to obtain the following one-round characteristic:

$$((\Omega_L \parallel 60\ 00\ 00\ 00) \Rightarrow (60\ 00\ 00\ 00 \parallel \Omega_L \oplus (00\ 80\ 82\ 00)))$$

Now that we have these two characteristics, we can combine them to create a fairly good three-round characteristic. To see how this is done, simply look at the previous characteristic, and assume that $\Omega_L = 00\ 80\ 82\ 00$.

In this case, we will have the following chain, using the second, first, and second characteristics in that order:

$$(00\ 80\ 82\ 00 \parallel 60\ 00\ 00\ 00)$$
$$\Rightarrow (60\ 00\ 00\ 00 \parallel 00\ 00\ 00\ 00)$$
$$\Rightarrow (00\ 00\ 00\ 00 \parallel 60\ 00\ 00\ 00)$$
$$\Rightarrow (00\ 80\ 82\ 00 \parallel 60\ 00\ 00\ 00)$$

This is an example of an iterative characteristic: It yields itself after several rounds. Therefore, these can be chained together to create larger and larger characteristics.

Cryptanalysis of DES itself using this characteristic, as well as a few others, gives us an approximation for enough of the cipher to start brute-forcing particular subkey bits.

7.8   Analysis

Now that we have seen exactly how to perform differential cryptanalysis, it's fair that we should attempt to analyze its operations and discuss some of its properties.

As we have shown, differential cryptanalysis has two primary features: It is a probabilistic attack, and it is a chosen-plaintext attack. Neither of these scenarios is ideal, but we are stuck with them.

The implications of this probabilistic attack are similar to the properties of other probabilistic problems. We aren't guaranteed to get good results, even with perfectly good inputs and a sufficient number of chosen plaintexts. The more chosen plaintexts we do have, however, the more likely we are to succeed.

Another disadvantage of this method is that we will come up with an answer no matter what; the answer will just be incorrect if we don't have a sufficient number of texts to test it against. Furthermore, there is no way to tell if the key bits derived are correct until we derive all the rest of the key bits and actually test encrypting the plaintext with the potential key (unless we know the answer ahead of time).

The fact that this algorithm is chosen plaintext is another step back: Chosen plaintexts represent some of the most stringent conditions of a cryptanalytic attack. They require the cryptanalyst to not only know and understand the cryptographic algorithm being used, have developed a plan of action against it, and collected a large amount of ciphertext with known plaintext values, but in addition have the ability to manipulate this plaintext! This is a fairly tall order and is a bit less practical than a known-plaintext attack or a ciphertext-only attack.

Finally, we have the fact that to execute the attack at all, we must store a large number of plaintext–ciphertext pairs. There are ways around this, in test scenarios at least, where we reverse the order that we do things. We first generate a new plaintext–ciphertext pair, XOR the plaintext to obtain the resultant ciphertext, and then try every possible subkey against it, incrementing their respective counts, as necessary. At the end of this computation, we can throw away the pairs and generate new ones. Thus, in some cases, we can mitigate this storage problem.

Moreover, the improvements in time over exhaustive search represent a tremendous breakthrough, even considering the strenuous requirements to implement the improvements.

Although differential cryptanalysis has several drawbacks, the overall concept has had a powerful impact on cryptanalysis. In the following sections, we examine some of the fundamental extensions of differential cryptanalysis.

7.9   Differential-Linear Cryptanalysis

An interesting combination of the two important algorithms presented in the last two chapters, **linear and differential cryptanalysis**, appeared in Reference [12], courtesy of Susan Langford and Martin Hellman.

The trick is to use a linear expression, developed in the way already shown, and to measure what changes in the plaintext do to the value of that linear expression. In this way, we aren't simply brute-forcing the subkey by calculating counts on the linear expression; rather, we are using carefully selected differentials that should produce fixed, expected probabilities of the two linear expressions being XORed being equal to 0. As before, we normally expect this to happen roughly half the time for any arbitrary linear expression and difference; thus, any deviation from this can be used.

A good example that the authors show is using a three-round linear approximation for DES. A normal linear expression proposed by Matsui is

$$L_{0[7,18,24,29]} \oplus R_{0[15]} \oplus R_{3[7,18,24,29]} \oplus L_{3[15]} = 0$$

This holds with a probability of either approximately 0.695 or 0.305.

The differential attack comes from noting that we can toggle bits 29 or 30 (or both) of the L_1 value, and this will produce no changes in the fourth-round linear approximation. This means, at this point, that our linear approximations XORed together have a probability of 1 of occurring.

Carrying this out to an eight-round approximation, the probability of the linear expression XOR becomes

$$0.695^2 + 0.305^2 = 0.576$$

We add the numbers together since we could either be right twice in a row or wrong with our expression twice in a row, and we can't really tell the difference. As the authors of the paper say, two wrongs make a right in binary arithmetic.

This means we have a bias of 0.076, giving us an approximate number of plaintext–ciphertext pairs:

$$8 \times (0.076)^{-2} \approx 1400$$

We can even pull another trick to reduce this number further.

Since we still have to get bits 29 and 30 to toggle in L_1, we will naturally have to toggle bits in the plaintext (L_0 and R_0). Toggling the same two bits in R_0 will perform this.

We will also toggle bits 1, 9, 15, and 23 of L_0: These are the output bits of the S-box S_1 (which is also affected by 6 bits of the key). Bits 29 and 30 are also used as the input to S_1 (and no other S-box in round 1); thus, our changes affect only S_1. This gives a total of 64 plaintexts, with their ciphertexts.

At first glance, none of these plaintext–ciphertext pairs are really "paired" in the way that differential cryptanalysis requires. However, it turns out that there are several such pairings. We can pair each plaintext value (there are 64) with three other plaintexts: one with bit 29 of R_0 toggled, one with bit 30 of R_0 toggled, and one with both bits toggled in R_0. This way, we have three pairs, for a theoretical total of $64 \times 3 = 192$ pairings. In reality, we get half as many (96), since half of the pairings are redundant.

This way, we are getting 96 pairings for 64 plaintexts (a ratio of 3-for-2), instead of the normal 1-for-2 of standard differential cryptanalysis because in differential cryptanalysis, we generate one plaintext, and then XOR it with a fixed value to obtain another plaintext. Thus, we have two plaintexts and one pairing, for a ratio of 1-for-2, which is approximately three times less efficient than combining the two techniques.

While this technique doesn't yield more key bits than either differential or linear cryptanalysis, it *does* allow us to derive these key bits with fewer plaintext–ciphertext pairs, while still maintaining a high success rate. There are some issues with scalability, though: This method works well for fewer numbers around and doesn't apply well to more rounds.

7.10 Conditional Characteristics

It is difficult to apply differential cryptanalysis to certain classes of ciphers. For example, if we have certain portions of the cipher modify the structure of the cipher itself based on the key, then we would not be able to effectively develop iterative characteristics to use in differential cryptanalysis. Ben-Aroya and Biham explore a particular method against two particular ciphers thought to be strong against differential cryptanalysis using a technique called **conditional characteristics** [1].

One of the ciphers they analyze is called **Randomized DES (RDES)**. Many cryptologists thought that a way to limit the susceptibility of DES to differential cryptanalysis was to swap the left and right halves during some of the rounds: which rounds depended on the key value. Since there are 16 different rounds, there would be $2^{16} = 65,536$ different combinations of swapping and not swapping, thereby making normal differential analysis extremely difficult.

Naturally, there is one problem. For a certain number of keys (one out of every 2^{15} of them), there would be no swapping at all! If subjected to a known-plaintext attack, the entire right half would not be affected by the encryption, passing through the rounds untouched. Similarly, for another set of one out of every 2^{15} keys, there would only be a swap on the last round, allowing us to easily derive most of the key bits using simple analysis of the inputs and outputs of the round function.

The rest of the keys is where the concept of a conditional characteristic comes in handy. A **conditional characteristic** is a characteristic that is dependent on the key being used. Typically, the characteristic is only effective against keys with certain properties (such as certain bits being set). The number of keys that the conditional characteristic is good for, divided by the total number of keys, is called the **key ratio**.

The attack uses two different round function characteristics of DES:

$$(0 \Rightarrow 0)$$

$$(19 \ 60 \ 00 \ 00 \Rightarrow 0)$$

When combined, they provide a two-round iterative characteristic:

$$((19 \ 60 \ 00 \ 00 \ 00 \ 00 \ 00 \ 00) \Rightarrow (00 \ 00 \ 00 \ 00 \ 19 \ 60 \ 00 \ 00))$$

In DES, we can iterate this characteristic many times, but owing to the swapping and non-swapping portions of RDES, we can't use this one as is.

We can, though, use the individual components. Essentially, we use the first characteristic $(0 \Rightarrow 0)$ on the first round and the next characteristic after the first swap. From then on, we alternate at every swap. This will construct a characteristic for the entire cipher.

We can produce a second characteristic for the entire cipher in a very similar way, only starting with the second round characteristic in the first round, and then using the first round characteristic after the first swap, and alternating to fill the rest of the cipher (using a new characteristic for each swap).

At least one of these characteristics will have a probability of $(1/234)^r$, where r is the number of rounds of the characteristic (or, equivalently, the number of swaps).

In this way, we will have to produce characteristics for all of the 2^{15} possible swapping scenarios. However, we have only two characteristics per swapping scenario, requiring us to have only about twice as many chosen plaintext–ciphertext pairs as normal differential cryptanalysis.

But the advantage is, if there are less than 13 swaps, then the probability will be much greater than the normal DES probability, decreasing the cost of the attack. At 13 swaps, the complexity of the attack is 2^{46}. It turns out that 98 percent of the keys will generate 13 swaps or less. Since this leaves only $1/50$ keys left, we can do an exhaustive search of these if the above attack fails, leaving only a 2^{50} attack, which is still better than DES.

Therefore, using conditional characteristics, we have proved that the security of RDES is always less than DES, and in many cases, is significantly worse.

7.11 Higher-Order Differentials

Differential cryptanalysis is the study of normal differentials, where we have two texts, X_1 and X_2, and we use information about the difference of those two texts:

$$\Omega_X = X_1 \oplus X_2$$

This difference allows us to analyze how the cipher changes.

There was some effort to start arming ciphers to become immune to these differential attacks, for example, by using S-boxes with more uniform differences, as well as other techniques [10, 15].

One of the responses to this trend is the concept of **higher-order differentials** [9, 11]. If we have a difference of plaintexts, for example, why stop at just this one difference? Why not have a difference of the difference of the plaintexts, and see if we can use this to determine any information? This would be a **second-order differential**. We can also have third-order, fourth-order, and so forth.

More formally, suppose that we have a differential, Ω_X, and another differential, Ω'_X. We can define a second-order input differential, say, Ω^2_X, where

$$\Omega^2_X = \Omega_X \oplus \Omega'_X$$

This requires us to have four ciphertexts, say, X_1, X_2, X_3, and X_4, such that the first-order differentials are

$$\Omega_X = X_1 \oplus X_2, \quad \Omega'_X = X_1 \oplus X_3, \quad \Omega'_X = X_2 \oplus X_4$$

Then the second-order input differential is

$$\Omega_X^2 = \Omega_X \oplus \Omega_X'$$

However, the output differential (of F, which could be a round function, or one or more rounds) is normally referred to as the second-order differential. For the first-order output differentials, we would then have

$$\Omega_Y = F(X_1) \oplus F(X_2), \quad \Omega_Y' = F(X_1) \oplus F(X_3) = F(X_2) \oplus F(X_4)$$

And for the second-order output differential:

$$\Omega_Y^2 = \Omega_Y \oplus \Omega_Y'$$

This would give us the second-order characteristic:

$$(\Omega_X^2 \Rightarrow^2 \Omega_Y^2)$$

I use the symbol ''$\Rightarrow^2$'' to represent that this is not an ordinary characteristic.

This process can be extended further to create higher-order differentials. Formally, for these, we can use a slightly different notation from Reference [9], as the above notation can quickly become a bit cumbersome. Furthermore, the above notation applies only to standard binary ciphers. For ones that take place, for example, in finite fields, we need a slightly different notation, since the operation to take the difference might be different from the one to add a difference.

Let a first-order differential of the output of a round function F of an input point X be denoted

$$\Delta_{A_1} F(X) = F(X + A_1) - F(X)$$

where A_1 is the differential of the input. For a second-order differential, we have

$$\Delta_{A_1, A_2}(F(X_1)) = \Delta_{A_2}(\Delta_{A_1}(F(X)))$$

We'll expand this so it is a little clearer:

$$\Delta_{A_2}(\Delta_{A_1}(F(X)))$$
$$= \Delta_{A_2}(F(X + A_1) - F(X))$$
$$= F(X + A_1 + A_2) - F(X + A_1) - F(X + A_2) + F(X)$$

This technique of higher-order differentials can be very useful. In Reference [9], Knudsen shows that the round function $f(x + k)^2 \bmod p$, where p is prime (and has a block size of twice the number of bits in p), has no useful first-order differentials. However, if we use second-order differentials, we can break the round function very easily.

7.12 Truncated Differentials

In standard differential cryptanalysis, we take a fixed difference in the input and rely on this difference producing a chain reaction of a step-by-step series of differences, which eventually trickle down to a point that we can measure. When we measure at this point, we are looking for an exact difference between two ciphertexts: We count these exact differences, and ignore any plaintext–ciphertexts pairs that do not have this difference in the ciphertext.

To be more specific, in the above standard differential attacks, we would check to see if there was a difference by XORing the two values and checking the value of the output. If it matched what we expected, then it's a hit. Otherwise, it's not, even if all of the bits we expected to be flipped were, but some extra bits were also flipped.

The concept of **truncated differentials** relaxes the constraint that we need to look for the entire difference to be exactly what we use (in the input difference) or what we predict (in the output difference). If we have a normal characteristic, with two differentials:

$$(\Omega_X \Rightarrow \Omega_Y)$$

then we have a truncated differential:

$$(\Omega'_X \Rightarrow \Omega_Y)$$

where Ω'_X and Ω'_Y, respectively, represent subsets of the differentials Ω_X and Ω_Y. The term *subsets* here means that just some (or possibly all) of the bits that are different in characteristics will be different in the truncated differential.

For example, DES itself has known truncated round characteristics of probability 1.

Knudsen in Reference [9] gives a simple attack on a five-round Feistel cipher with an n-bit round function (and, therefore, a $2n$-bit block size). Let the Feistel round function be F. Assume we have a non-zero input truncated differential Ω_a, using only some of the bits:

1. Let T be a table, potentially up to size 2^n, of all zeros.

2. For every input value of x (all 2^n of them), calculate $x + \Omega_a$, and set the entry corresponding to the output differential equal to 1, that is, set

$$T[F(x) \oplus F(x \oplus \Omega_a)] = 1$$

This way, all possible output differentials corresponding to the truncated differential are marked and known.

3. Choose a plaintext at random, P_1. Calculate $P_2 = P_1 \oplus (\Omega_a \parallel 0)$, that is, the right half of the difference is 0, and the left half is Ω_a.

4. Calculate the encryptions of P_1 and P_2, setting them to C_1 and C_2, respectively.

5. For every value of the fifth round key, k_5, do the following:

   (a) Decrypt one round of C_1 and C_2 using k_5, and save these intermediate ciphertexts as D_1 and D_2.

   (b) For every value of the fourth round key, k_4, do the following:

      i. Calculate $t_1 = F(D_1^R \oplus k_4)$ and $t_2 = F(D_2^R \oplus k_4)$, where the R represents the right half of the D-values.

      ii. If $T[t_1 \oplus t_2 \oplus D_1^L \oplus D_2^L]$ is greater than 0, then output the values of k_4 and k_5 (where the L represents the left half of the D-values). Here, we are measuring if the truncated differential was seen.

This will generate a list of keys proportional to the number of key bits in the truncated differential. Repeating this a sufficient number of times, we will have only a single set of keys come out each time.

We can use this same attack on any number of rounds by doing the exact same analysis, except for the first three rounds. Naturally, with each application, we have to do more work and will have less precision.

Truncated differential analysis is a potentially powerful technique. It has been done on the Twofish Algorithm [17] in Reference [14], although it has not been used in a successful attack as yet [16].

7.13   Impossible Differentials

Impossible differentials were used successfully to cryptanalyze most of Skipjack [19] (31 out of 32 rounds) by Biham, Biryukov, and Shamir [4].

The idea is fairly simple: Instead of looking for outcomes that are as highly probable as possible, we look for events that cannot occur in the ciphertext. This means that, if we have a candidate key (or set of key bits) that produces a differential with a probability of 0, then that candidate is invalid. If we invalidate enough of the keys, then we will be left with a number reasonable enough to work with.

As Biham et al. [4] point out, events that should be impossible have been historically used in other events [5]. For example, with a German Enigma machine, it was not possible for any plaintext character to be encrypted to itself. Therefore, any potential solution of a ciphertext must not have a character of plaintext be the same as the corresponding character in the ciphertext.

The particular attack Biham et al. [4] explain is a miss-in-the-middle attack on Skipjack. If we feed an input differential into round 5 of $(0, a, 0, 0)$ [into (w_5, w_6, w_7, w_8)], then we can check for an impossible output differential in (the output of) round 28: $(b, 0, 0, 0)$. We will write this impossible differential as

$$(0, a, 0, 0) \nrightarrow (b, 0, 0, 0)$$

This differential is impossible if a and b are both not 0. (The rounds are numbered from 1 to 32.)

This is a miss-in-the-middle attack because, if we analyze the differentials from round 5 and round 28, we can trace them all the way to the output of round 16 (or, equivalently, the input of round 17); two effects of each differential meet: The input differential says that the round value should be (c, d, e, 0), while the output differential says that the round value should be (f, g, 0, h). Specifically, e and h cannot be 0, and therefore there is a contradiction. Figure 7-2 graphically depicts the impossible differential attack.

For the exact details of the full attack, including complete details on a key recovery attack, see Reference [4]. However, I'll outline the attack below.

This technique can be used to derive a key in the following way. We use the above differential [(0, a, 0, 0) $\nRightarrow$ (b, 0, 0, 0)] to ferret out all of the invalid subkeys. We launch an attack very similar to a standard differential attack, where we expect to predict the key by using the plaintext–ciphertext to test a differential as above. However, instead of selecting the subkey with the most hits, we instead eliminate any key that ever shows an impossible difference. Repeating this enough times, we will eventually be left with a single candidate subkey. Repeat this a sufficient number of times for different subkeys, and we will eventually be left with a reasonable number of keys to check through brute-force. Performing a 25-round attack can recover the full key in about 2^{27} steps. However, when we hit 26 rounds, this becomes 2^{49} steps and gets worse from there.

The above key recovery attack, unfortunately, only seems to work for up to about 26 rounds of the full 32-round Skipjack. With 31 rounds, Biham et al. [4] instead found that they would have to check every single key. Luckily, checking every single key does not require performing the complete encryption or decryption: It can be limited to a handful of computations of the G-function. Since a full encryption works by using several G-function computations, as long as we keep the number of G computations down below the amount required for a full encryption, we are still doing less work than would be required on a normal exhaustive attack. The authors predict about 2^{78} steps, with 2^{64} bits of memory (2,048 petabytes). This is still faster than an exhaustive attack, which would require 2^{80} steps.

One of the most important contributions of the concept of impossible differentials is that the normal method of "proving" cipher secure against differential cryptanalysis — that by creating a very low upper bound on probabilities of differentials in the components — is flawed. If there are a sufficient number of zero or low-probability differentials, then the impossible differential attack can be carried out.

Furthermore, this same attack can be applied with conditional characteristics and differentials, as well as linear cryptanalysis.

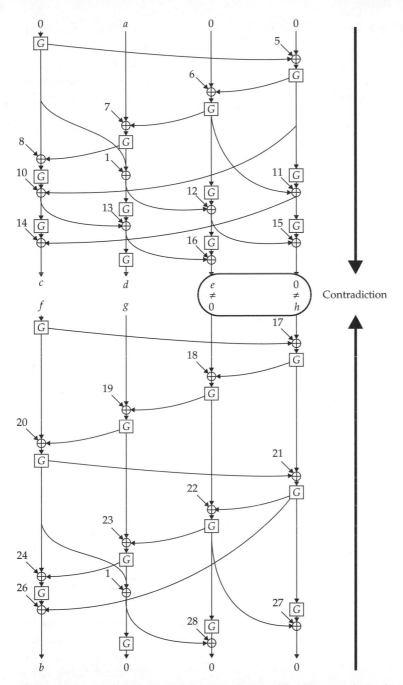

Figure 7-2 A graphical depiction of the impossible differential attack on Skipjack, based on a diagram from Reference [4]. The rounds have been "unrolled" from the shift register mechanism, allowing us to more easily see the mechanism. We can see the differentials missing in the zero, as one side predicts a zero, and the other side predicts a non-zero intermediate.

7.14 Boomerang Attack

So far, we have been focusing almost entirely on top-down approaches to cryptanalysis: Our attacks work by taking information about the plaintext, and deriving some feature of the ciphertext that we will test. How often the test succeeds gives us a likelihood that a key is correct.

The above attack with impossible differentials, as well as the previously discussed meet-in-the-middle attack, shows us that this view may be missing out on some advantages to working both ends at once. Linear cryptanalysis even uses some of this symmetry to help derive more key bits.

The **boomerang attack** is another differential meet-in-the-middle attack [20].

The basic premise uses four pairs of plaintexts and their associated ciphertexts:

$$(P_0, C_0), (P_1, C_1), (Q_0, D_0), (Q_1, D_1)$$

Using the premises of Reference [20], let's break the encryption operation (E) into two subparts: E_0 (the first half of the encryption) and E_1 (the second half of the encryption). For example:

$$C_0 = E(P_0) = E_1(E_0(P_0))$$

I'll denote the inverse operations of E_0 and E_1, as in, the decryption operations, as E_0^{-1} and E_1^{-1}, respectively. From the above, we would also have

$$P_0 = E_0^{-1}(E_1^{-1}(C_0))$$

Here, we will have to develop two characteristics, one for the first half of the encryption, E_0, and one for the second half's decryption, E_1^{-1}:

$$\begin{aligned} E_0 : &\quad (\Omega \Rightarrow \Omega^*) \\ E_1^{-1} : &\quad (\omega \Rightarrow \omega^*) \end{aligned}$$

Note that the E_1^{-1} characteristic works from the ciphertext to the intermediate ciphertext (outside inwards). The differentials are used in the following relations:

$$\begin{aligned} P_0 \oplus P_1 &= \Omega \\ C_0 \oplus D_0 &= \omega \\ C_1 \oplus D_1 &= \omega \end{aligned}$$

Using these two characteristics, we can then derive a new characteristic for the intermediate encryption of Q_0 and Q_1:

$$\begin{aligned} &E_0(Q_0) \oplus E_0(Q_1) \\ =\ &E_0(Q_0) \oplus E_0(Q_1) \oplus (E_0(P_0) \oplus E_0(P_0)) \oplus (E_0(P_1) \oplus E_0(P_1)) \\ =\ &E_1^{-1}(D_0) \oplus E_1^{-1}(D_1) \oplus E_1^{-1}(C_0) \oplus E_0(P_0) \oplus E_1^{-1}(C_1) \oplus E_0(P_1) \\ =\ &(E_0(P_0) \oplus E_0(P_1)) \oplus (E_1^{-1}(C_0) \oplus E_1^{-1}(D_0)) \oplus (E_1^{-1}(C_1) \oplus E_1^{-1}(D_1)) \\ =\ &\Omega^* \oplus \omega^* \oplus \omega^* \\ =\ &\Omega^* \end{aligned}$$

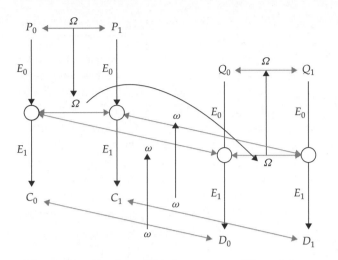

Figure 7-3 Derivation of the boomerang differential $P_0 \oplus P_1 = \Omega$ leading to $Q_0 \oplus Q_1 = \Omega$, based on a diagram in Reference [20]. (Light gray lines) XOR's; (dark gray lines) how the differentials propagate from the P's to the Q's; (black lines) encryption.

Hence, we have derived a new characteristic for the Q values:

$$E_0^{-1} : (\Omega^* \Rightarrow \Omega)$$

This characteristic can then be measured by calculating $Q_0 \oplus Q_1 = \Omega$. Figure 7-3 shows a graphical representation of how this characteristic occurs.

From the diagram and the derivation above, we can see why this is called the *boomerang attack*: If we construct the differentials correctly, the differential Ω will come back and hit us in $Q_0 \oplus Q_1$.

We construct the boomerang differential by taking a seed plaintext P_0 with our Ω differential and creating $P_1 = P_0 \oplus \Omega$. We then encrypt P_0 and P_1 to obtain C_0 and C_1, respectively. Next, we calculate new ciphertexts with our ω differential, so that $D_0 = C_0 \oplus \omega$ and $D_1 = C_1 \oplus \omega$. We then decrypt D_0 and D_1 to obtain Q_0 and Q_1. Some percentage of the time, the moons will align and the differentials will all line up, allowing us to measure to see if $Q_0 \oplus Q_1 = \Omega$. When all four differentials hold, we refer to this as a **right quartet**.

What is the significance of this attack? Well, many algorithms have been deemed to be "secure" against differential cryptanalysis because of the lack of any good characteristics on the full cipher. Normally, as the number of rounds increases, the probability of the differential decreases, thereby requiring more and more plaintext–ciphertext pairs.

The above boomerang attack lets us develop an attack using only the characteristic for the first half of the cipher, bypassing the latter half. If sufficiently strong characteristics exist, then we have a good attack. We use the characteristics just as before to derive the key. With the characteristic properly set in the final (and first) rounds, we can brute-force the keys that affect the differential, measure it, and select the most likely candidate key bits.

After this first layer is stripped away, we can continue developing characteristics to get more key bits, or just perform an exhaustive search on the remaining key bits.

Wagner [20] uses exactly this premise against the COCONUT98 algorithm [18]. COCONUT98 has a 256-bit key and was developed specifically to defeat differential cryptanalysis by having no useful characteristics. Despite this, COCONUT98's key can be derived using the boomerang attack with 2^{16} chosen plaintext–ciphertext sets, with 2^{41} offline computations (equivalent to 2^{38} encryptions, according to Reference [20]).

In addition to its attack on COCONUT98, Reference [20] also mounts an incredibly successful attack against FEAL (Section 4.7) and Khufu, a 64-bit block cipher with a 512-bit key [13].

7.15   Interpolation Attack

Many of these differential techniques are extensions of standard, continuous techniques of calculus, such as the derivative. As a matter of fact, differentials are sometimes referred to as **derivatives**. The primary difference is that, instead of applying the techniques to continuous spaces, like real or complex numbers, we are applying the techniques to discrete spaces — in our case, integers between 0 and 2^n.

Another technique many learn is **interpolation**: If we wish to find a line between two points, or a parabola between three, or, in general, a polynomial of degree $n-1$ that passes between n points, there is a simple formula to calculate this polynomial. These formulas can be used to analyze the relationship between various points or to find additional points lying in between points.

For example, for a simple line between two points (x_0, y_0) and (x_1, y_1) we can see that the following line includes both points:

$$p(x) = y_0 \times \left(\frac{x - x_1}{x_0 - x_1} \right) + y_1 \times \left(\frac{x - x_0}{x_1 - x_0} \right)$$

If we plug in x_0, we get y_0, and if we plug in x_1, we get y_1. The function is linear because it contains only the variable x.

In the general case, for points (x_i, y_i), for $i = 1, \ldots, n$, our **interpolating polynomial**, $p(x)$, is given by

$$p(x) = \sum_{i=1}^{n} y_i \prod_{1 \leq j \leq n, j \neq i} \left(\frac{x - x_j}{x_i - x_j} \right)$$

This is merely an extension of our previous case to produce a polynomial of degree $n - 1$. This is called the **Lagrange interpolating polynomial**.

This technique can also be applied to the discrete world of bits and bytes, as shown by Jakobsen and Knudsen [7]. We simply apply the above definitions to discrete functions, where the x- and y-values will be plaintext and their associated ciphertexts, respectively.

We can apply this technique by noting that 32-bit XOR operations are identical to algebraic addition in the finite field GF (2^{32}) (since it has characteristic 2, i.e., 2 is equivalent to 0, so that $1 + 1 = 0$).

Constructing this polynomial will not immediately yield the key, however. Given sufficient pairs, it can actually yield a polynomial that emulates the encryption function: It produces valid ciphertexts from given plaintexts.

To actually get key bits, we instead try to find a polynomial for the plaintext and the next-to-last round of ciphertext. Similar to the way we have done before, we decrypt some portion of the last round by guessing the last round key. When we have done this for a sufficient number of plaintext–ciphertext pairs, we will have enough plaintext and intermediate ciphertext pairs to attempt to construct a polynomial. We check the polynomial against another value that wasn't used in the construction to test it. If the polynomial produces the correct result, then we have guessed the key bits.

The interpolating attack is a bit academic in nature, but it provides an interesting avenue of attack. For certain ciphers that provably secure against traditional differential cryptanalysis, the interpolating attack produces a very reasonable method for deriving the key, as shown in Reference [7].

7.16 Related-Key Attack

Finally, we want to look at a completely different way of viewing differential cryptanalysis. In the previous sections, we analyzed ciphers by examining how differences in the plaintexts and ciphertexts propagate to determine key bits. This was accomplished through the use of chosen-plaintext attacks.

One avenue unexplored is that of attacking the key itself. After all, we have considered the key to be out-of-bounds for modifications. It hasn't been part of our model to modify it, since it is what we are trying to derive. Furthermore, doesn't the ability to change the key automatically mean that we know the value of it?

Actually, no. As Kelsey, Schneier, and Wagner [8] point out, many key exchange protocols leave themselves vulnerable in two ways. The first way is that they do not check the integrity of the key before they start using it to encrypt plaintext into ciphertext encrypted — meaning that, immediately after exchanging the keys, they immediately encrypt some plaintext and send the ciphertext to the other party.

Secondly, many key exchange protocols use simple XOR structures to pass along the key. For example, assume that there is a pre-shared secret key, K_m. A new session key may be generated by sending a message:

$$(M, E_{K_m}(M) \oplus K_s)$$

This two-part message will hide the actual value of the key. However, if we have the ability to modify the message in transit, then we could corrupt the key the first time around with a known difference. Now, one party will send a message encrypted with one key, and the other will send a message encrypted with the key XORed with a fixed, chosen difference.

Typically, we also address this attack as a chosen plaintext, so that both parties would attempt to encrypt the same plaintext with the XORed keys.

Owing to the difficulty of achieving such an attack, this scenario has often been disregarded. However, the above key-exchange scenario should provide some conjecture that the above attack is very possible.

Naturally, the XOR difference will have to be significant, usually to exploit a weakness in the key-scheduling algorithm. Attacks that rely on such weaknesses are called **related-key attacks**, since the attack relies on so-called "related keys" in the schedule. Indeed, many ciphers use schedules in which key bits are copied or have a linear relationship to many other bits.

7.16.1   Related-Key Attack on GOST

Sometimes the related-key attack can be carried out with a normal differential attack. In Reference [8], the authors exploit a key scheduling weakness in the GOST 28147-89 cipher, a Soviet cryptosystem [6]. The key schedule they specify takes a 256-bit key and breaks it into eight 32-bit subkeys, $K_0, \ldots, K_7$, generating subkeys (sk_i) for use in the 32 rounds by

$$sk_i = \begin{cases} K_{i \bmod 8} & \text{if } i < 24 \\ K_{(7-i) \bmod 8} & \text{else} \end{cases}$$

We can use this key schedule in a clever manner.

Say that we have an interesting differential for the plaintext on this algorithm, Ω. Since the keys (in most ciphers, actually) are directly XORed in at some point, we should be able to choose a related key to the original that will counteract the Ω for the first round. This could be done simply by taking $K_0 = K_0 \oplus \Delta$, for some appropriate value of Δ.

Note that the subkeys for the next seven rounds ($i = 1, \ldots, 7$) don't rely on K_0. This means that the difference for each of these rounds from the original plaintext is zero! The differences will then start with the eighth round. In essence, we skipped the first eight rounds of the cipher and can instead mount a much simpler 24-round attack.

7.16.2   Related-Key Attack on 3DES

A very interesting use of a related-key attack is on 3DES, using three separate keys [8]. We recall that 3DES uses the standard DES encryption function three times in succession, each time with a different key. (The decryption, naturally, decrypts with the keys in the exact opposite fashion.) This allows us to virtually triple the total key space, while not changing the underlying structure of DES at all.

Assume that we have a DES encryption of a plaintext P to a ciphertext C, using keys K_a, K_b, and K_c as follows. Let the E-function represent DES encryption, and the D-function represent DES decryption. Then,

$$C = E_{K_c}(D_{K_b}(E_{K_a}(P)))$$

Now, assume that we have a related key, with $K'_a = K_a \oplus \Delta$. We select to have the original C decrypted to give us a new plaintext, P', or

$$P' = D_{K_c}(E_{K_b}(D_{K'_a}(C)))$$

Note that the decryption to P is

$$P = D_{K_c}(E_{K_b}(D_{K_a}(C)))$$

That is, the decryption to P and P' differs only in the last step, allowing us to write

$$P' = D_{K'_a}(E_{K_a}(P))$$

We can then treat this as a known-plaintext attack and attack it via an exhaustive search, for 2^{56} work, deriving K_a in the process.

Once we have K_a, we can then obtain $E_{K_a}(P)$, allowing us to look at it, along with C, as a known plaintext–ciphertext pair of double DES. We may recall that double DES is susceptible to a meet-in-the-middle attack with 2^{57} work.

With a related-key attack, we have then broken 3DES to be no better than normal DES. Note, however, that this works only when all three keys are independent. The most common form of 3DES, with the first and third keys the same, is immune to this attack, as the differential would carry into the first and last steps of both encryption and decryption.

Finally, the authors of Reference [8] give some guidance on how to avoid related-key attacks.

First, avoid using key-exchange algorithms that do not have key integrity; always check the key before using it blindly to encrypt something and broadcasting it.

Second, making efforts to not derive round keys in such linear manners will go a long way. The authors make a very good suggestion of running the key first through a cryptographic hash function, such as SHA-1, and then using it to derive a key schedule. Any sufficiently strong hash function will obliterate any structures that may have been artificially induced, preventing them from meaningfully modifying the ciphertext.

7.17   Summary

In this chapter, I demonstrated many modern differential attacks against modern ciphers. The standard differential attack has been extended and studied extensively over the past two decades and continues to be in conferences and papers every year.

There is always more to learn in the field of cryptanalysis. This book only covered some of the more popular and influential topics in the field. To the reader wanting to learn even more about the field, you can look through the archives and current issues of *The Journal of Cryptology, Cryptologia*, the proceedings of conferences such as CRYPTO, EUROCRYPT, ASIACRYPT, Fast Software Encryption, and many others.

Again, we must reiterate, though: The best way to become a better cryptanalyst is to practice, practice, practice!

Exercises

Exercise 1. Change the S-box and P-box of the EASY1 cipher to randomly generated values. Use the analysis in this chapter to create a differential attack on this for three rounds.

Exercise 2. Use the basic one-round version of the cipher from the previous exercise as a round function to a simple Feistel cipher. Use a simple key schedule, such as using the same 36-bit key every round.

Use differential cryptanalysis to break this Feistel cipher for eight rounds. Give analysis for how many plaintext–ciphertext pairs this will require.

Exercise 3. Perform a differential analysis of the S-boxes of DES. Discuss your results.

Exercise 4. Perform a differential analysis of AES. How successful would you guess a standard differential attack against AES might be based on this analysis?

Exercise 5. Attempt an impossible cryptanalysis attack against the cipher you created in Exercise 1. Try again with the Feistel cipher in Exercise 2.

Exercise 6. Mount a boomerang attack against the cipher you created in Exercise 2, but extend the number of rounds to 16.

References

[1] I. Ben Aroya and E. Biham. Differential cryptanalysis of lucifer. In *Advances in Cryptology – Crypto '93*, (ed. Douglas R. Stinson), pp. 187–199. Lecture Notes in Computer Science, Vol. 773. (Springer-Verlag, Berlin, 1993).

[2] E. Biham and A. Shamir. Differential cryptanalysis of DES-like cryptosystems (extended abstract). In *Advances in Cryptology – Crypto '90*, (eds. Alfred J. Menezes and Scott A. Vanstone), pp. 2–21. Lecture Notes in Computer Science, Vol. 537. (Springer-Verlag, Berlin, 1990).

[3] E. Biham and A. Shamir. Differential cryptanalysis of Feal and N-hash. In *Advances in Cryptology – EuroCrypt '91*, (ed. Donald W. Davies), pp. 1–16. Lecture Notes in Computer Science, Vol. 547. (Springer-Verlag, Berlin, 1991).

[4] Eli Biham, Alex Biryukov, and Adi Shamir. Cryptanalysis of skipjack reduced to 31 rounds using impossible differentials. *Journal of Cryptology* **18**(4): 291–311 (2005).

[5] Cipher A. Deavours and Louis Kruh. *Machine Cryptography and Modern Cryptanalysis,* Artech House Telecom Library. (Artech House Publishers, Norwood, MA, 1985).

[6] Government Standard 28147-89. (Government of the USSR for Standards, 1989).

[7] Thomas Jakobsen and Lars R. Knudsen. The interpolation attack on block ciphers. In *Fast Software Encryption: 4th Interntional Workshop, FSE '97*, (ed. Eli Biham), Lecture Notes in Computer Science, pp. 28–40. Lecture Notes in Computer Science, Vol. 1267. (Springer-Verlag, Berlin, 1997); http://citeseer.ist.psu.edu/jakobsen97interpolation.html.

[8] J. Kelsey, B. Schneier, and D. Wagner. Key-schedule cryptanalysis of IDEA, G-DES, GOST, SAFER, and triple-DES. In *Advances in Cryptology – Crypto '96*, (ed. Neal Koblitz), pp. 237–251. Lecture Notes in Computer Science, Vol. 1109. (Springer-Verlag, Berlin, 1996).

[9] Lars R. Knudsen. Truncated and higher order differentials. In *Fast Software Encryption: Second International Workshop, Leuven, Belgium, December 14–16, 1994*, (ed. Bart Preneel), pp. 196–211. Lecture Notes in Computer Science, Vol. 1008. (Springer-Verlag, Berlin, 1995); http://iteseer.ist.psu.edu/knudsen95truncated.html.

[10] Kenji Koyama and Routo Terada. How to strengthen des-like cryptosystems against differential cryptanalysis. *IEICE Transactions on Fundamentals*

of Electronics Communications and Computer Sciences **E76-A**(1): 63–69 (1993).

[11] Xuejia Lai. Higher order derivatives and differential cryptanalysis. In *Proceedings of Symposium on Communication, Coding and Cryptography* (Monte-Vina, Ascona, Switzerland, 1994).

[12] S. K. Langford and M. E. Hellman. Differential-linear cryptanalysis. In *Advances in Cryptology – Crypto '94*, (ed. Yvo Desmedt), pp. 17–25. Lecture Notes in Computer Science, Vol. 839. (Springer-Verlag, Berlin, 1994).

[13] R. C. Merkle. Fast software encryption functions. In *Advances in Cryptology – Crypto '90*, (eds. Alfred J. Menezes and Scott A. Vanstone), pp. 476–501. Lecture Notes in Computer Science, Vol. 537. (Springer-Verlag, Berlin, 1990).

[14] Shiho Moriai and Yiqun Lisa Yin. *Cryptanalysis of Twofish (II)*; http://www.schneier.com/twofish-analysis-shiho.pdf.

[15] K. Nyberg and L. R. Knudsen. Provable security against differential cryptanalysis. In *Advances in Cryptology – Crypto '92*, (ed. Ernest F. Brickell), pp. 566–574. Lecture Notes in Computer Science, Vol. 740. (Springer-Verlag, Berlin, 1992).

[16] Bruce Schneier. *Twofish Cryptanalysis Rumors*. (2005); http://www.schneier.com/blog/archives/2005/11/twofish_cryptan.html.

[17] Bruce Schneier, John Kelsey, Doug Whiting, David Wagner, Chris Hall, and Niels Ferguson. *The Twofish Encryption Algorithm: A 128-Bit Block Cipher*. (John Wiley, New York, 1999).

[18] S. Vaudenay. Provable security for block ciphers by decorrelation. In *STACS 98: 15th Annual Symposium on Theoretical Aspects of Computer Science, Paris, France, February 25–27, 1998, Proceedings*, (eds. Michel Morvan, Christoph Meniel, and Daniel Krob). Lecture Notes in Computer Science, Vol. 1373. (Springer-Verlag, Berlin, 1998).

[19] U.S. Government. *SKIPJACK and KEA Algorithm Specifications*. (1998).

[20] David Wagner. The boomerang attack. In *Fast Software Encryption: 6th Interntional Workshop, FSE '99*, (ed. Lars R. Knudsen), pp. 156–170. Lecture Notes in Computer Science, Vol. 1636. (Springer-Verlag, Berlin, 1999); http://citeseer.ist.psu.edu/wagner99boomerang.html.

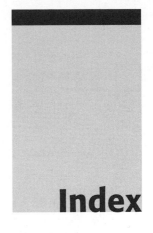

Index